IMAGES
of America
SAN LUIS

ON THE COVER: The civic stature of this building in 1913 is the perfect backdrop for this group of unidentified men to assemble for a historic photograph. Musicians and patriotic horsemen join together with an unknown council, possibly the Sociedad Protección Mutua de Trabajadores Unidos (SPMDTU) chapter, for what appears to be an organizational meeting. In response to public outcry from citizens, the county commissioners signed a contract on July 6, 1883, with masonry contractor John Farrington and project superintendent Samuel Tucker to build a suitable courthouse. It was completed that same year for the cost of $12,600. Dedicated in 1883, the Costilla County courthouse is representative of adobe territorial style architecture. It is one of only two intact historic adobe courthouses in the state of Colorado. (Courtesy of Darryl E. Garcia.)

IMAGES
of America

SAN LUIS

Dana Maestas

ARCADIA
PUBLISHING

ISBN 978-1-4671-3247-3

Published by Arcadia Publishing
Charleston, South Carolina

Printed in the United States of America

Library of Congress Control Number: 2014950706

For all general information, please contact Arcadia Publishing:
Telephone 843-853-2070
Fax 843-853-0044
E-mail sales@arcadiapublishing.com
For customer service and orders:
Toll-Free 1-888-313-2665

Visit us on the Internet at www.arcadiapublishing.com

For my children: Bianca, Derrick, Aubin, and Dyami;
and grandchildren, Amyas and Soleil.

Para la gente de San Luís.
For the people of San Luis.

Contents

Acknowledgments

The traditions and culture of San Luis de la Culebra are important parts of Colorado history. This book was made possible through the people of San Luis who have preserved their family history. I am grateful to the following people who have provided photographs and stories about their ancestors: Theresa B. Vigil, Ida Valdez, the Candido Olivas Sr. family, Josephine and Eugene Lobato, Adolfo Lobato, Diana Cortez, Demostenes Vigil II, the Olivia Maestas family, the Lee Madrid family, Francisco Gallegos, Hope Gallegos Yost, the Nesrala Zegob family, Pat and Lorraine Gallegos, Cathy Serna-Egana, Wanda Vigil, Randy Pijoan, Marcella Pacheco, Charlie Jaquez Jr., the Dario Gallegos family, Dana EchoHawk, Ben Doon, Mathew Valdez, Evan Valdez Jr., Pat Trujillo VanZandt, Darryl E. Garcia, Conrad and Acela Garcia, Theresa Medina, Frankie Sanchez, Josito Espinoza, Joetta E. Frost, Victoria Quintana, Monica and Carmen Olguín, Julia Valdez, Iva L. Gallegos, Augustin and Dora Padilla, Beatrice Marquez, Clarence and Casilda Vigil, Larry and Rita Vigil, Maria Mondragon Valdez, Kenneth Gardner, and the Land Rights Council. Thanks to Jessy Randall of Tutt Library at Colorado College, Melissa VanOtterloo and the staff at the Stephen H. Hart Library and Research Center–History Colorado, and my editor Stacia Bannerman and publisher Jeff Ruetsche.

Much respect and gratitude goes to Brenda Vialpando and Richard de Olivas y Cordova, who are my "go-to" people when I need information, and to 92-year-old Libby Rivera, whose feisty nature and humor gives me a glimpse of a past well loved.

A very special thank-you goes to Huberto Maestas and Maria Valdez Bloomfield, who are a tremendous source of support, vision, and encouragement as we journey toward understanding the history of the place we call home.

In memoriam for Henrietta Mascarenas, whose recollections of her father, mother, and grandfather made for a remarkable and memorable day. This work is also in special memoriam for Evan A. Valdez and Louisa Arellano Valdez, whose gifts of love of learning, *familia*, and faith were my inspiration to share this story.

Original Town Ordinance of San Luis

The ordinance is dated May 11, 1863, twelve years after the settlement began.

All the inhabitants shall have the use of pasture, wood, water, and timber and the mills that have been erected shall remain where they are, not interfering with the rights of others. No stock shall be allowed in said lands, except for household purposes. All those who come as settlers shall agree to abide by the rules and regulations and shall keep as good citizens and be provided with the necessary weapons for the defense of the settlement.

Rules for the Town of San Luis of the Culebra are as follows: Inasmuch as no civilized society can endure in good, order, peace and union, which constitutes the happiness of the civilized peoples and establishes the superiority and advantage which Christian people enjoy over the manners of the barbarians, we come to propose to establish the following rules viz:

1st To maintain the cleanliness of the town and not consent that there be placed therein any nuisance.

2nd That drunken revels will not be permitted in the presence of the families of the town, nor fights nor similar disorders.

3rd That no person from outside will be admitted to live in the town, without having previously presented himself before the Judge or Justice of the Peace and received his permission, whether or not he may have acquired property in the town.

4th It will not be permitted that any obstruction be placed in the entrances and outlets of the town.

5th Every one who wishes to take a dwelling or lots in the town, will have to request it of the Judge paying its value which will remain for the benefit of the chapel.

—Charles Beaubien

Introduction

Entering the town of San Luis is like journeying to a different era and culture. Established on April 5, 1851, the traditions in Colorado's oldest town remain largely unchanged after 160 years.

At the northernmost area of Spanish exploration in the New World, about 18 pioneers migrated north from New Mexico into the largest alpine valley in the world—the San Luis Valley. Settlers had come before, but the Utes, who had called the valley home for more than 10,000 years, had discouraged Spanish expansion into their territory.

In the spring of 1851, the following heads of families and single men founded San Luis de la Culebra on the Culebra River (*culebra* is the Spanish word for "snake"): Vallejos, Vigil, Gallegos, Martinez, Pacheco, Jacquez, Valencia, and Valdez.

This beautiful village was settled on the Sangre de Cristo Land Grant. In 1843, Carlos Beaubien petitioned the Mexican government for the grant for his son Narcisco and Stephen Luis Lee. Upon the death of his son and Lee in the Taos Pueblo uprising, Beaubien inherited the grant. Recruited by Beaubien and enticed by the promises of La Merced (the Spanish land grant system), pioneers established Colorado's first permanent settlement. In 1863, Beaubien set aside close to 900 acres of fertile lowland pasture east of town for use as a *vega*, a common grazing area. Still in use today, La Vega remains the last true commons in the United States.

Following the pattern of the land grant system, Beaubien gave the people of San Luis and the communities of Chama, San Francisco, San Pablo, San Pedro, and San Acacio the rights to use La Sierra, the nearby mountain tract. Unique to southern Colorado and northern New Mexico, the *acequias*, an irrigation system, were designed in a way to guarantee agricultural prosperity. This access to communal land and water is not only a necessity but also an ancestral right that benefits all users. It sustains a way of life and preserves a culture in this highly isolated desert region.

The traditions of music, dance, *cuentos* (stories), Las Posadas, the Sociedad Protección Mutua de Trabajadores Unidos (or "Mutual Protection Society of United Workers," SPMDTU, the longest-standing Hispanic fraternal organization), and *penitentes* (penitents) housed in adobe *moradas* (meeting houses) continue to live on today thanks to those families who remain the keepers of culture.

The history of San Luis is bound together by an isolation that sets the Culebra villages apart, a language dating back to 16th-century Castilian Spanish, and a deep faith that places the church at the heart of the community.

The land, the water, and the arts reflect a rich cultural mosaic, representative of the people who live in and around San Luis de la Culebra. Generations have experienced the unchanging treasure of spiritual values and ecological and cultural traditions that are the sacred center of San Luis's landscape.

One

Historic San Luis Merchants and Schools

The settlement of San Luis de la Culebra consisted of Culebra de Medio, Upper Culebra San Acacio, and Lower Culebra San Pablo. A fort was built in San Pablo to protect the village from Indian attacks. The heads of families who settled these fertile lands were Antonio José Vallejos, Mariano Vallejos, Miguel Vallejos, Francisco Vallejos, Juan Miguel Vigil, Nacasio Gallegos, Antonio Vigil, José Antonio Martinez, Mariano Pacheco, Juan Ignacio Jacquez, Juan Pacheco, Ricardo Vigil, Salome Jacquez, Desiderio Valencia, Juan Julian Martinez, José Maria Martinez, Juan Oeracio Jacquez, and José Ilario Valdez.

The first plaza was built just north of the People's Ditch and south of the present town. The settlers built their homes around an L-shaped *placita* for protection. Out of necessity and an entrepreneurial spirit, several took on the challenge of running their own businesses. One of the most diverse was the F.W. Posthoff/Ferdinand Meyer Store, considered one of the first chain stores, with seven locations in the region. Antonio Alcario (A.A.) Salazar was a young employee of Meyer who after four years moved to San Luis to work in the first mercantile business established by Dario Gallegos in 1857. In 1895, the building was destroyed by fire, and in 1947, a second disastrous fire burned it to the ground. Since rebuilding, this store has remained the oldest mercantile business in continual operation by the same family in the state of Colorado.

Siblings Antonio and Rose Zegob peddled dry goods out of a suitcase before opening their store in 1905. Antonio's nephew Nesrala later became his partner in the store. Nesrala Zegob Jr. took over the store in July 1952. Other mercantile stores emerged throughout the San Luis area, including the Barela Store, Olguín General Mercantile, Maxwell Store, San Pablo Cash Store, and the Chama Mercantile Store.

El Molino, also known as the San Luis Roller Mill, opened in 1890 and operated under the ownership of the Parrish family until 1949. Located at the south end of San Luis, the mill was where people brought their wagonloads of wheat to be ground into flour.

There are several versions of the origin of the name San Luis. One is that it was named in honor of San Luis (or Aloysius) Gonzaga, on whose feast date the settlers reached this site. Another is that it was named after Saint Louis; Louis IX, king of France; or the city of St. Louis, Missouri, from which the early settlers obtained their goods by oxen train.

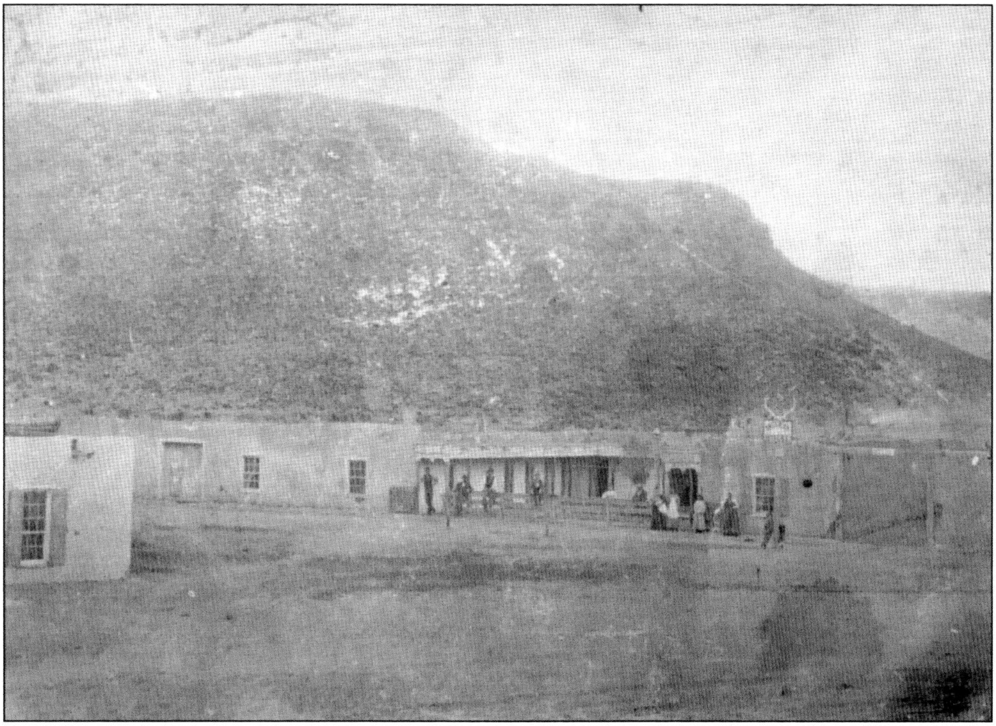

Several men, women, and children pose for this photograph within a territorial-style courtyard along a plaza area at the foot of San Pedro hills at San Luis de la Culebra in 1881. The plaza settlement pattern was built to focus on the extended family and for protection from the Ute tribes. Nearly 30 years after the establishment of the community, the settlers have built adobe plazas, a mercantile store, and the American House, a possible dwelling for out-of-town lodgers. The sign that one of the youngsters leans on rises above the flat rooftops and sports a large elk horn beckoning weary travelers to stop and rest. (Courtesy of History Colorado.)

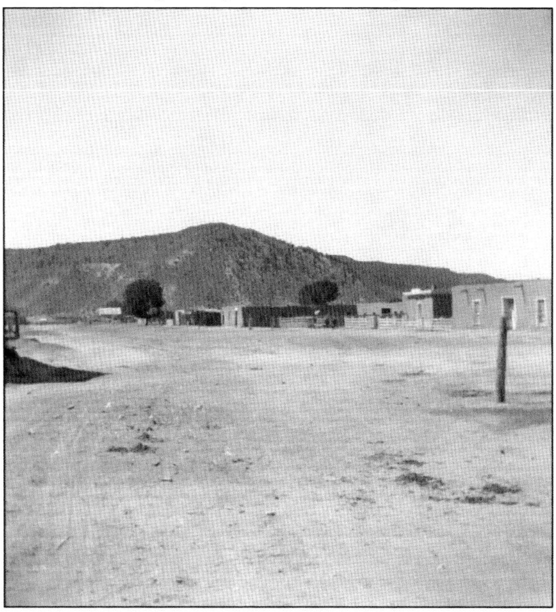

This view, facing to the south of San Luis de la Culebra in 1899, reveals a peaceful village founded on the Sangre de Cristo Land Grant. Its houses were all one-story *jacal* (a form of mud and log construction in which four- to six-inch diameter logs were placed upright in the ground, plastered with several layers of mud on both sides, and then covered by a thick clay finish) and adobe constructions in a central plaza. Founded in 1851, the original site of San Luis de la Culebra was three-quarters of a mile south of the present one. The plaza was called Plaza del Medio, or center village. This was the first plaza built in San Luis de la Culebra and is on the Culebra (Snake) River just north of the People's Ditch. (Courtesy of History Colorado.)

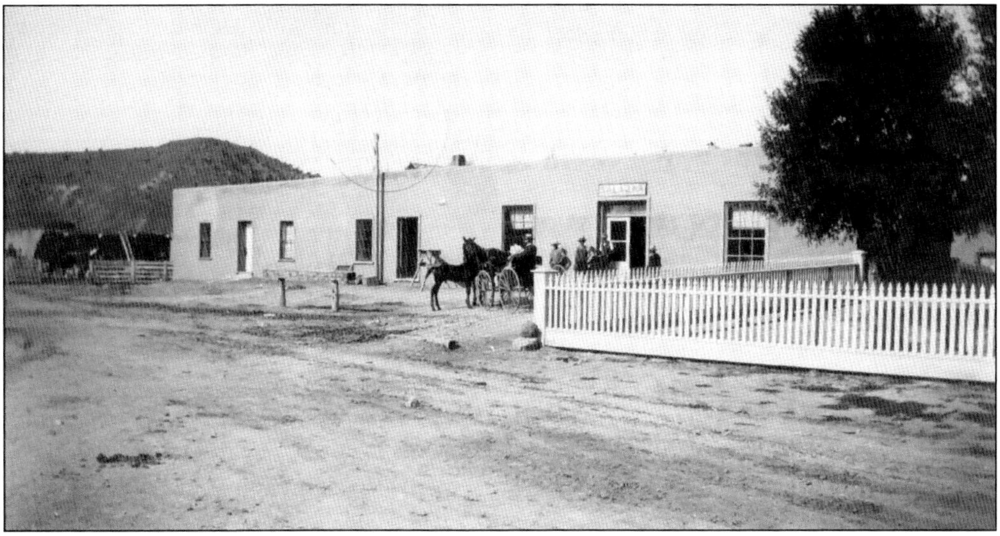

The first mercantile business was opened in San Luis in May 1857 by Dario Gallegos. The capital investment in the new venture was $452 and consisted of three 150-pound bags of green coffee, unrefined or brown sugar that originally came from Mexico, and white and blue corn meal. In the original stock were also sun dried apples from New Mexico, chocolate, salt, peas, corn, tobacco, and an assortment of fabrics like calico and unbleached muslin. In the spring of 1858, Gallegos sent four wagons and ox teams to St. Louis, Missouri, to acquire dry goods, boots, and shoes for the store. The round trip took 11 months. (Courtesy of Dario Gallegos family.)

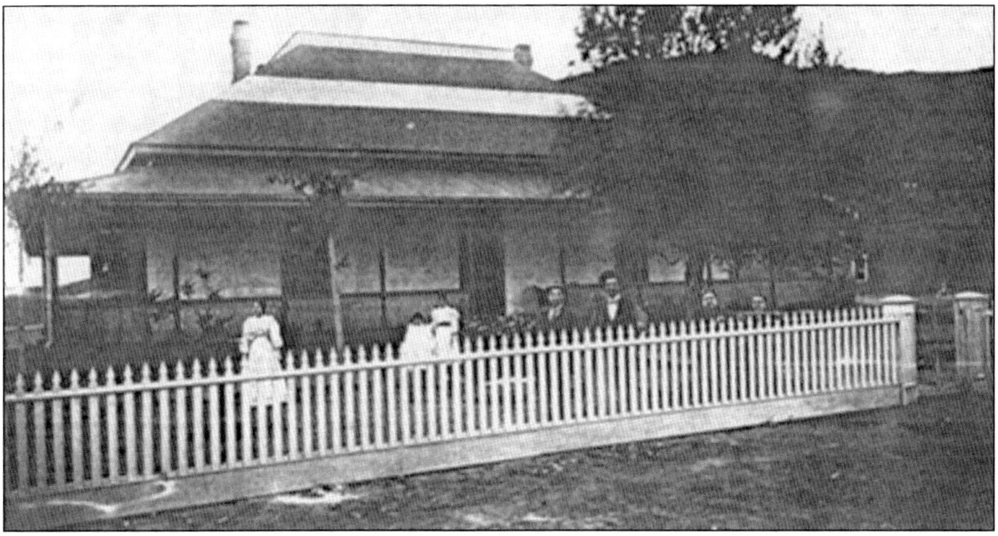

This home was built in 1860 for Dario Gallegos and his wife, Maria Eulogia Valdez Gallegos. They are pictured in front of their home in San Luis with one of their three sons, José Felico, Gaspar, or Donaciano; their two daughters, Genoveva and Maria Refugio; and an unidentified girl. The home sits next to the Gallegos-Salazar Store with a picketed fence surrounding it. This large home with seven fireplaces was a feed store in the early 20th century and later became the Valencia Hotel in the 1930s and 1940s. It was lived in by Mike Joseph, owner of the Liberty Theatre, whose daughter Jane inherited the home, raised five daughters here, and ran a local bus depot next door. In recent years, the home has become an art gallery and is presently owned by author Dana Valdez Maestas and her husband, Huberto. (Courtesy of Dario Gallegos family.)

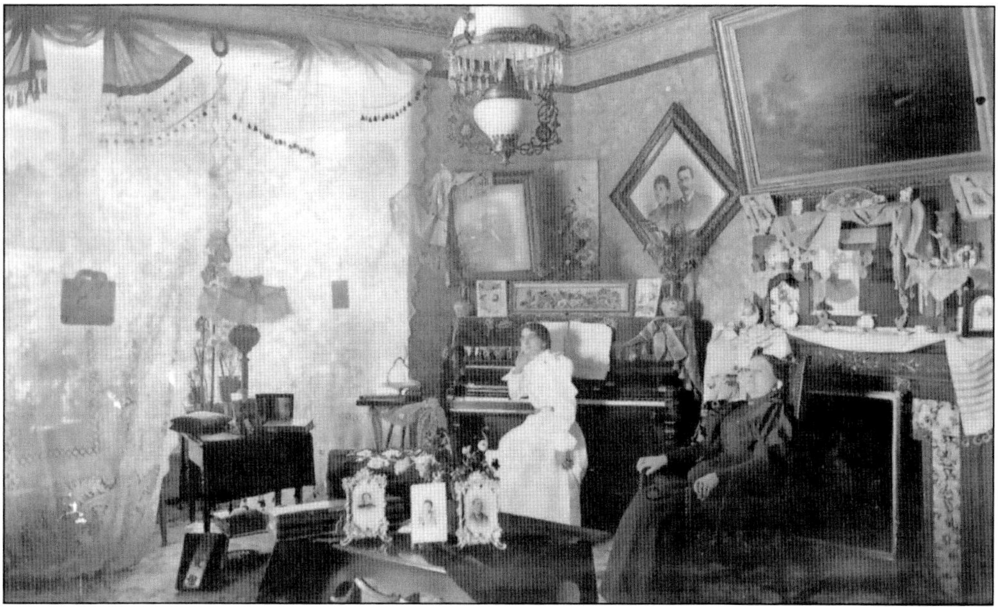

In this photograph of the front parlor off the foyer in the Gallegos home, Doña Maria Eulogia Valdez Gallegos sits on a rocker in front of the carved mahogany fireplace. Her daughter Genoveva is seated on a corner piano bench. A sign of the family's tastes and social class, the parlor was a showcase of family possessions, as seen by the family photos in the background. The lady of the home, Doña Eulogia was responsible for furnishing the parlor with expensive lamps, doilies, tapestries, statuettes, and flowers. The parlor was also a gathering space for family and friends. (Courtesy of Dario Gallegos family.)

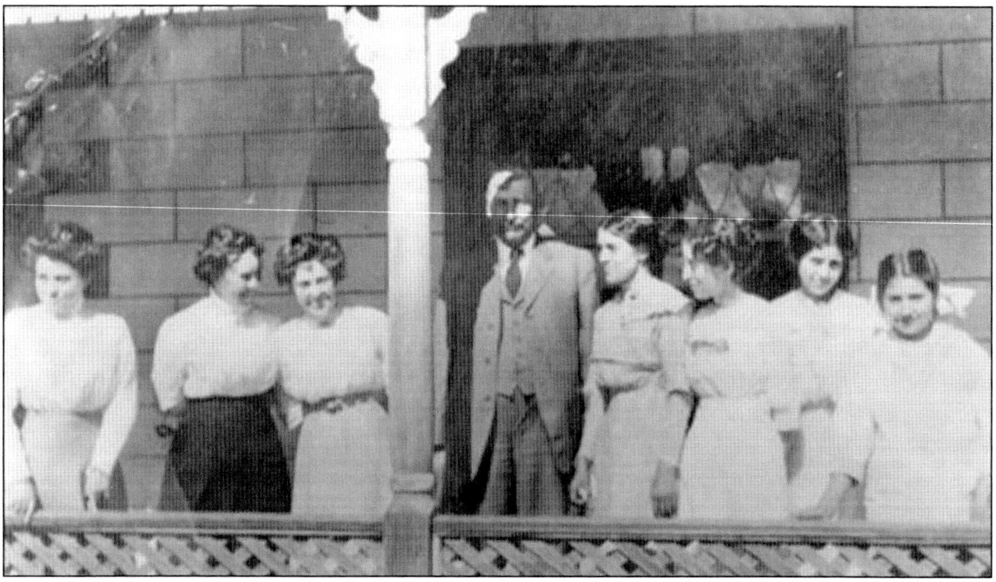

Pictured in front of this Spanish territorial style portal and home is A.A. Salazar and his seven daughters. In 1874, Salazar married one of Dario Gallegos's daughters, 14-year-old Genoveva. He bought an interest in the town's first mercantile store and livestock to form the partnership of Salazar and Gallegos. A.A. Salazar bought Gallegos's interest in 1894 and resumed the business as A.A. Salazar. (Courtesy of Diana Cortez.)

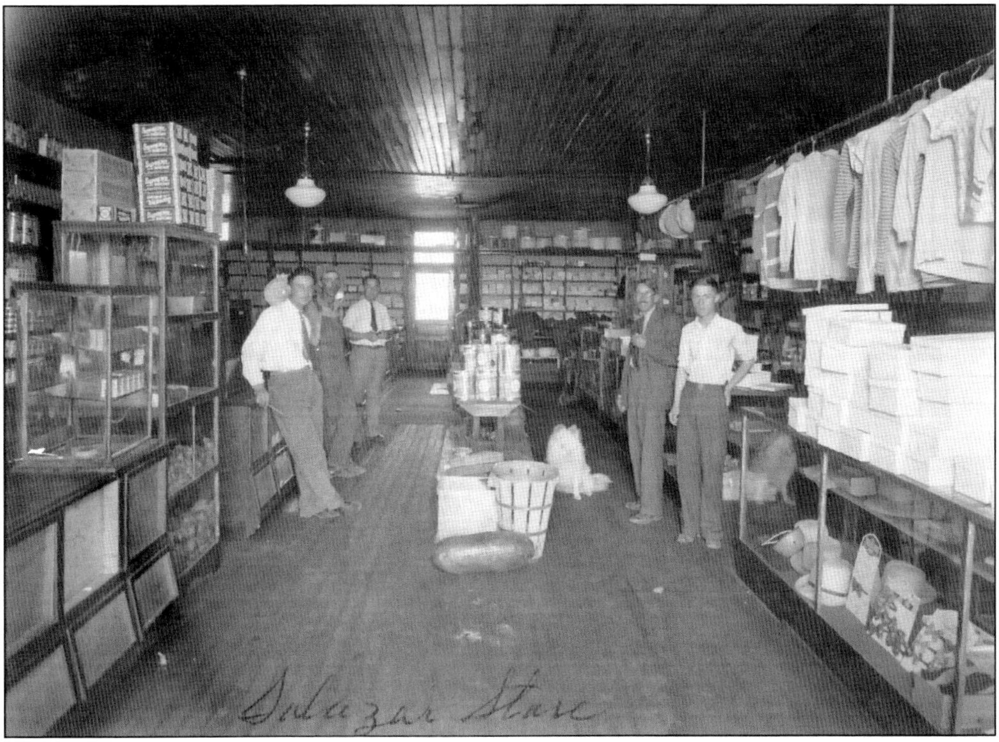

Unidentified men pose inside the Salazar store in 1929. Possibly, one of the men pictured is owner Delfino Salazar, whose improvements to the store included added floor space for storing machinery and hardware. In addition to carrying dry goods, clothing, and shoes, the business expanded to the handling of sheep, lamb, and wool and raising vegetable crops. (Courtesy of Dario Gallegos family.)

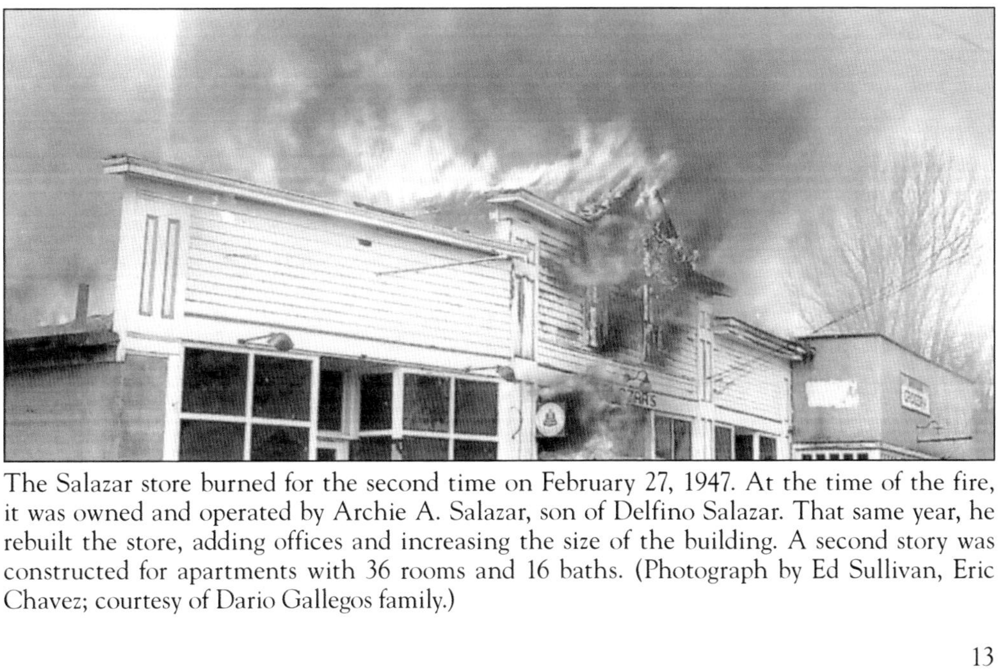

The Salazar store burned for the second time on February 27, 1947. At the time of the fire, it was owned and operated by Archie A. Salazar, son of Delfino Salazar. That same year, he rebuilt the store, adding offices and increasing the size of the building. A second story was constructed for apartments with 36 rooms and 16 baths. (Photograph by Ed Sullivan, Eric Chavez; courtesy of Dario Gallegos family.)

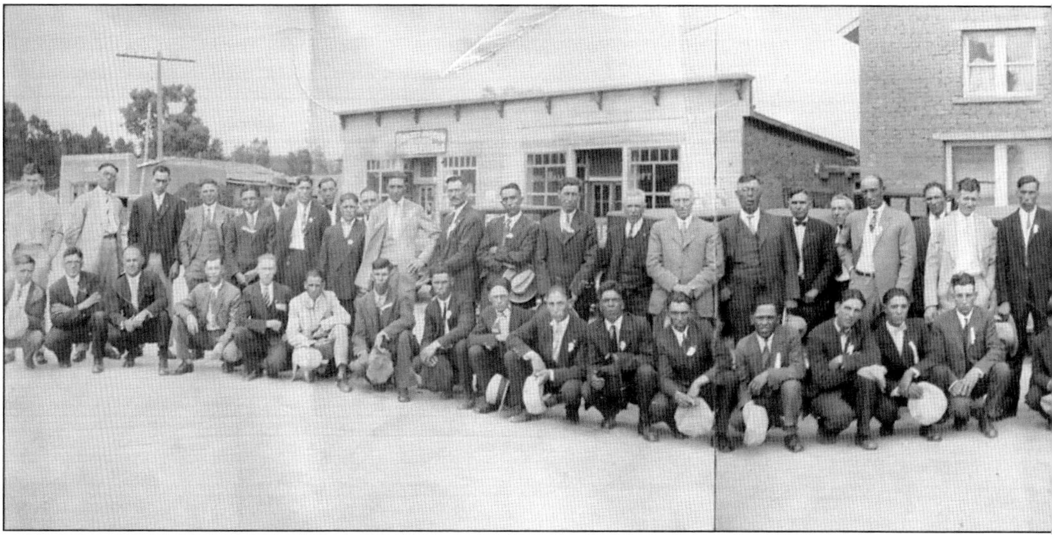

This group of gentlemen pictured in front of the local SPMDTU building (currently Sam's Covered Wagon Hall) is the Knights of Columbus Council No. 2620. Looking to garner sponsors for membership, the council drew together delegates from the Culebra River villages for the first Knights of Columbus initiation on August 12, 1927. From the left in the first row are Nesrala Zegob Sr. (third), Rosendo Jaquez (fifth), David Vialpando (11th), Anastacio Sanchez (12th), Juan

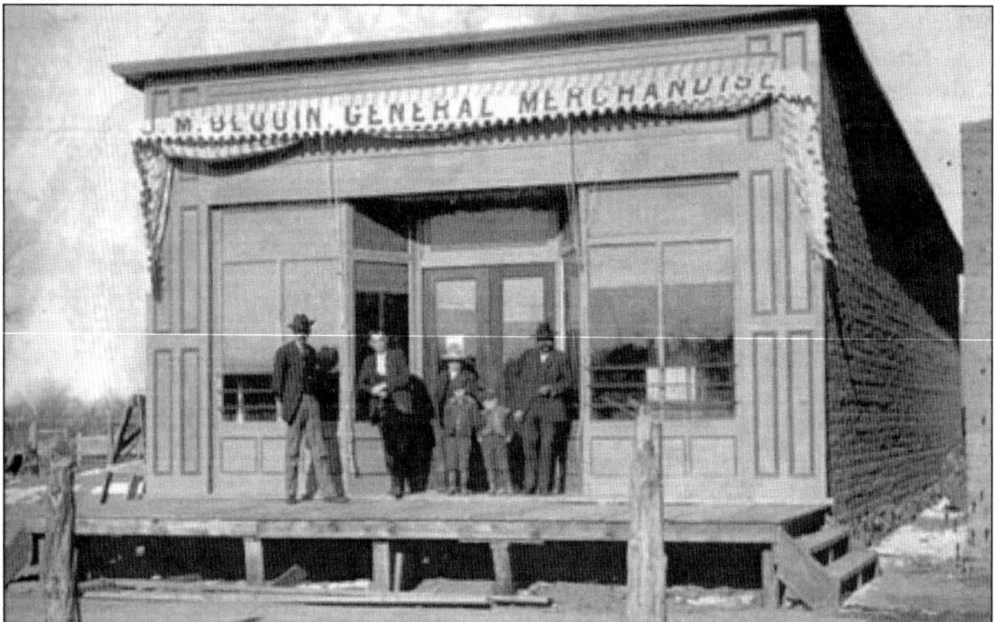

Pictured in 1910 in front of Olguín General Merchandise in San Luis are, from left to right, Armand Choury, Miguel Martinez, Rosendo Valdez, Diego Gallegos (child), Maclovio Gallegos (child), and Jesús Maria "J.M." Olguín, the owner of the mercantile. Olguín ran the business with his brother-in-law and store clerk, Miguel Martinez. In the early 1920s, before Prohibition, J.M. Olguín II had a partnership in a restaurant here with other family members. They were the first business to get a liquor license in San Luis after waiting on the sidewalk for hours in Denver. The store was later called Olguín SAV-U-MOR. The store closed in 1953. (Courtesy of Francisco A. Gallegos.)

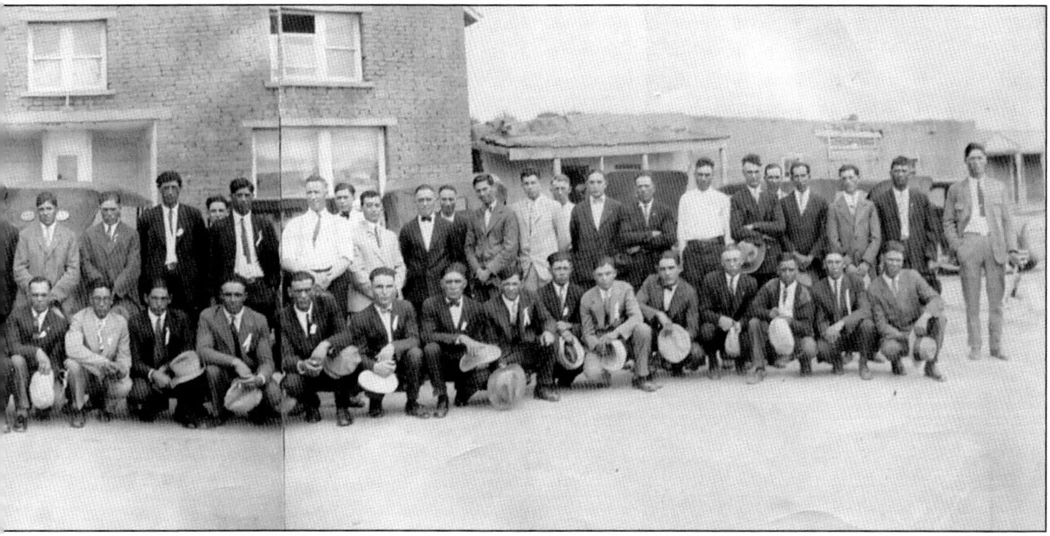

Estevan Medina (15th), Mariano Sanchez (16th), Eutimio Vialpando (18th), Antonio Sanchez (19th), Moises Vialpando (20th), Manuel Espinoza Sr. (21st), Ernesto Cardenas Sr. (24th), and Agapito Olivas (27th). Standing at far right in the second row is Fred Mascarenas, and standing 25th from right is Alejandro Vialpando (the author's paternal great-grandfather). The other men are unidentified. (Courtesy of Pat and Lorraine Gallegos.)

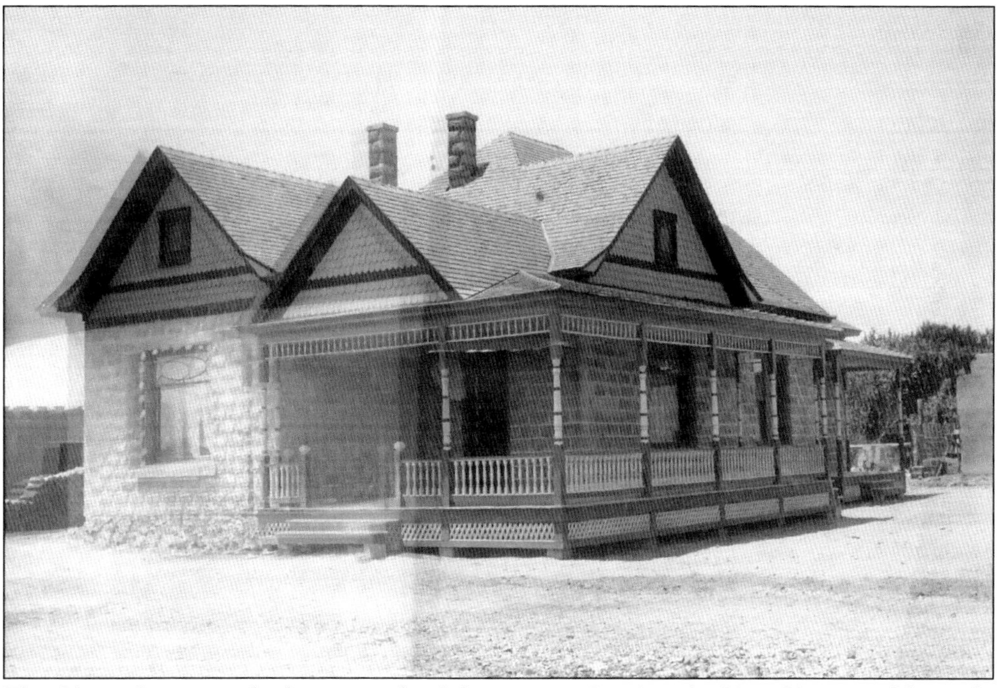

The Olguín home was built just south of the store in San Luis by J.M. Olguín and his wife, Beatrice Valdez Olguín. While this territorial style adobe home with surrounding portal was being built, the family lived in the back in the original adobe plaza, where they stored goods for the store. The Olguín family sponsored and raised local youngsters to send them to school to be educated. Siblings Felix Maestas and Pablita Maestas-Jaquez were two children raised by the Olguín family. (Courtesy of Henrietta Mascarenas.)

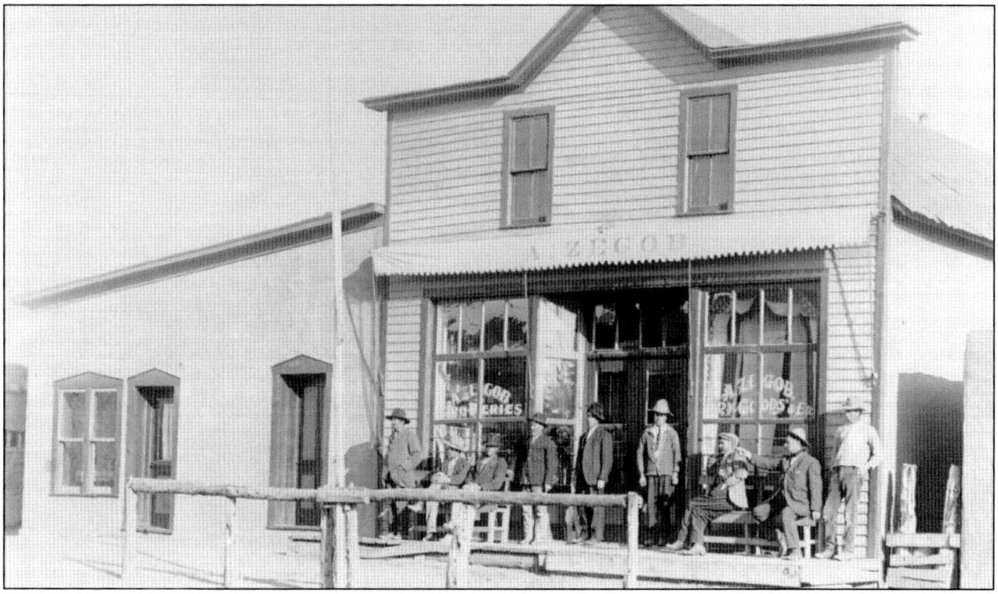

Pictured above are Antonio Zegob, his nephew Nesrala, and a group of companions gathered in front of the A. Zegob store in the 1920s. As a child, Antonio Zegob came to the United States with an uncle from Tripoli, Lebanon, and became an American citizen. Many years later, Antonio's mother and three sisters came to the United States. One sister, Rose, and her husband, Michael Tabar, came with their two-year-old son, Nesrala. In 1898, Rose gave birth to a daughter, Olga, in Stamford, Connecticut. In time, her husband returned to Lebanon. In search of their brother, Antonio, sisters Rose, Bahia, and Adla ventured into the vast San Luis Valley. Once they found him, both Antonio and Rose peddled dry goods out of suitcases door-to-door. In 1905, the bishop of Denver and Father Joseph Garcia of Most Precious Blood Catholic Church sold Antonio land to build his store. Antonio's sister Bahia operated a candy and ice cream shop in the adjacent adobe house. In 1906, Rose died of cancer. Antonio and his wife, Margarite Salazar Zegob, adopted Rose's two children, who both took the name Zegob. The young children grew up in the mercantile business, and in the 1920s, Nesrala Zegob became a partner in the store. He married Edna Vigil in 1921. Below, Antontio Zegob proudly stands in the interior of his store around 1910. (Both, courtesy of Zegob family.)

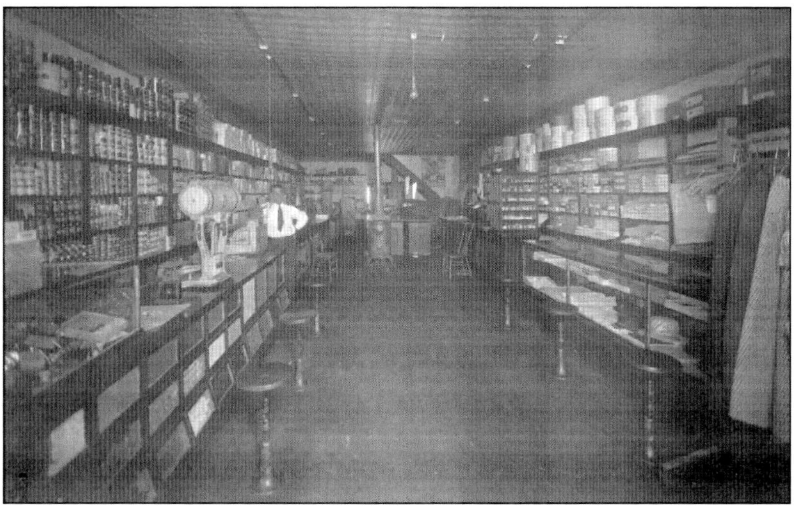

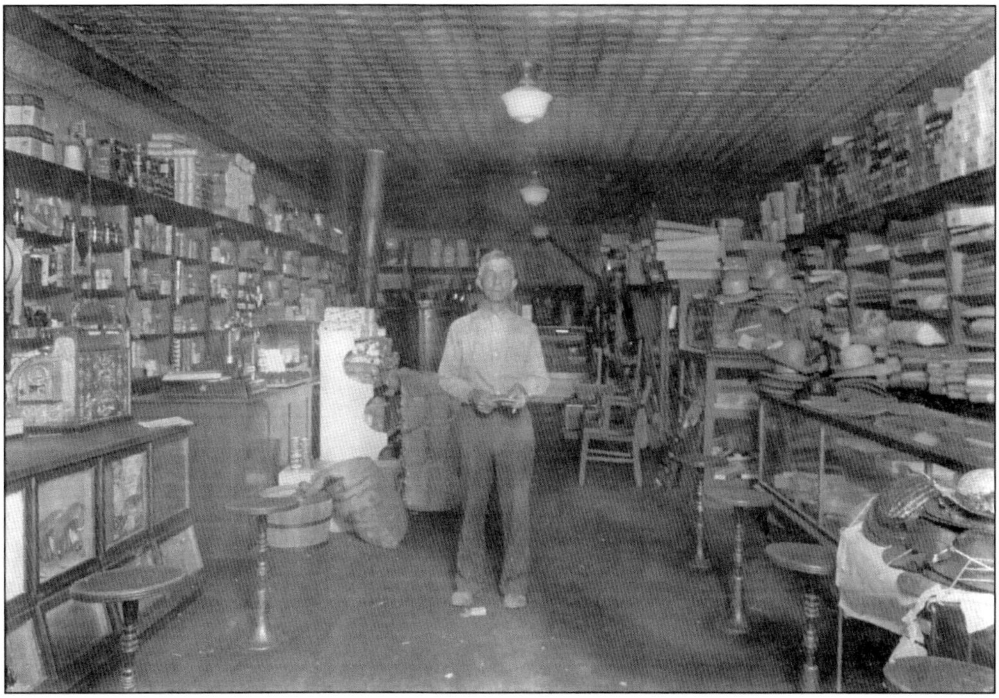

Surrounded by dry goods and groceries, Nesrala Zegob Sr. poses within his store. The young man gained a controlling interest in the business in 1936. Older residents referred to Nesrala Sr. as "Mestrario," and the store as La Tienda de Mestrario. (Courtesy of Zegob family.)

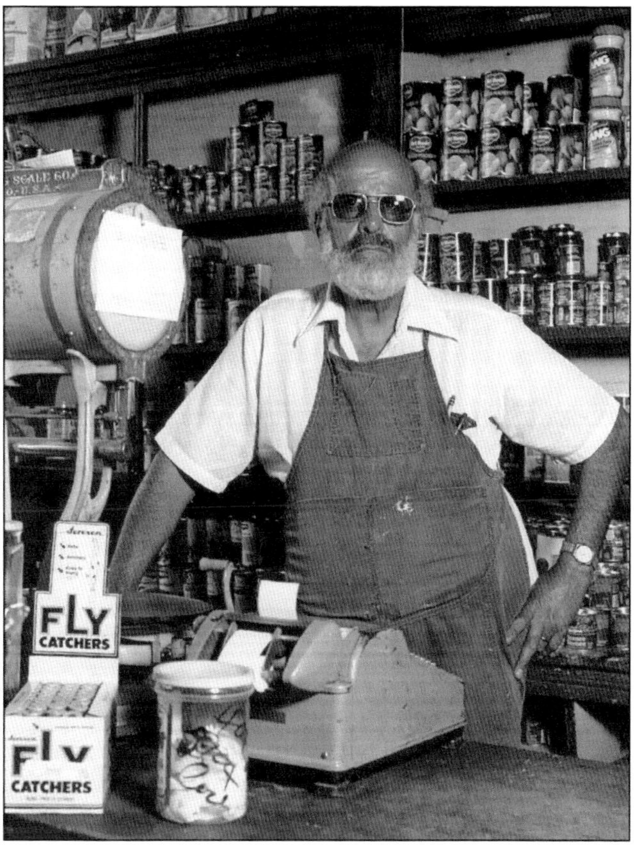

Nesrala Zegob Jr. married Mary Jane Eichman in June 1952, and he took over the store in July of that year. He is pictured here around 1970. The iconic scale pictured next to Nesrala is fondly remembered by many San Luis residents. (Courtesy of Zegob family.)

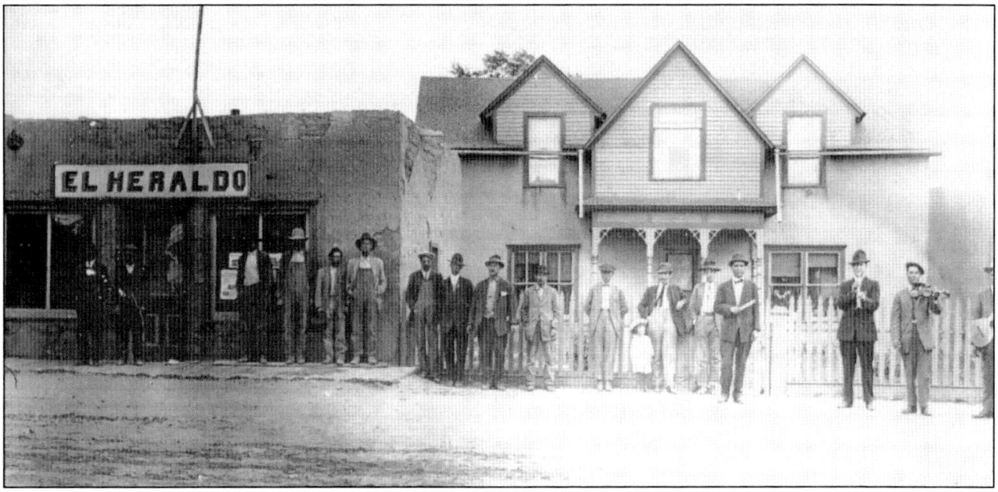

The office of the local newspaper, *El Heraldo del Valle*, was a meeting place and hub for information and regional news in the early 1900s. Pictured in the center around 1916 with a black tie and leaning against the fence is editor and publisher Juan Ramos Valdez. Valdez ran the newspaper from the late 1800s to 1940. The child next to him is his son, Ruben Valdez, born in 1912. Ruben later continued as editor and publisher of the newspaper from 1940 to 1949. The man to the left of his son is José Candelario de la Luz "J.C.K." Valdez, who served as Costilla County treasurer, justice of the peace, and sheriff. The tall man fourth from the left is José Torres, who is related to Cordy Arellano and lived in the Cordillera. The man with the violin is Ross Valdez's father, Flaviano Valdez. The home in the background belonged to the family of Juan Ramos and Gavinita Rodriquez Valdez. (Courtesy of Dora and Augustin Padilla.)

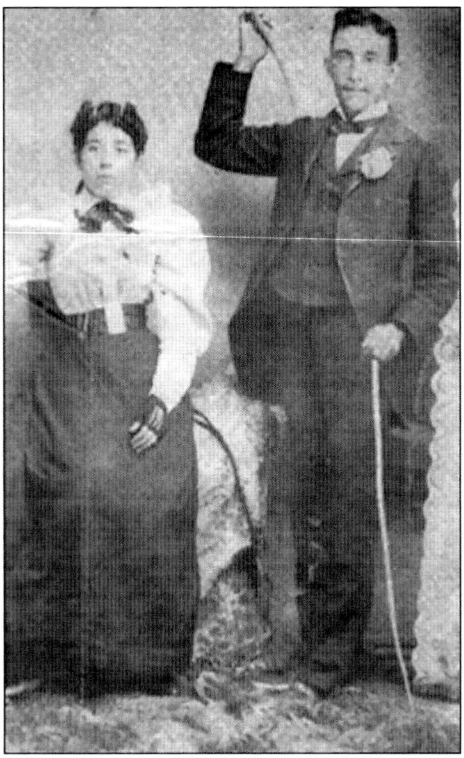

This is Juan Ramos Valdez and his wife, Gavinita Rodriguez Valdez, around 1901. Juan Ramos was a newspaper man who started *El Heraldo del Valle* in the late 1800s. The Valdez family had seven children, four of whom died in infancy, one at seven years of age. The only surviving son, Ruben, continued in his father's footsteps, and in 1940, became editor and publisher of *El Heraldo.* (Courtesy of Charlie Jaquez Jr.)

Friends and well-known businessmen Emilio Lobato Sr. and Juan Ramos Valdez, editor of *El Heraldo del Valle*, pose for a *Life* magazine photographer in 1961. Valdez, a man well educated on the history of San Luis, was 90 years old when this photograph was taken. The local politician and newspaper editor and publisher are pictured in the Costilla County courthouse. The Lobato family always said that Don Ramos was giving Lobato a lecture. (Courtesy of Henrietta Mascarenas.)

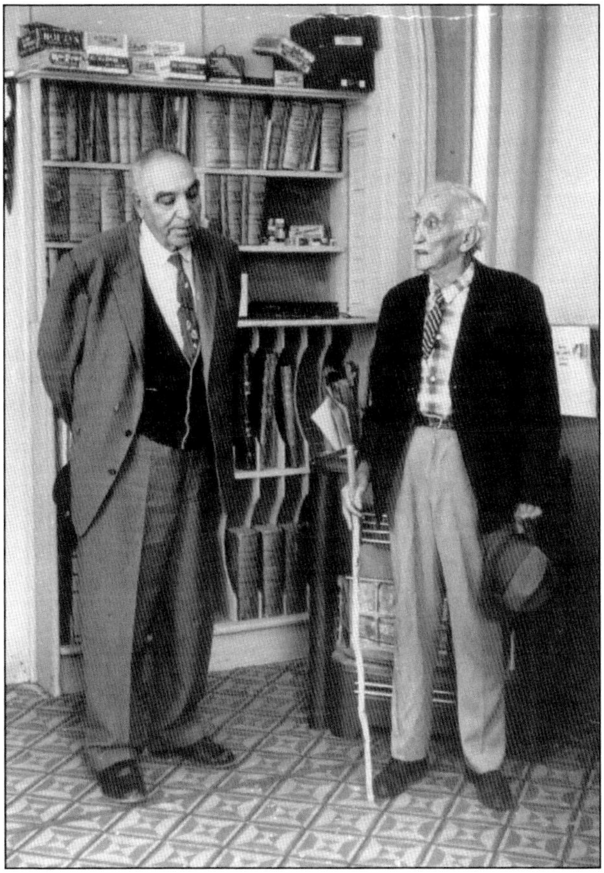

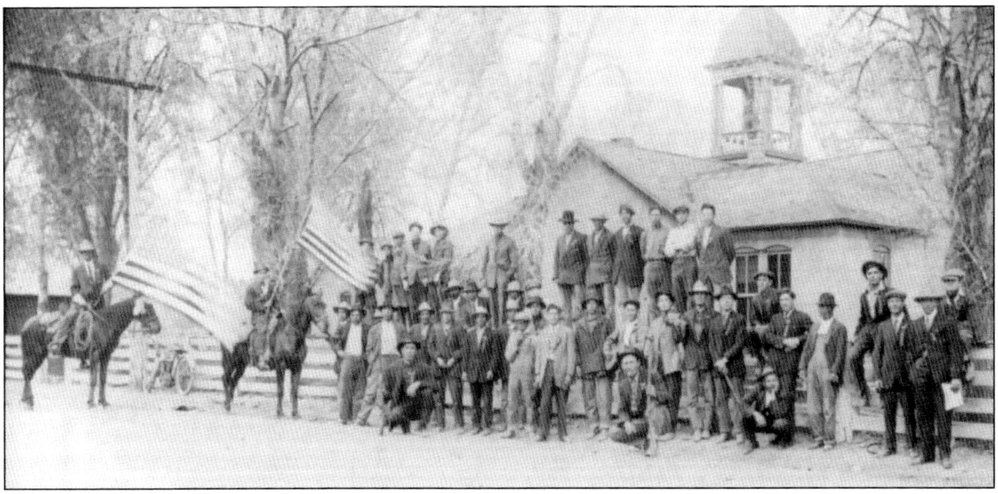

An unidentified group of men, possibly members of the Hispanic fraternal organization SPMDTU, gathered in 1913 for a picture in front of the Costilla County courthouse in San Luis. Significant to Colorado history, the building is the state's oldest courthouse structure. A public use building constructed of adobe, the courthouse marks the center of the community. On November 1, 1861, the Act of the first Colorado Territorial Assembly approved the construction of county courthouses for Colorado's 16 counties. (Courtesy of Darryl E. Garcia.)

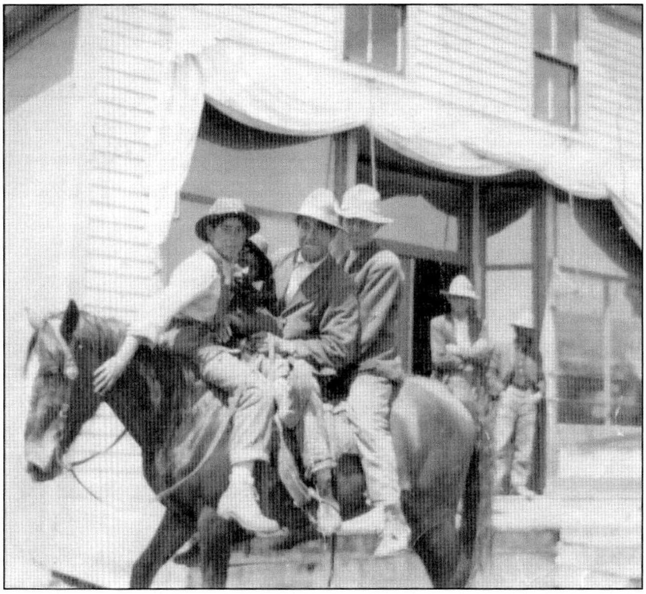

A group of locals pose in front of the Chama Mercantile Store in Chama, Colorado, in 1912. The store was opened by Emilio Lobato Sr. in 1907. He owned the store for 36 years. The Lobatos sold farm equipment, groceries, household items, clothing, and shoes during the Depression. They volunteered time with the Office of Price Administration to give certificates for cans of food during World War II. When the store closed, the owners allowed the community members to help themselves to the remaining items. (Courtesy of Henrietta Mascarenas.)

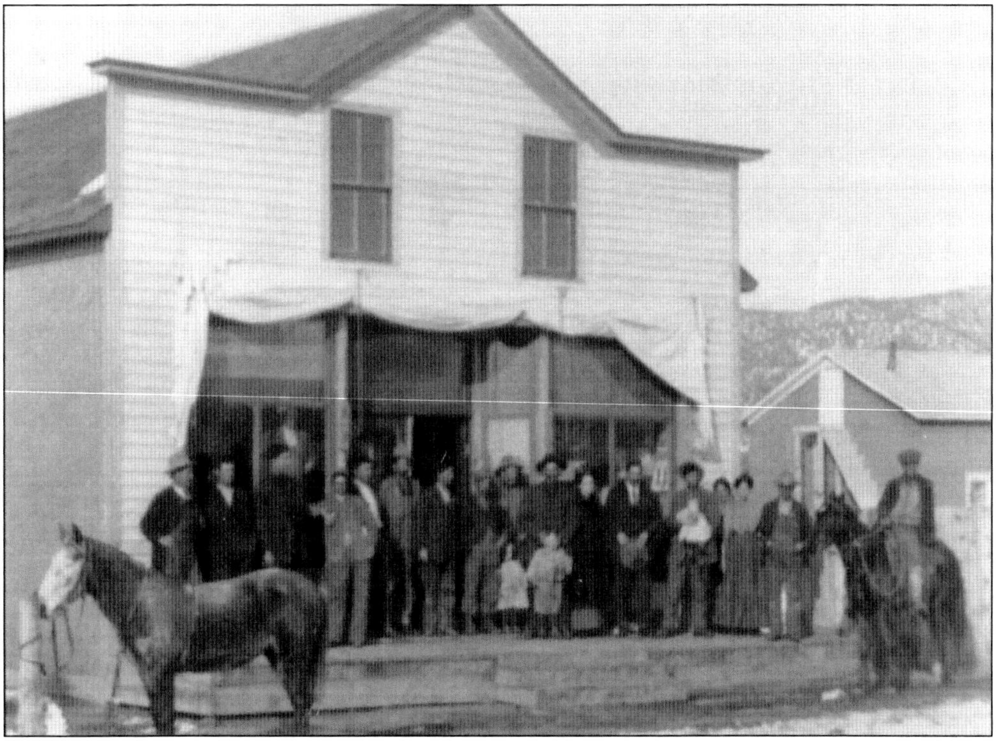

Another group in front of the store in 1913 are, from right to left, Adolfo Vialpando (on the horse), Farris Jaquez (white hat), Elvina Vialpando (wife of Felipe Vialpando), Crucita Sanchez Lobato, Felipe Vialpando (holding an unidentified baby boy), Emilio Lobato Sr., wife Enriqueta Choury Lobato, and father José Francisco Lobato (the owners of the store), Adrian Lobato (Francisco's son standing in front), Antonio Albert, Demetrio Jaquez (second to the last), Enrique Lobato (Francisco's son), and others. (Courtesy of Eugene and Josie Lobato)

Pictured here is Emilio Lobato Sr. with his wife, Enriqueta, holding their first born child, Elizabeth (Bessie) Concepción Lobato, born on November 4, 1912. The photograph was taken in front of their Chama home in 1913 in celebration of the child's baptism. (Courtesy of Henrietta Mascarenas.)

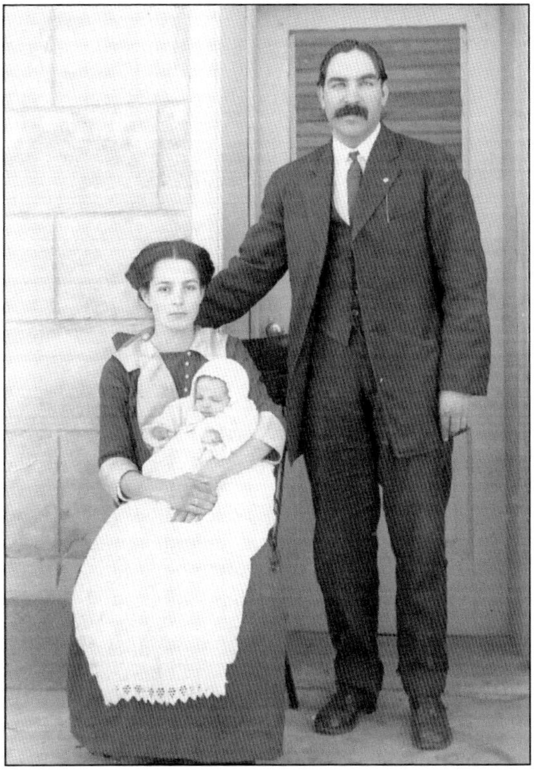

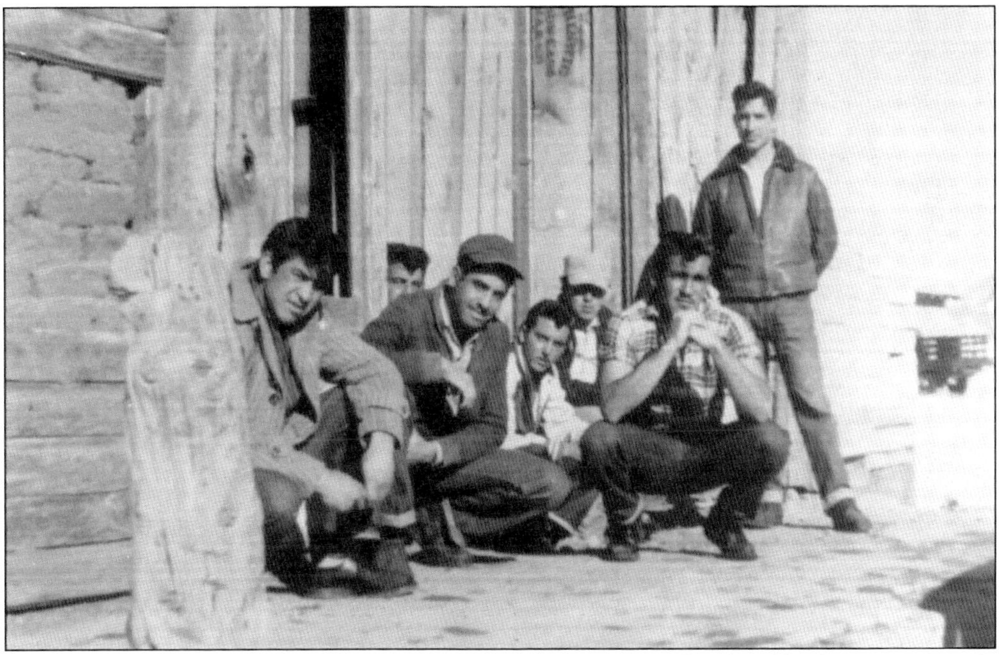

These young men gathered in front of the local hangout, La Sala, the old Chama Mercantile Store in Chama, around 1957. From left to right are Fred "Chispas" Sanchez, 17-year-old Marcos Lobato (back), Elisardo Espinoza, Elmer Valdez, Gilbert Albert, Bonifacio "Bonnie" Lobato, and James "Jaime" Mascarenas (standing). (Courtesy of Henrietta Mascarenas.)

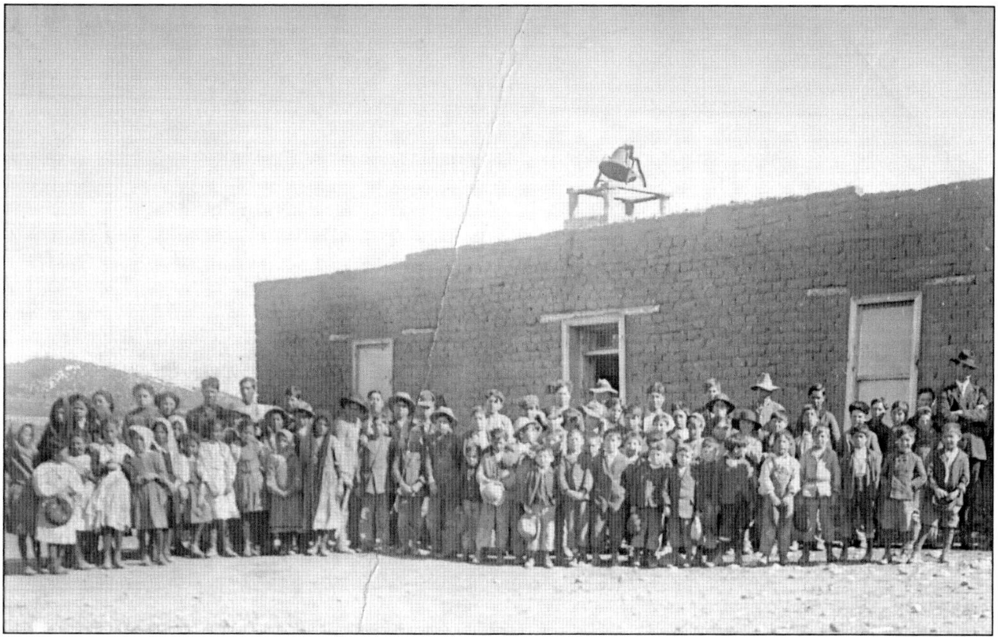

School-age children pose with their teacher, Robert Choury (the tall man at back right) in front of the Chama School around the late 1920s. The school building, with exposed adobe bricks, served students from the first to eighth grades. Soon after this photograph was taken, the school burned down. It was rebuilt in 1940. In the interim, students attended school at the local dance hall, Sala de Vale. (Courtesy of Henrietta Mascarenas.)

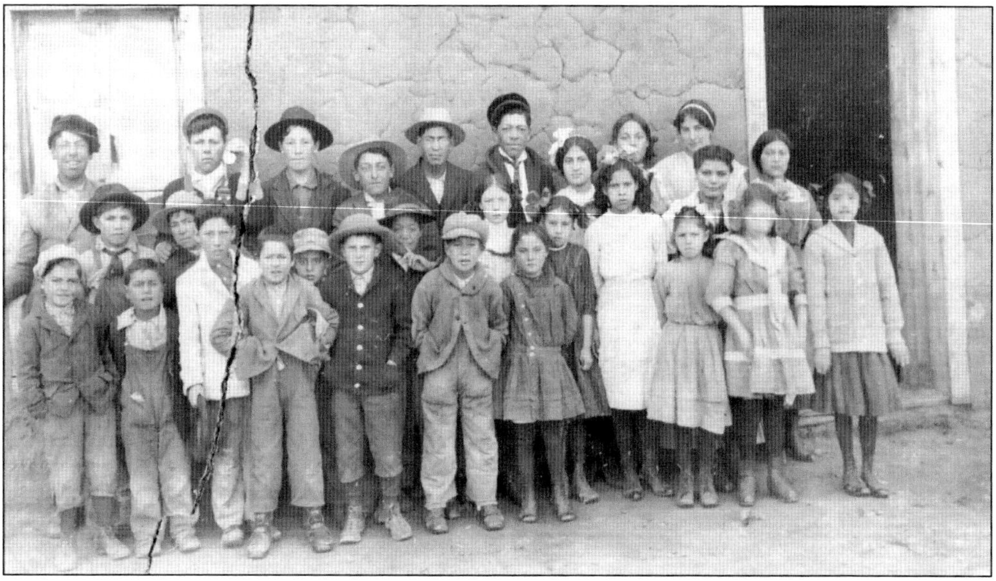

Young students are pictured around 1930 in front of the Corrillera School with their teacher, Clotilde Choury Wilson (back right with the white ribbon), age 22. The building was a multipurpose facility, used as a dance hall and meeting place. This public school was organized in 1885. The school was located in La Corrillera near the present home of the late George and Collie Valdez. (Courtesy of Henrietta Mascarenas)

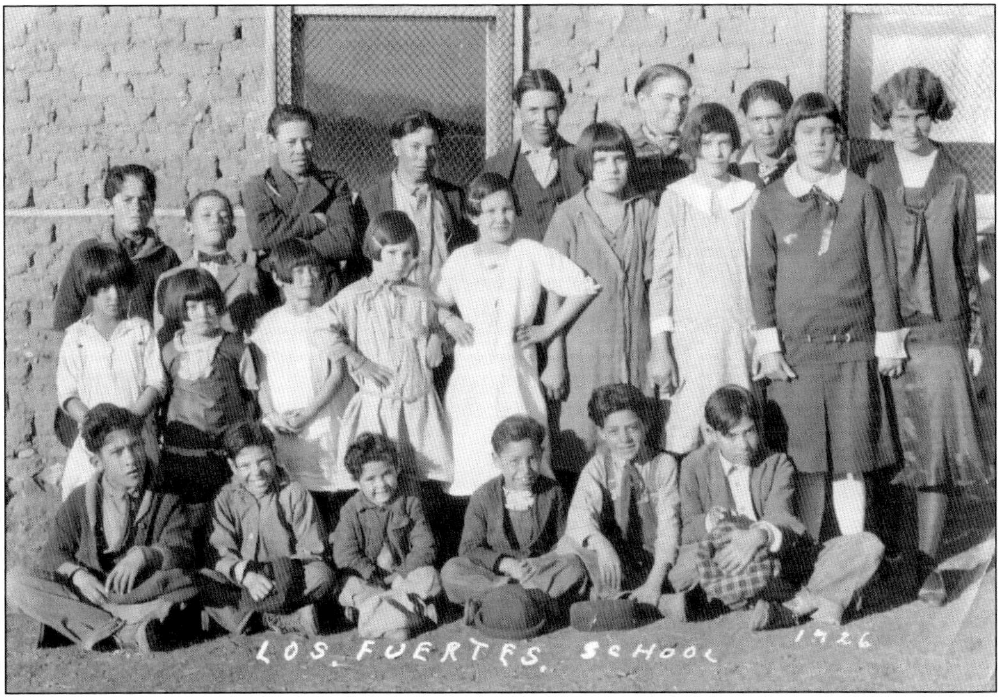

Pictured in 1926 at Los Fuertes School are, from left to right, (first row) Pablo Mondragon, Armando Valdez, Rosenaldo Mondragon, Charlie Vigil, Roberto Valdez, and Eleazar Valdez; (second row) Eduvigen Mondragon, Ramoncita Mondragon, Esther Valdez, Libby Medina, Bernarda Medina, Maclovia Mondragon, Beatriz Valdez, Celsa Valdez, and Clea Bailey (the teacher); (third row) Rosendo Mondragon, Charlie Taylor, Bernabe Medina, Felix Valdez, Charlie Medina, Edward Vigil, and Margarito Mondragon. The Los Fuertes School District was organized in 1858. (Courtesy of Pat Trujillo VanZandt.)

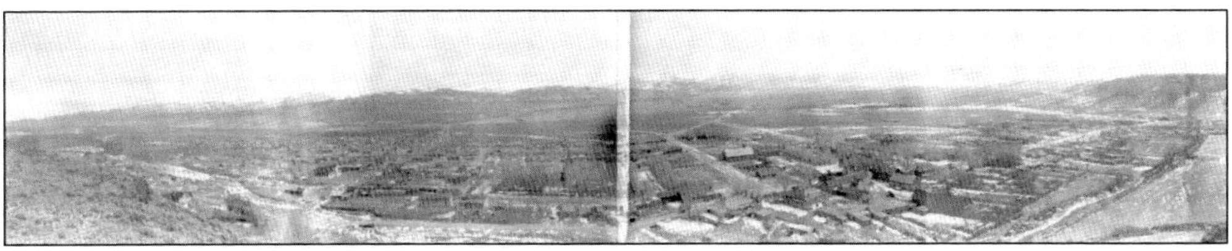

This 1928 panoramic photograph of San Luis by Mr. McDonald of Del Norte, Colorado, was taken from San Pedro Mesa looking toward the Sangre de Cristo Mountains to the east. The view of the town shows the Salazar house, the local school and tower in a residential area, an icehouse, Most Precious Blood Church, the Valencia Hotel, a livery and feed stable, the SPMDTU building, the Costilla County courthouse, the Zegob store, the Barela store, Olguín Mercantile, and the Salazar store. Prior to 1900, the Salazar family platted the Salazar addition east of what is now Highway 159. This area, known as Cuba, was built prior to 1920. (Courtesy of Huberto Maestas.)

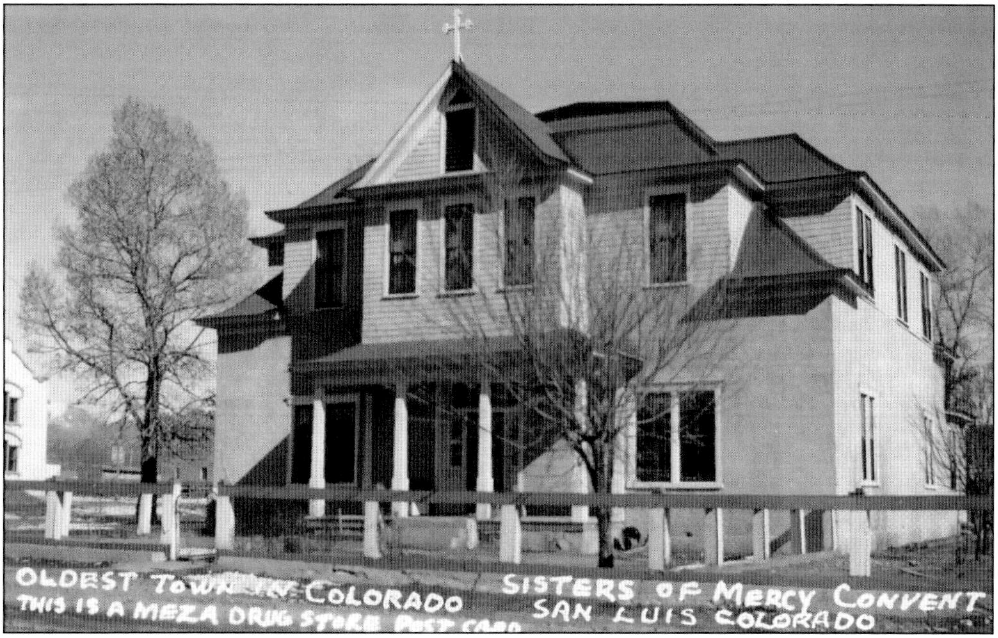

Father Samuel Garcia's ambitious construction project was the founding of a convent and school. In 1904, he established an elementary school, the same year he recruited the Sisters of Mercy to teach around 30 students in San Luis. A high school was started in 1909. The Sisters of Mercy convent housed the sisters in the upper level and a chapel, classrooms, kitchen, and common dining area on the lower level, which also served as the school. In the 1990s, the Sisters of Mercy Convent was renovated and converted into El Convento Bed & Breakfast. (Courtesy of Olivia Maestas family.)

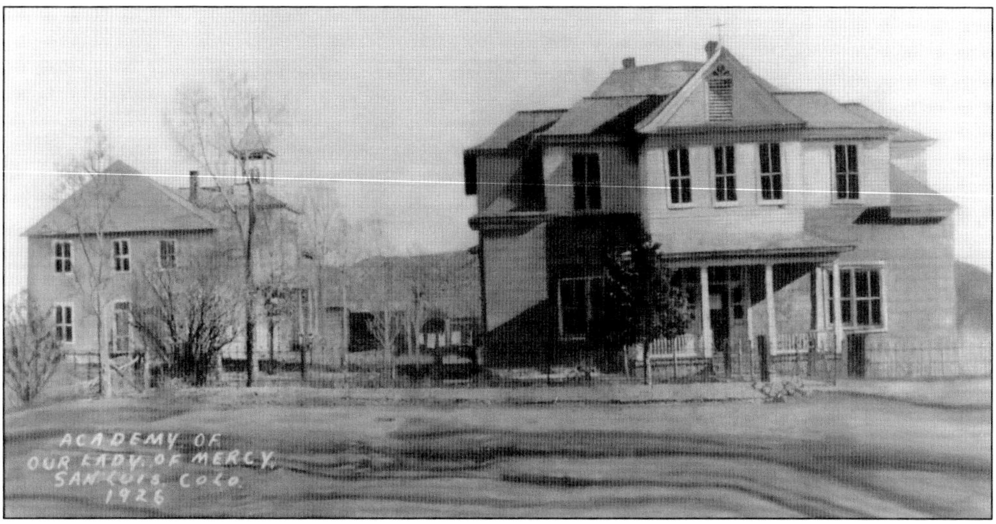

The Academy of Our Lady of Mercy in 1926 was a convent and school run by the Sisters of Mercy from the St. Louis Province. Pictured at left is Mercy High School, which was constructed because the old convent could not house the growing number of students. The building had several rooms and a large auditorium. The schools in the outlying Culebra villages generally taught classes up to the eighth grade. If students wished to further their schooling, they had to attend Mercy High School in San Luis or go elsewhere. (Courtesy of Sangre de Cristo Parish.)

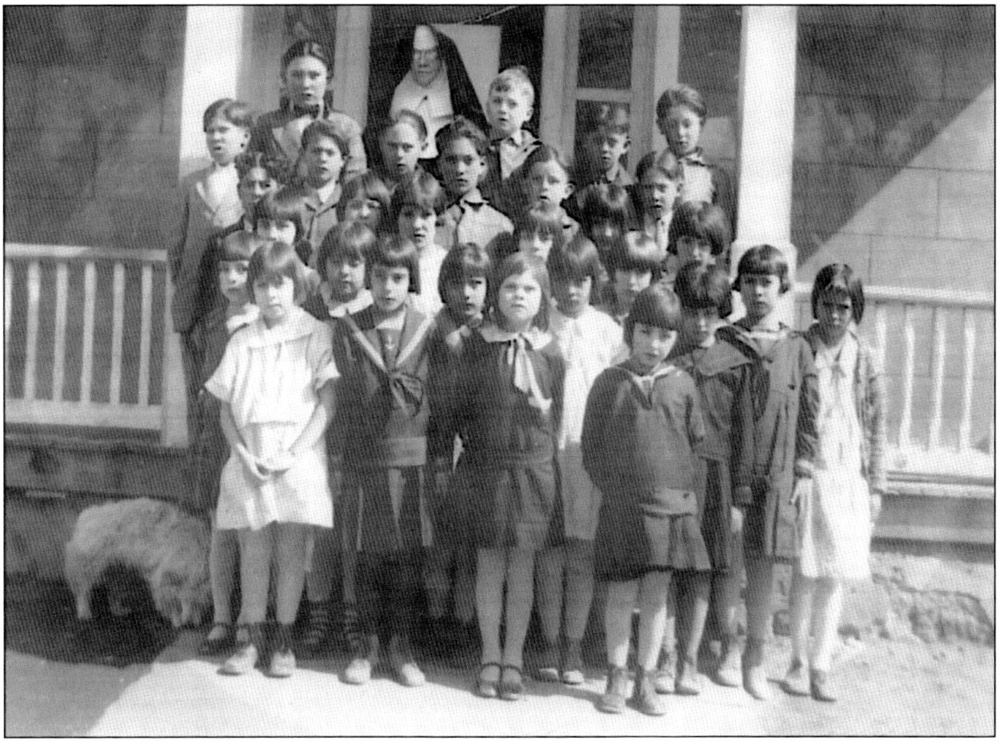

A Sister of Mercy teacher and her students pose in front of Academy of Our Lady of Mercy in San Luis in the 1920s. The Sangre de Cristo Parish established Mercy Academy in 1904–1905, and it was the only high school in the county until 1953. School District No. 1 was organized in San Luis in 1856. The Sisters of Mercy were strict disciplinarians, usually tolerating no nonsense. The students had to learn English first in order to study the three Rs. (Courtesy of Sangre de Cristo Parish.)

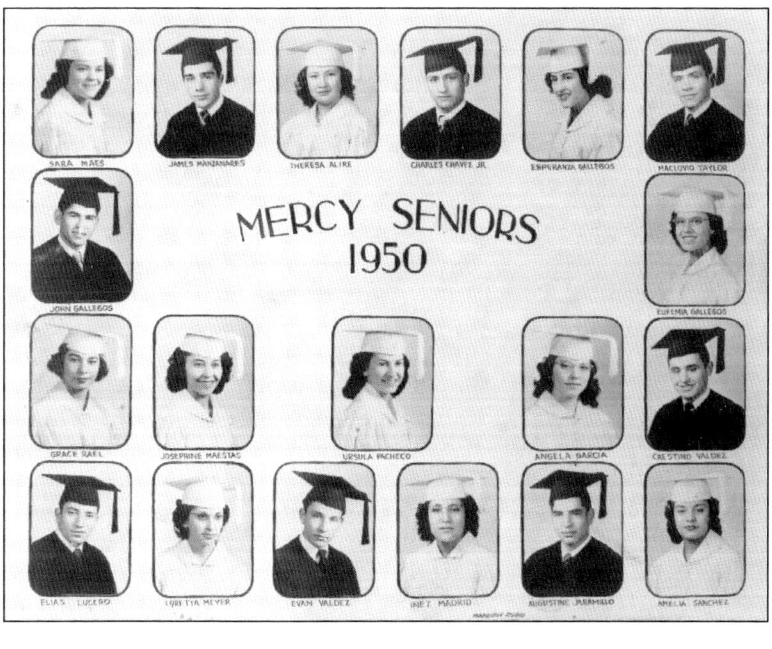

Mercy High School seniors are pictured in this composite of the graduating class of 1950. Students from the surrounding Culebra villages would attend Mercy High School in San Luis. (Courtesy of Evan A. Valdez.)

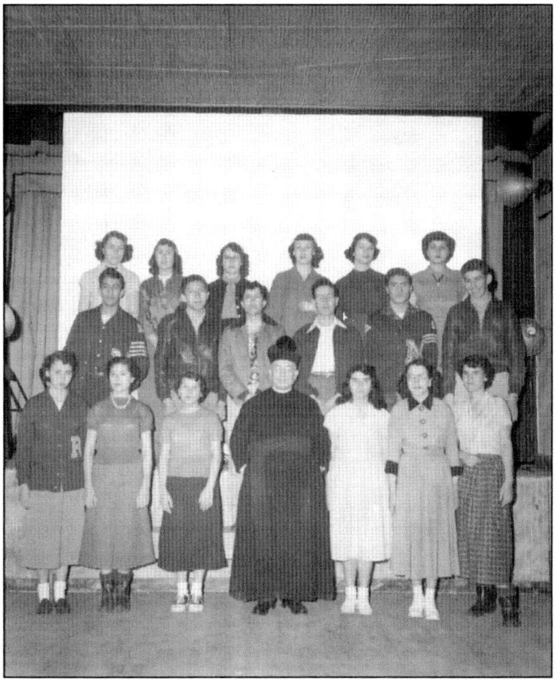

Eighteen students were part of the 1952 senior class of Mercy High School in San Luis. Pictured with Father Onofrey "Humphrey" Mortorell (first row, center) are, from left to right, (first row) Joan Vigil, Helen Olivas, Lisaida Garcia, Casilda Segura, Henrietta Lobato, and Carmel Jaramillo; (second row) Procopio Vigil, Abel Medina, Fred Sanchez, Rudy Madrid, Fermin Cordova, and Eloy "Easy" Cordova; (third row) Julia Gallegos, Ruth Vigil, Cecelia Vigil, Patricia Pacheco, Mariella Pacheco, and Anna Maria Sanchez. Not pictured are Damion Velasquez, Leo Rael, and Eugene Lobato. (Courtesy of Henrietta Mascarenas.)

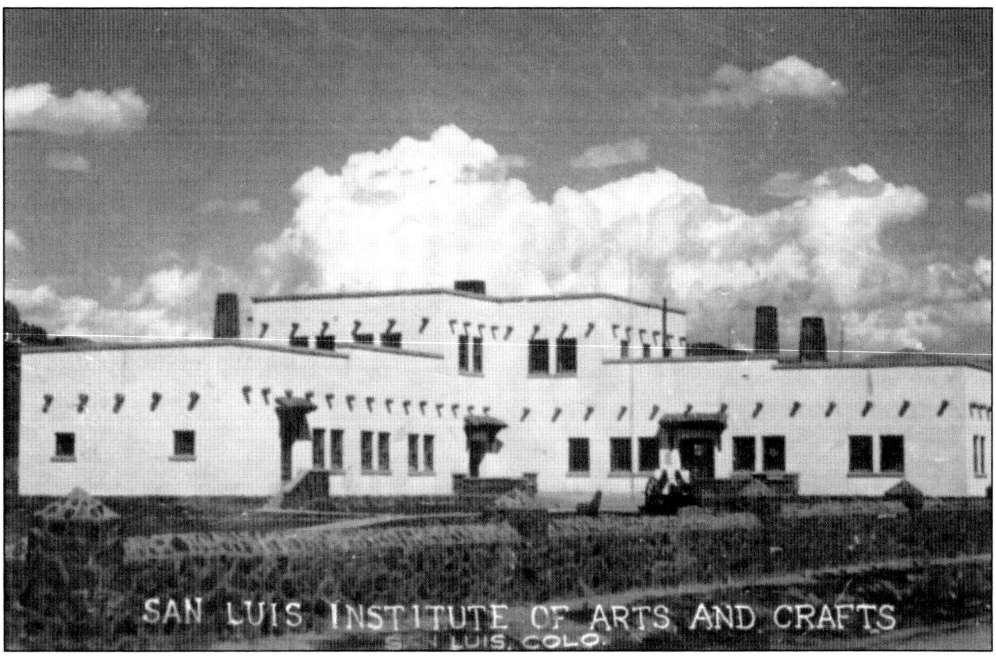

The San Luis Institute of Arts and Crafts opened as an extension of Adams State Teachers' College in November 1943. The building, an old Works Progress Administration (WPA) building given to the state at no cost, was used as a division of the college and was improved upon with help from faculty, students, and volunteers. A vital asset to the community, the school aided in furthering the education of many Spanish American students. The building is presently being restored to house the Sangre de Cristo Heritage Center. (Courtesy of Richard de Olivas y Cordova.)

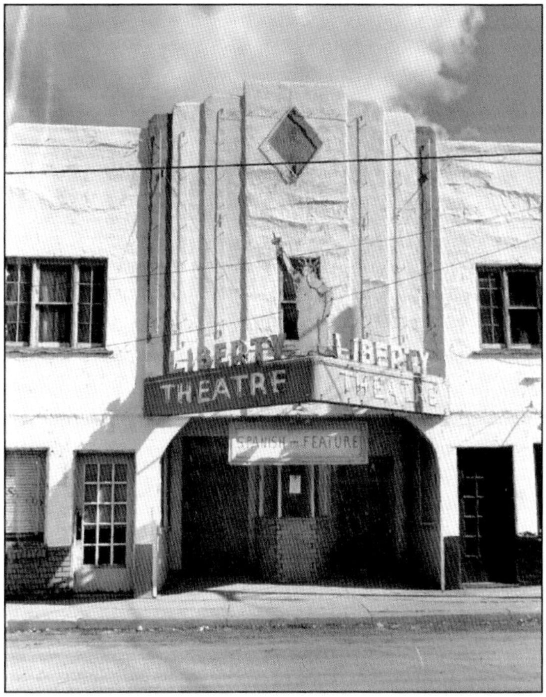

Owned by Mike Joseph, the Liberty Theatre was one of two theaters located in the central business district of San Luis, the other being the San Luis Theatre across the street by R&R Market. Families attended the movies on Sunday afternoons for 25¢ per person. It cost 10¢ for the movie and 15¢ for a drink and popcorn. Newsreels, such as those produced during World War II, would come on before the featured movie. The theater had a mezzanine, and many times was standing room only. The theater building was destroyed in the 1980s. (Courtesy of Sangre de Cristo Heritage Center)

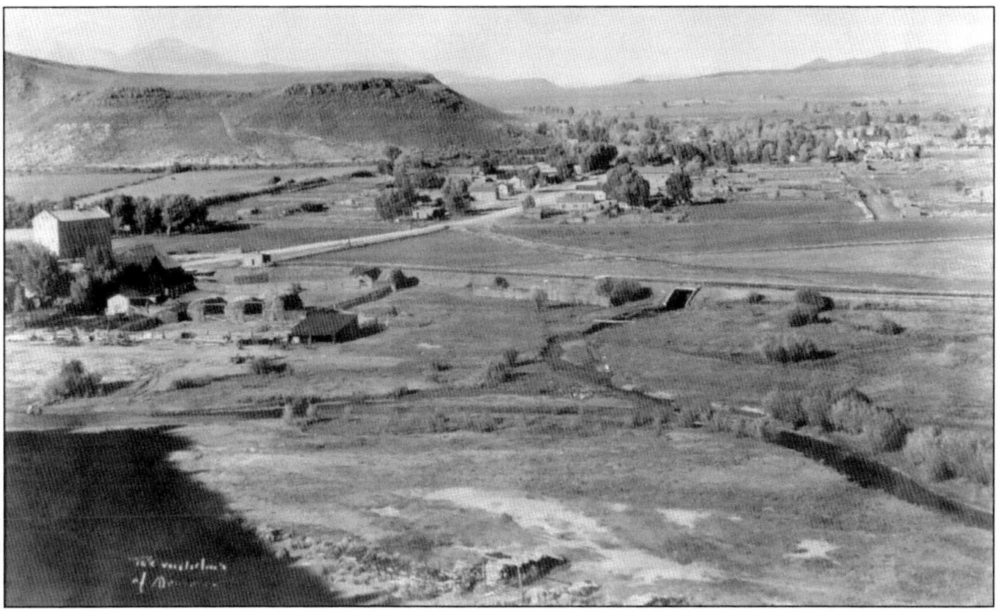

This view of San Luis looking north from San Pedro Mesa shows the village of San Luis de la Culebra in 1929. In the foreground is Colorado's first modern flour mill, the St. Vrain–Easterday Flour Mill, established in 1859. The San Luis Mill (El Molino) supplied flour to mining camps in the northern parts of Colorado, the Denver region, and military forts north of El Paso. In 1860, within a year of establishing the mill, business partner Harvey Easterday told Ceran St. Vrain that the mill needed an official mailing address. According to historian Maria Mondragon Valdez, "he petitioned the Post Master General to grant the town a post office and call it San Luis." (Courtesy of Randy Pijoan and Marcella Pacheco.)

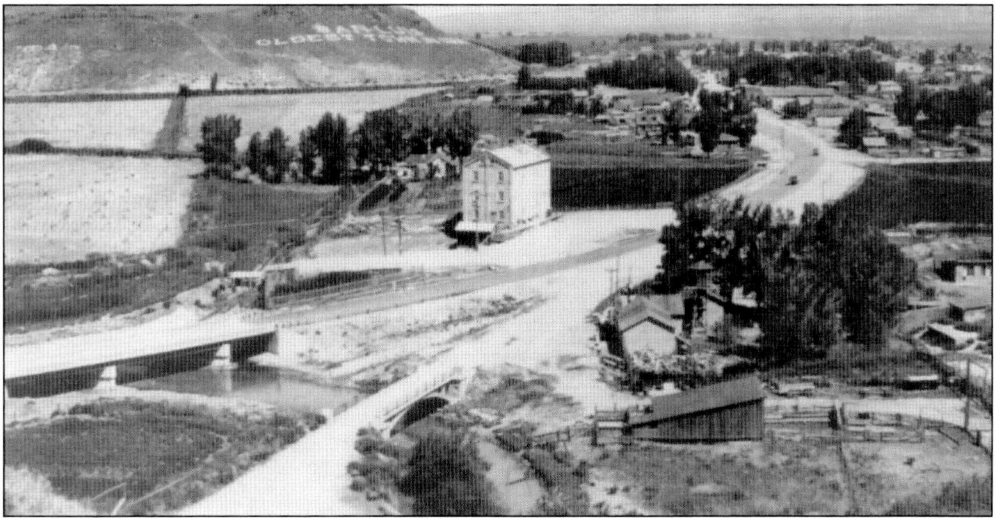

This c. 1937 photograph shows the mill next to the Culebra River and one of the earliest bridges in the area. When the mill was first built, it obtained water rights to 44 feet of water flow from the Culebra River. The mill structure was eventually moved west across the road. The new three-story building was constructed of cement. During the WPA era, self-taught artist and muralist Rafael Lucero created the rock inscription "San Luis, Oldest Town in Colorado," using whitewashed basalt rocks arranged across San Pedro Mesa, seen in the background. (Courtesy of Olivia Maestas family.)

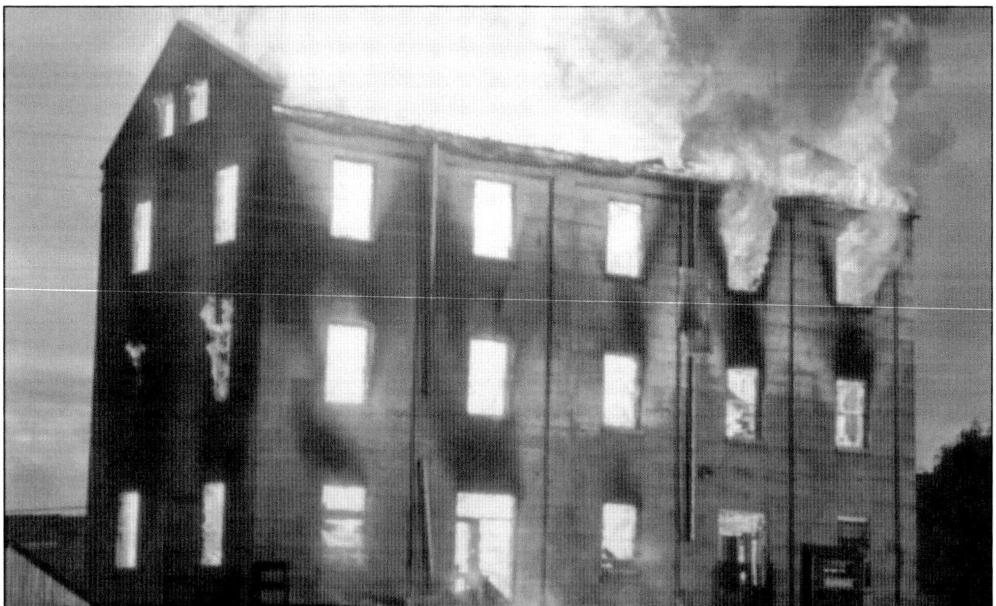

Between 1890 and 1949, the San Luis Roller Mill was under the ownership of the William S. Parrish family and later William's son, Bill Parrish. The three brands of flour sold were Pride of Our Valley, Colorado's Best, and Indian Made. People, including the Taos Pueblo natives, would come in their wagons to the mill, bringing wheat to be ground into flour. It burned in the early 1960s, and eventually, the remnants of Colorado's first modern flour mill had to be destroyed. (Courtesy of Darryl E. Garcia.)

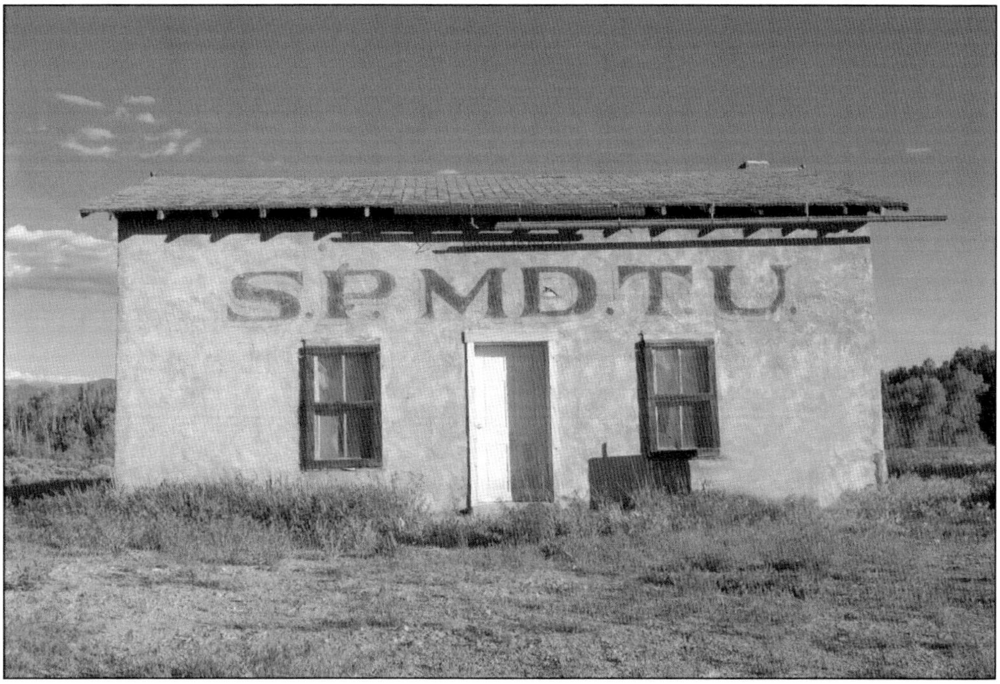

This adobe building in Chama was the local meeting lodge for the Sociedad Proteccion Mutua de Trabajadores Unidos. The SPMDTU is a mutual aid society that started in order to mobilize Spanish Americans against discrimination. It is the longest-standing Hispanic organization in the United States. The organization offered its members insurance policies, sickness subsidies, help with burial services, and unemployment benefits. The members (*mutualistas*) must be Latino males between 18 and 60 years of age, mentally competent, and practice *hermanismo*, or brotherhood. (Above, courtesy of Huberto Maestas; right, courtesy of Richard de Olivas y Cordova.)

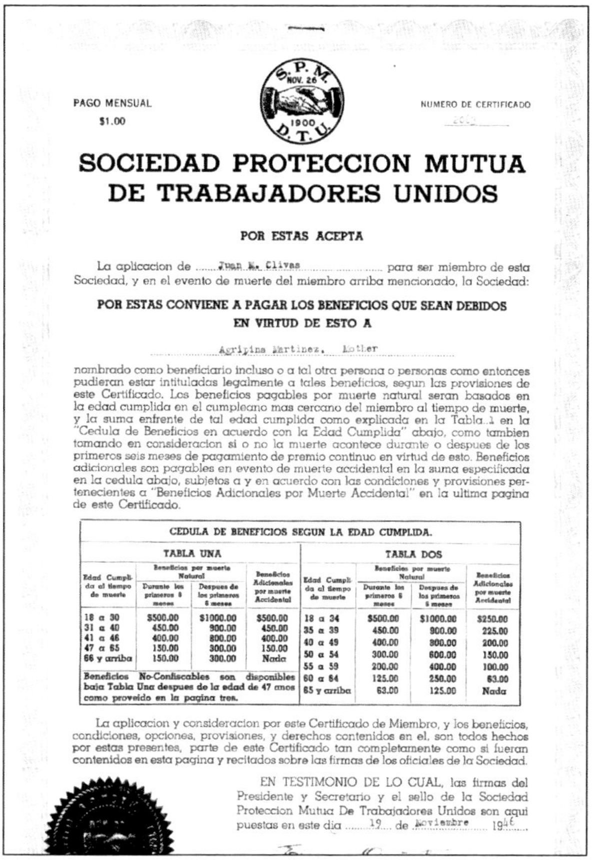

PAGO MENSUAL
$1.00

S.P.M. NOV. 26 1900 D.T.U.

NUMERO DE CERTIFICADO

SOCIEDAD PROTECCION MUTUA DE TRABAJADORES UNIDOS

POR ESTAS ACEPTA

La aplicacion de Juan M. Olivas para ser miembro de esta Sociedad, y en el evento de muerte del miembro arriba mencionado, la Sociedad:

POR ESTAS CONVIENE A PAGAR LOS BENEFICIOS QUE SEAN DEBIDOS EN VIRTUD DE ESTO A

Agripina Martinez, Mother

nombrado como beneficiario incluso o a tal otra persona o personas como entonces pudieran estar intituladas legalmente a tales beneficios, segun las provisiones de este Certificado. Los beneficios pagables por muerte natural seran basados en la edad cumplida en el cumpleano mas cercano del miembro al tiempo de muerte, y la suma enfrente de tal edad cumplida como explicada en la Tabla 1 en la "Cedula de Beneficios en acuerdo con la Edad Cumplida" abajo, como tambien tomando en consideracion si o no la muerte acontece durante o despues de los primeros seis meses de pagamiento de premio continuo en virtud de esto. Beneficios adicionales son pagables en evento de muerte accidental en la suma especificada en la cedula abajo, subjetos a y en acuerdo con las condiciones y provisiones pertenecientes a "Beneficios Adicionales por Muerte Accidental" en la ultima pagina de este Certificado.

CEDULA DE BENEFICIOS SEGUN LA EDAD CUMPLIDA.

TABLA UNA			
Edad Cumplida al tiempo de muerte	Beneficios por muerte Natural: Durante los primeros 6 meses	Beneficios por muerte Natural: Despues de los primeros 6 meses	Beneficios Adicionales por muerte Accidental
18 a 30	$500.00	$1000.00	$500.00
31 a 40	450.00	900.00	450.00
41 a 46	400.00	800.00	400.00
47 a 65	150.00	300.00	150.00
66 y arriba	150.00	300.00	Nada

Beneficios No-Confiscables son disponibles baja Tabla Una despues de la edad de 47 anos como proveido en la pagina tres.

TABLA DOS			
Edad Cumplida al tiempo de muerte	Beneficios por muerte Natural: Durante los primeros 6 meses	Beneficios por muerte Natural: Despues de los primeros 6 meses	Beneficios Adicionales por muerte Accidental
18 a 34	$500.00	$1000.00	$250.00
35 a 39	450.00	900.00	225.00
40 a 49	400.00	800.00	200.00
50 a 54	300.00	600.00	150.00
55 a 59	200.00	400.00	100.00
60 a 64	125.00	250.00	63.00
65 y arriba	63.00	125.00	Nada

La aplicacion y consideracion por este Certificado de Miembro, y los beneficios, condiciones, opciones, provisiones, y derechos contenidos en el, son todos hechos por estas presentes, parte de este Certificado tan completamente como si fueran contenidos en esta pagina y recitados sobre las firmas de los oficiales de la Sociedad.

EN TESTIMONIO DE LO CUAL, las firmas del Presidente y Secretario y el sello de la Sociedad Proteccion Mutua De Trabajadores Unidos son aqui puestas en este dia 19 de Noviembre 1946

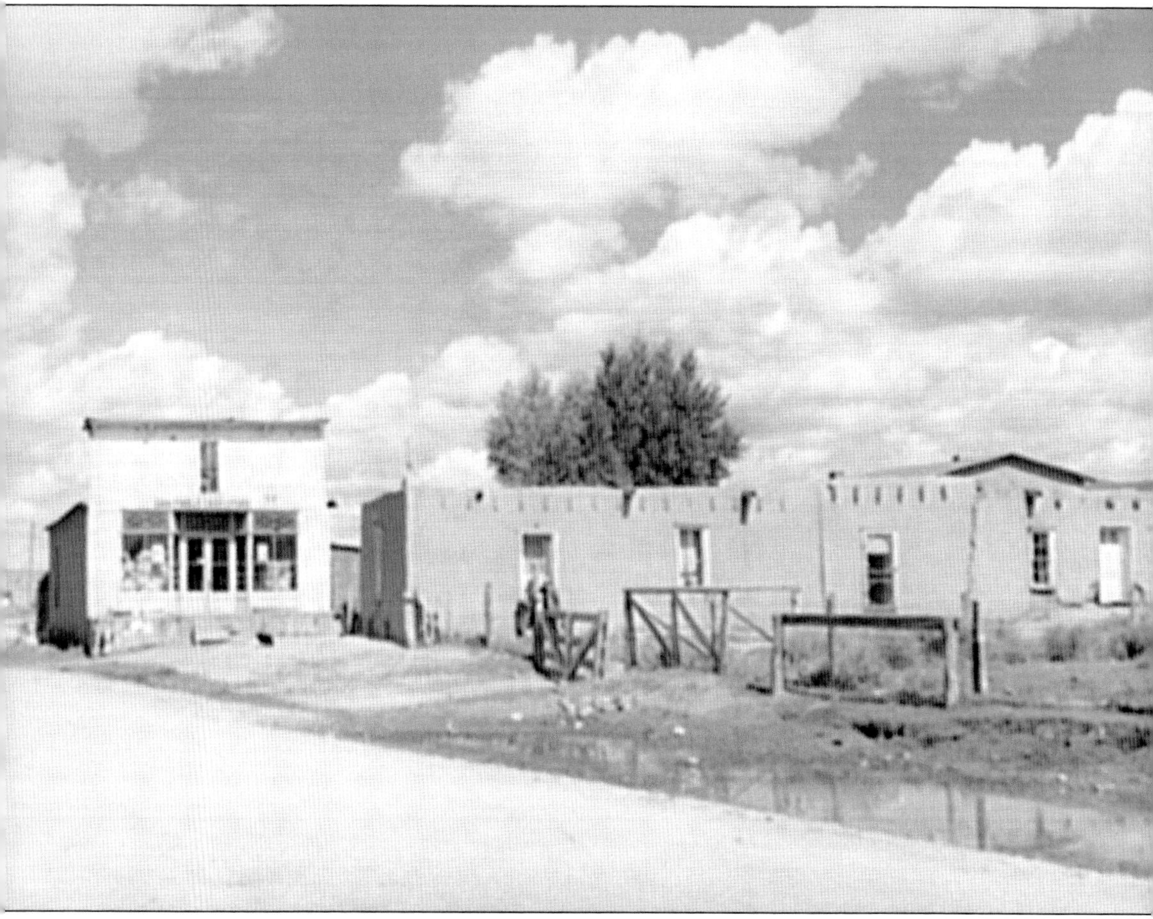

The San Pablo Cash Store, pictured in October 1939, was owned by José E. Sanchez and his wife, Dorothea Meyer Sanchez. Sanchez worked as a clerk for Ferdinand Meyer, who operated a chain of stores in northern New Mexico and southern Colorado during the late 1800s. After Sanchez married Meyer's daughter Dorothea, Meyer helped the couple open their own store in San Pedro, Colorado. At that time, there were two other stores nearby, the José Manuel Pacheco Store and Alta Vista Grocery. (Photograph by Arthur Rothstein; courtesy of Kenneth Gardner and Library of Congress.)

Two

Land and Water

The Sangre de Cristo Land Grant was one of the largest and most valuable land grants made by the Mexican government to encourage settlement, development of natural resources, and colonization of its frontiers. In their petition to Gov. Don Manuel Armijo to obtain the land, Narcisco Beaubien and Stephen Luis Lee stated they had found here "fertile land for cultivation, and abundance of pasture and water, all that is required for its settlement and the raising of horned and woolen cattle."

Three years after the grant had been placed in their possession, Lee and Beaubien were killed in the Taos Uprising of 1847. Carlos Beaubien inherited his son's interest in the land and purchased Lee's portion of the grant. In 1858, Beaubien filed to get congressional confirmation of the grant to protect Mexican land holders as provided by the Treaty of Guadalupe Hidalgo. On June 21, 1860, confirmation was granted. On May 11, 1863, Beaubien issued a deed to all the settlers for use rights to the mountain tract. The communal use of these mountain lands served as the lifeblood for the Culebra villages, providing meat from hunting and fishing, herbs for medicinal purposes, wood for fuel, timber for building homes, pasture for cattle and sheep, and, most importantly, water, the essence of life.

As the settlements in the area began to form, the settlers began to follow the custom of Spanish colonial law, called *el ejido*. This specified that common land was to be shared equally by the people in San Luis and neighboring towns, farms, and ranches. The cultivated land could be held in private, but mountain land could not. This was land that belonged to everyone.

In 1902, the Costilla Estates Development Company tried unsuccessfully to deny the settlers their rights to the grant. In 1960, land developer Jack Taylor purchased the mountain tract, began logging, and fenced the land, and in October 1965, convinced the U.S. District Court to revoke all rights to the mountain tract. The struggle continues to this day, despite the fact that access use rights were granted by the Colorado Supreme Court in June 2002.

Located in the Culebra River basin, 77,000 acres of La Sierra is the source of three rivers and 16 tributary streams. This irrigation system of acequias supports a historical agricultural base. La Acequia Madre, the mother ditch, nourishes the land while a series of smaller ditches—the *espinazos*, or spine—nourish the area's fertile valley. The San Luis People's Ditch, the oldest continuously used irrigation ditch in Colorado and the state's first decreed water rights, dating from April 10, 1852, is characteristic of the culture.

As integral to the community as the granting of land for colonial settlement, water and land access rights, the heirs of the original settlers maintain, are essential to the economic viability and cultural integrity of the communities of the Culebra River.

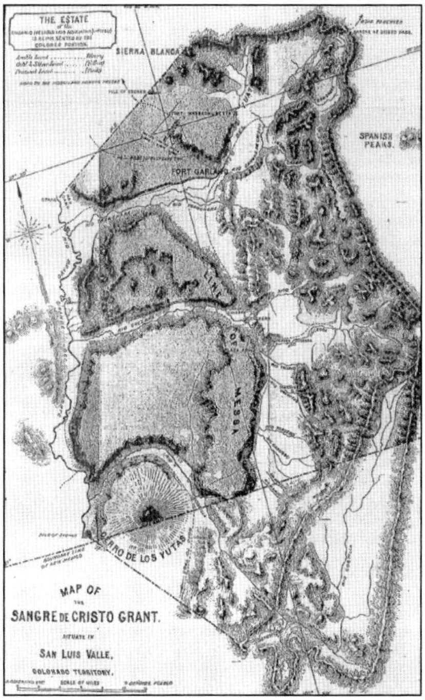

This is a survey map of the Sangre de Cristo Land Grant, located in southern Costilla County in the Rio Culebra basin. It was made by William Gilpin and William Blackmore in their early plans to subdivide the land grant. The traditional Spanish method of piling stones as markers is shown. Land grant owner Charles (Carlos) Beaubien enticed settlers to establish a community along the Costilla and Culebra Rivers. An agreement between Beaubien and Gilpin specified that the settlers' rights to the land would be protected, but the laws of the Colorado Territory and Spanish-Mexican law have interpreted the land use rights differently. The mountain tract is historically a portion of the communal lands granted by Beaubien to the *pobladores* (settlers). (Courtesy of History Colorado.)

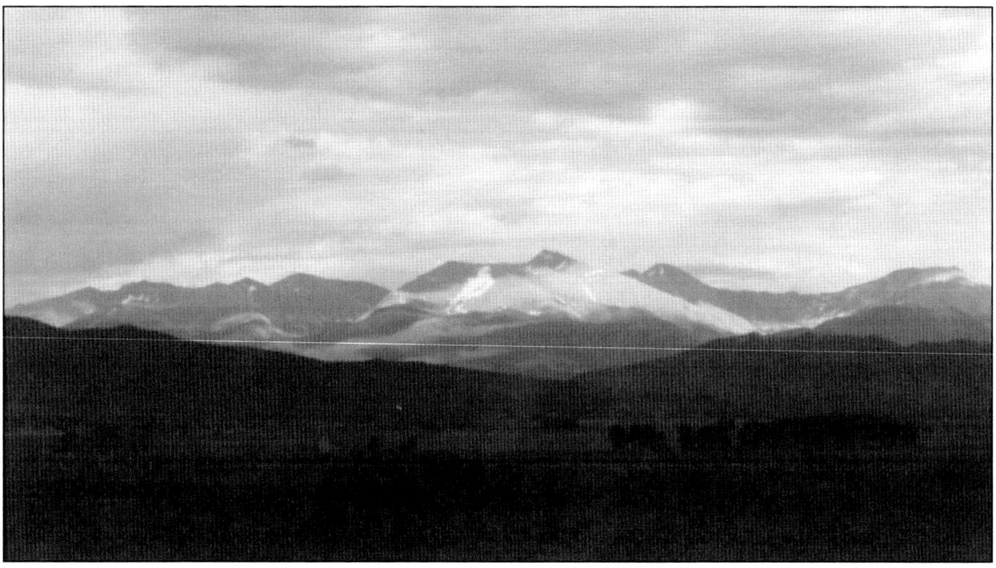

The mountain tract is known as Culeba Massif; to locals the uplands are La Sierra, or "the mountain." Over 14,000 feet high and totalling 77,524 acres, La Sierra is the source of three rivers and 16 tributary streams. This portion of land was originally granted to Luis Lee and Narciso Beaubien on December 27, 1843, as the Sangre de Cristo Land Grant. In their land claim to Gov. Don Manuel Armijo, they wrote, "We have seen with sufficient care the rivers of Costilla, Culebra, and Trinchera embrace the Rito [little river], and confluence with the Rio del Norte, and finding it the qualities of fruitfulness, fertile lands for cultivation, abundant pastures and water, and all that is required for its settlement and the raising of the larger kinds of stock and sheep." On December 30, 1856, legal title was granted to Charles Beaubien following the death of his son Narciso and Stephen Lee Luis at the Taos Uprising. (Courtesy of Marcella Pacheco.)

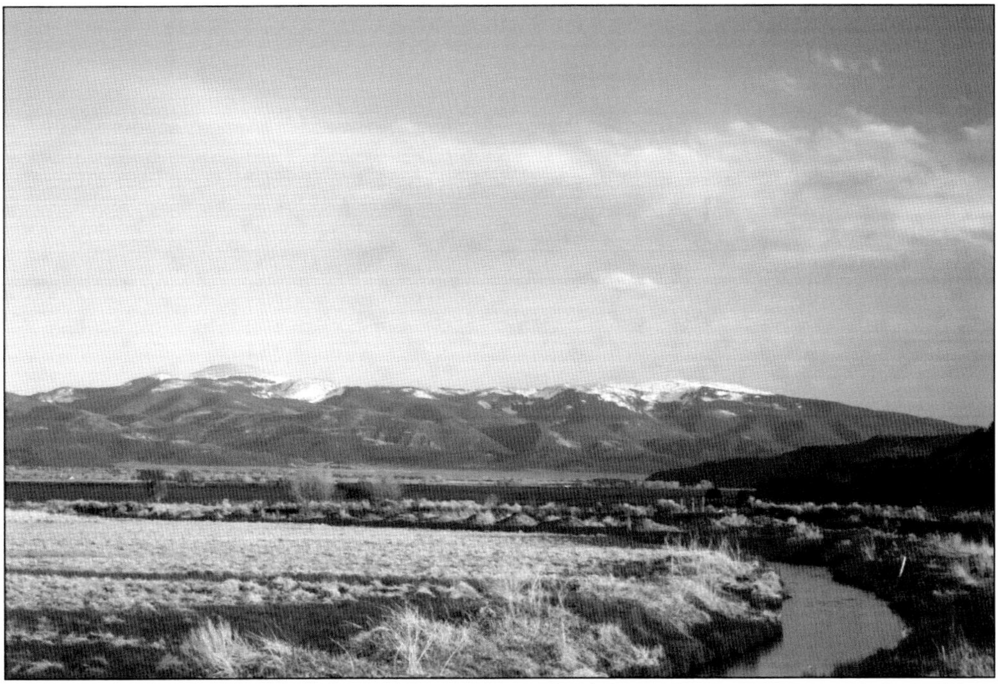

The San Luis Vega is a 633.32-acre ejido, or common land, located east of San Luis de la Culebra. Part of the Sangre de Cristo Land Grant, the land originally stretched 18 miles down to the New Mexico border. La Vega was designated by an 1863 covenant for villagers living in the Culebra basin, and continues to serve its original purpose of communal grazing today. The traditional rules dictate that the wetlands remain uncultivated since each family is allowed to graze four cattle or milk cows, horses, or mules. It is the only land grant commons in the United States. (Courtesy of Huberto Maestas.)

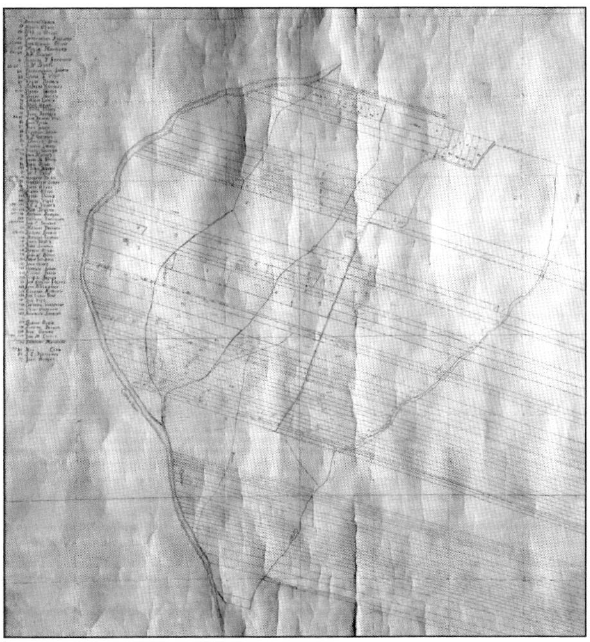

This land conveyance map illustrates the *vara* strips. A Spanish unit of linear measurement, a vara is 32.909 inches, or about three feet. These long strips of land are an average of 200 varas wide and vary in length from a few varas to *extensiones*, which can be up to several miles long. For very little money, land grant owner Carlos Beaubien gave or sold titles of vara strips of land to around 115 of the early settlers. This method of deeding property was meant to provide the natural resources needed for survival. These strips of land extended from river bottom and grassy pasture to mountainous woods and was abundant in wildlife. (Courtesy of Randy Pijoan.)

This is a copy of an original *hijuela*, or deed, hand written by Carlos Beaubien and his wife, Maria Pablita Lobato de Beaubien, that was given to Blas and Ignicita Olivas on September 2, 1863. Beaubien, a grantor of the Sangre de Cristo Land Grant, promised land to grantees, the settlers who, in turn, had the obligation of establishing settlements along the Culebra River. The Olivases acquired the land through the Sangre de Cristo Land Grant, and the property still remains in the family after five generations. The farm has been designated as a centennial farm in the state of Colorado. It is owned by the original settlers' great-great-grandchildren, Earl, Eric, and Lori Valdez. (Courtesy of Candido Olivas Sr. family.)

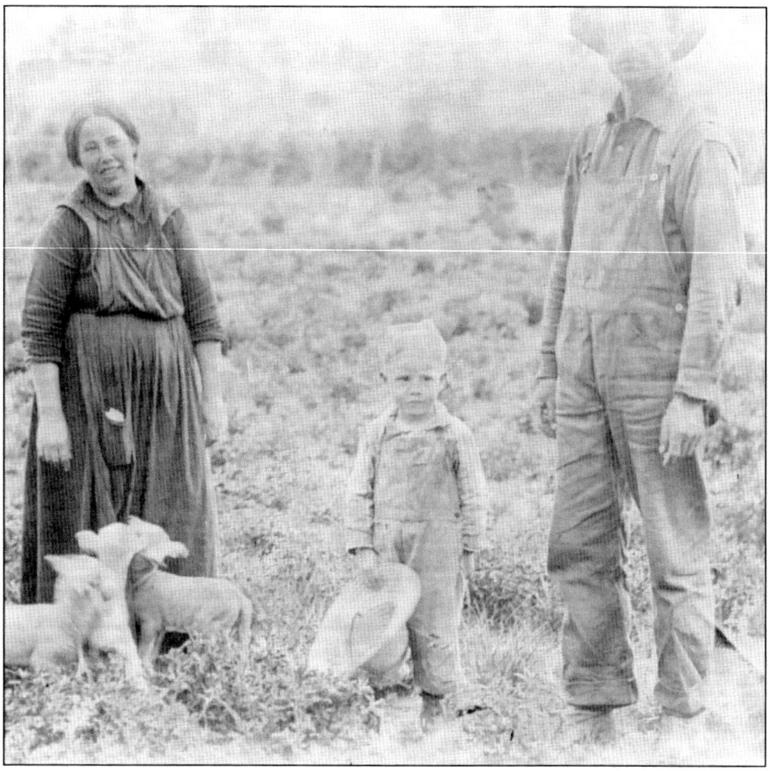

Pictured around 1915 on the family farm are Candido and Francesquita Olivas with their three-year-old son Ruben. They are tending to baby lambs, as farmers raised sheep for both wool for weaving and for food. Their land has been passed down through generations of the family who continue to raise and harvest hay and raise cattle and other farm animals. (Courtesy of Candido Olivas Sr. family.)

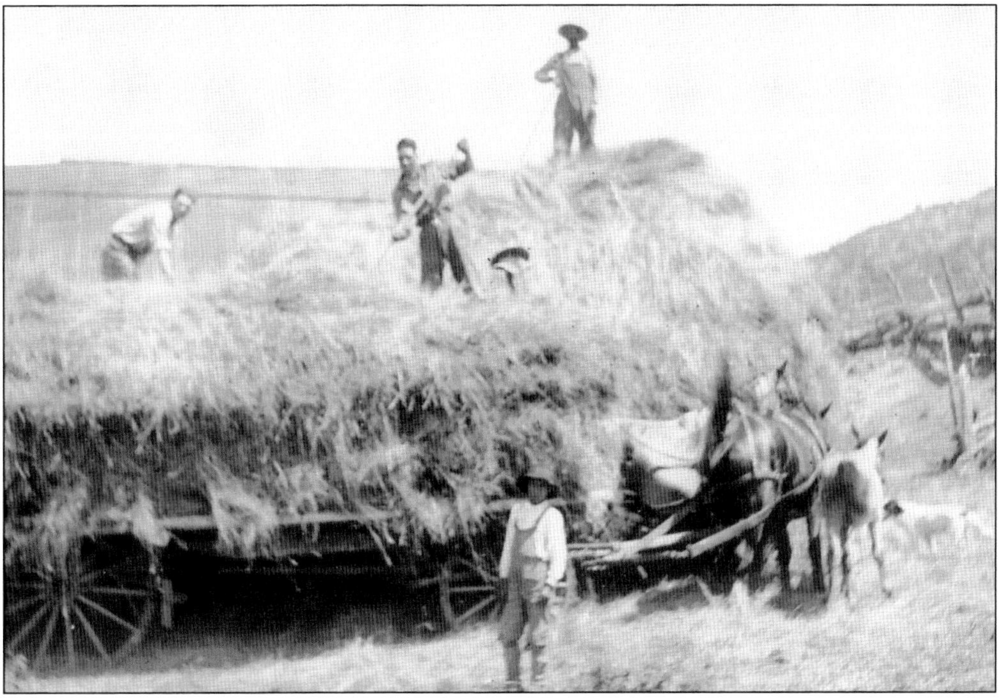

These four young men are gathering hay in the 1920s. Usually working with no machinery, the settlers of the area used pitchforks to throw the hay onto a horse-drawn flatbed wagon and have it pulled to a barn for storage. One would climb to the top of the haystack and pitch and move the hay around to make it strong. This photograph was taken at Joe Albert's farm in Cañon de Chama presently owned by Dale Quintana. (Courtesy of Brenda Vialpando.)

Farmers in the Culebra villages carry on the tradition of gathering loose hay with pitchforks and then stacking it on a horse-drawn flatbed wagon called a *guadana*. Pictured at the Sandoval family farm in San Pedro are Grandpa Zacarias Sandoval (center with rake) with grandsons Paul (pointing cap gun) and Ernest Jr. (back) on the hay stack. In front are grandchildren Edward, Cynthia, and Ron next to father, Ernesto Sr., Uncle Willie Rodriquez, and cousin Joann Rodriquez. Soon after this photograph was taken in the early 1950s, the cap gun went off, scaring their workhorse, Bonnie, forcing Ernesto Sr. to run after the hay wagon and calm the horse. (Courtesy of Carlos Sandoval.)

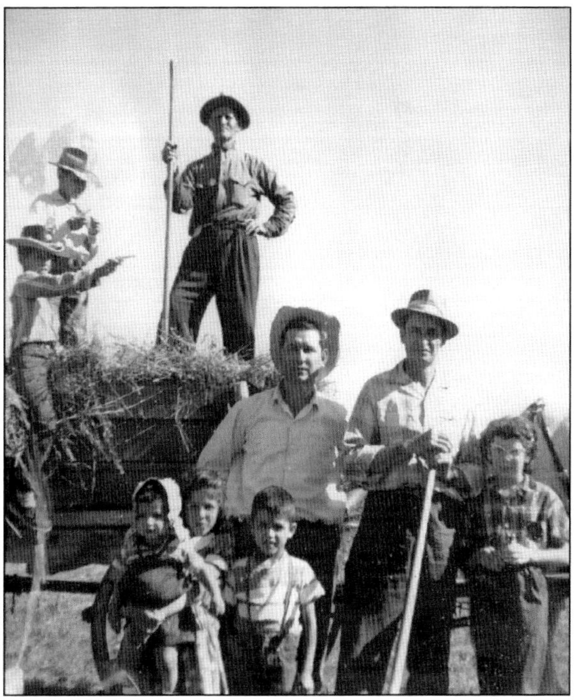

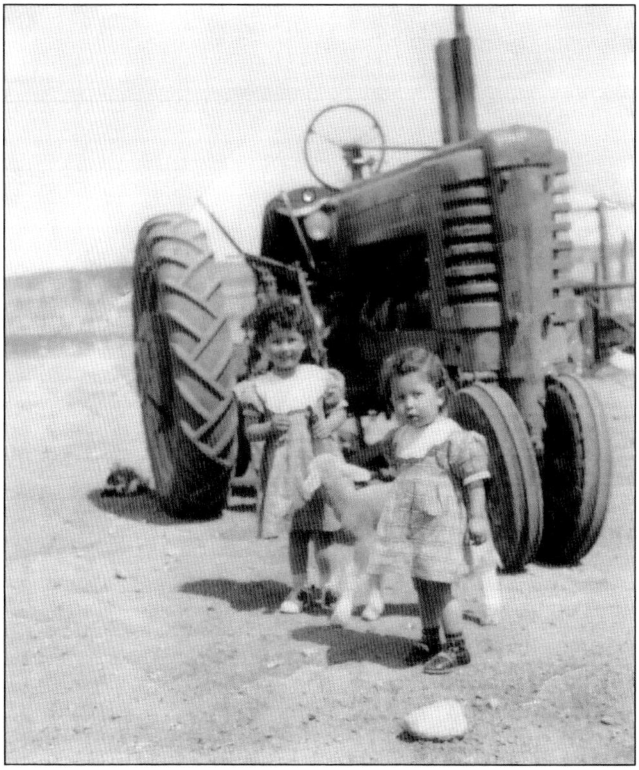

Pictured in front of a farm tractor are siblings Iva Lorraine and Jean Valdez in the early 1950s. Many times lambs were rejected by their mothers and were called "bum lambs." Family members would have to feed them with a bottle. Children especially enjoyed this chore. The farm is located at the Corrillera, a couple of miles east of San Luis de la Culebra near La Vega. (Courtesy of Julia Valdez.)

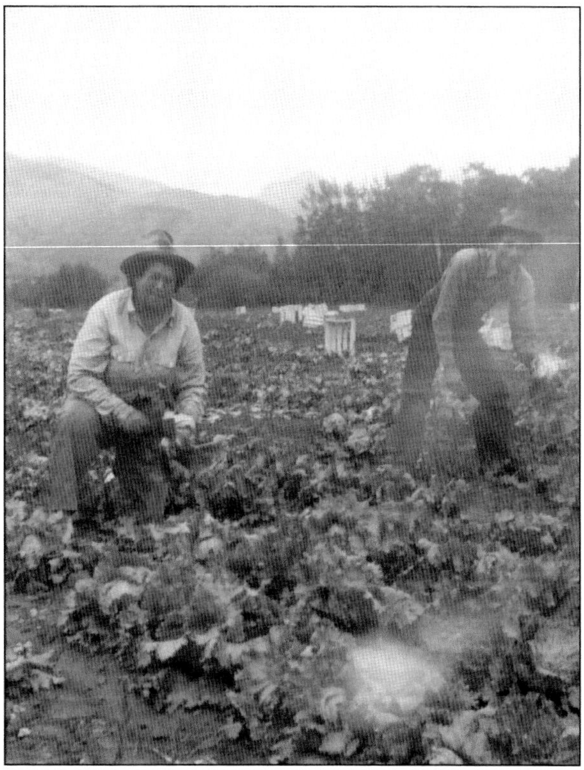

Demostenes Vigil and his wife, Aranita Jaramillo Vigil, are working in the lettuce fields in the 1930s. Farmers throughout the Culebra villages grew a variety of their own crops and had self-sustaining entrepreneurial family enterprises. By today's standards, the crops grown in the area were and continue to be organically produced. (Courtesy of Olivia Maestas family.)

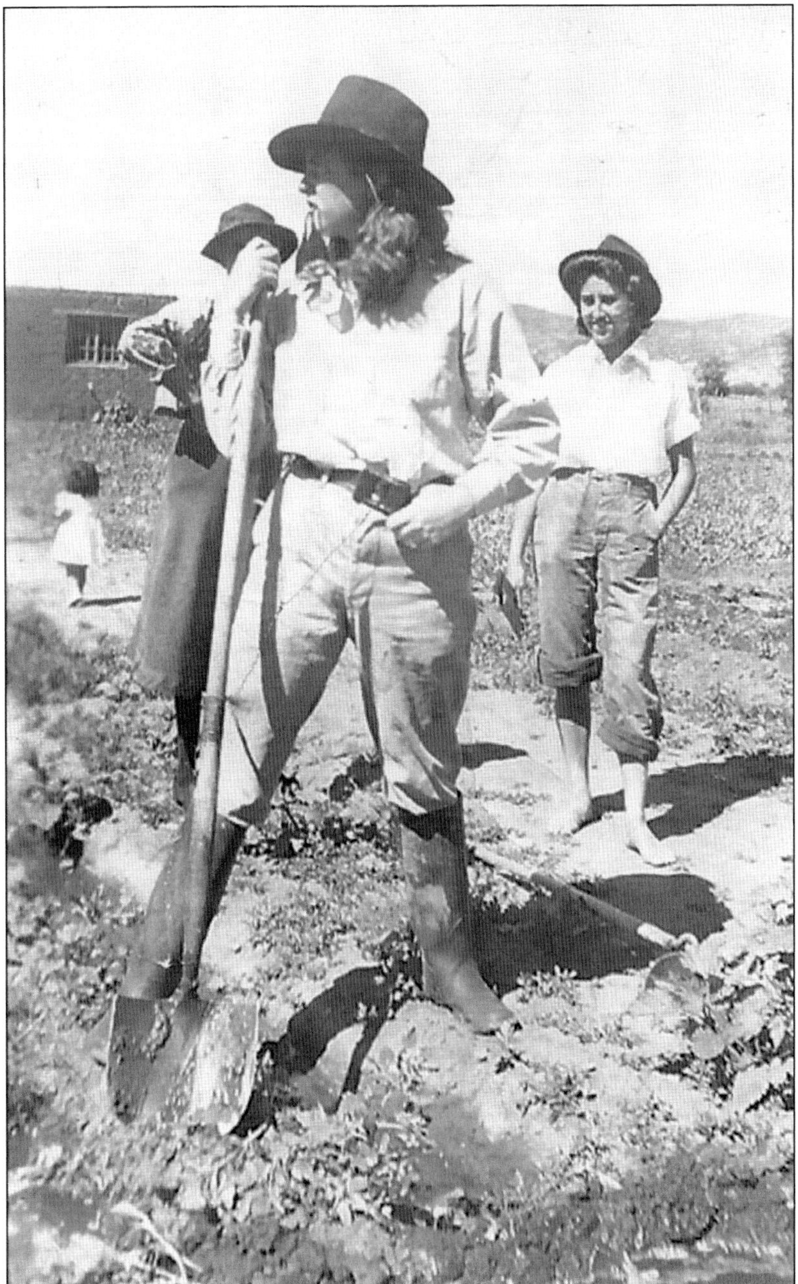

Eighteen-year-old Loretta Sanchez (center) is pictured with her 24-year-old sister, Dora Sanchez, assisting their mother, Tillie, on their homestead in 1942. The girls had the responsibility of irrigating the crops during the summer months. Tillie would plant a huge garden that was more like a field growing corn, squash, beans, peas, lettuce, and *calabazitas*. Tillie became a widow in her 30s and raised 10 children alone. The Sanchez farm in San Pedro became a family affair. As a young woman, Loretta worked with her mother while attending school. She became a schoolteacher and worked at the San Pablo School and the Redwing, Colorado, schools. (Courtesy of Kenneth Gardner.)

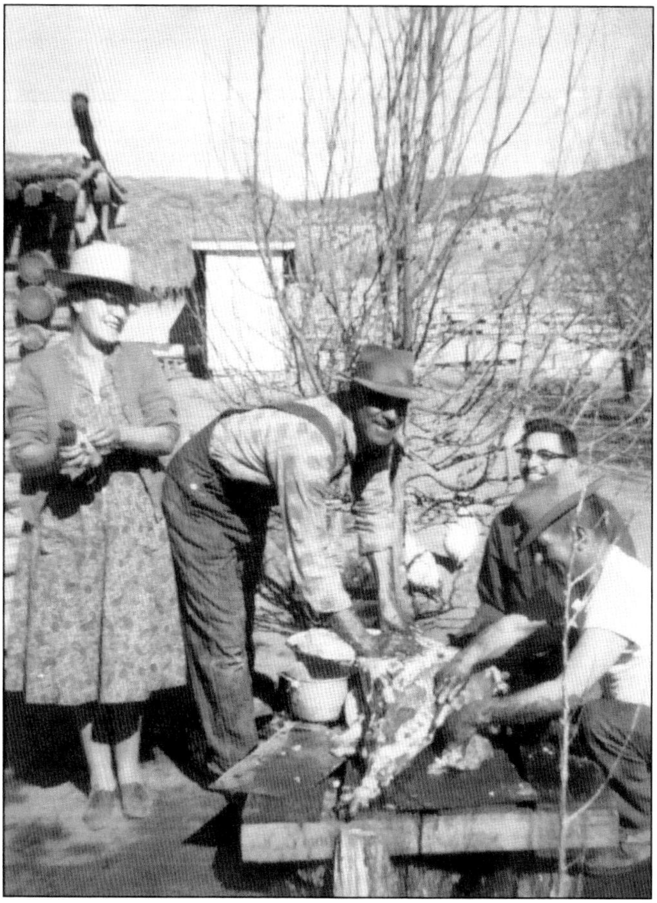

A long-held annual tradition observed every winter is the *matanza*, the slaughtering of a pig. Pictured at left in Chama on February 6, 1962, are Isabelita Vialpando, Frank Vialpando (husband), Floyd Espinoza, and Daniel Sanchez. Pictured below in San Luis in November 1955 are Abel Gallegos (standing), Diego Gonzales, Lee Madrid, Claude Belmontez, Juan D. Madrid (leaning over the pig), and Felix Barela. The matanza would yield meat for cooking and for *empanaditas*, a turnover filled with meat, nuts, and dates. Especially coveted are the *chicharrones* (pork cracklings—small cubes of fat with meat). They are prepared in a large cauldron over an open fire and are delicious served with a warm tortilla. (Left, courtesy of Brenda Vialpando; below, courtesy of Lee Madrid family.)

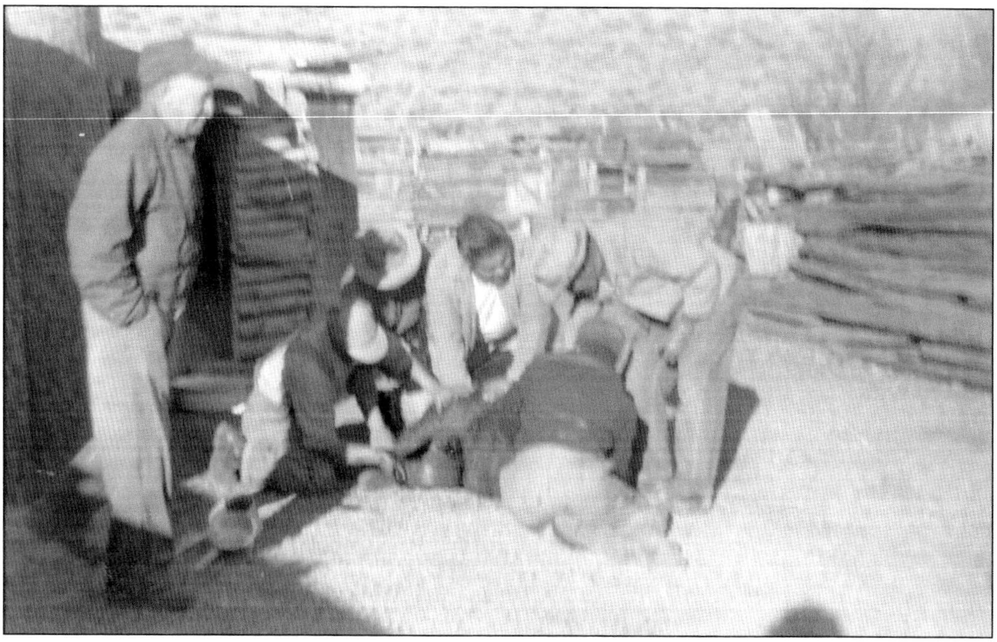

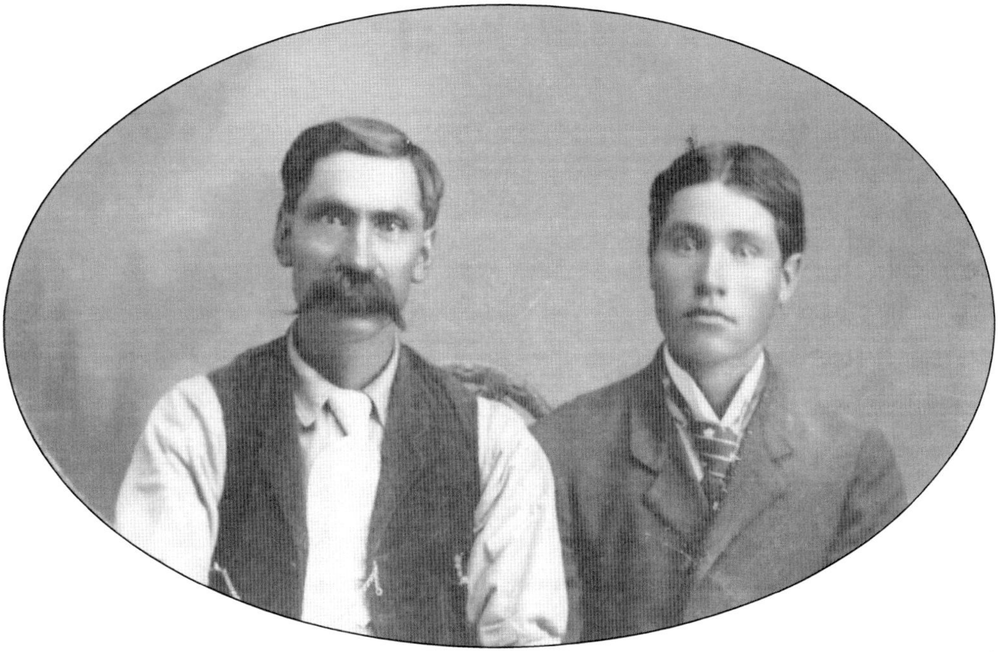

This portrait of brothers-in-law Juan de Dios Vialpando and Feliberto Lopez was taken around 1915. Juan de Dios married Maria Crestina Lopez on December 1, 1894. Feliberto Lopez married Magdalena Crestina Valdez. The young men were farmers and ranchers in the Chama area. (Courtesy of Brenda Vialpando.)

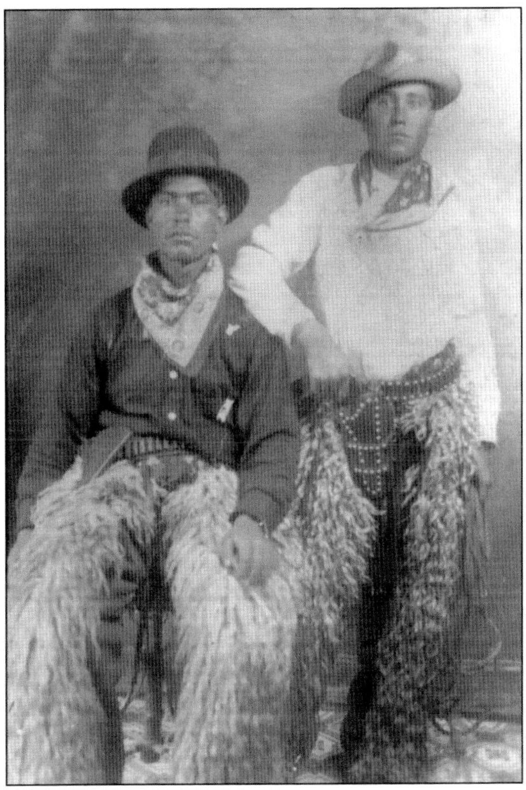

Pictured around 1920 with their cowboy outfit of hats, bandanas, and woolen chaps are Roman Vialpando (seated), born in 1896, and an unidentified friend. Roman was a sheepherder by trade and passed away at the young age of 25. (Courtesy of Brenda Vialpando.)

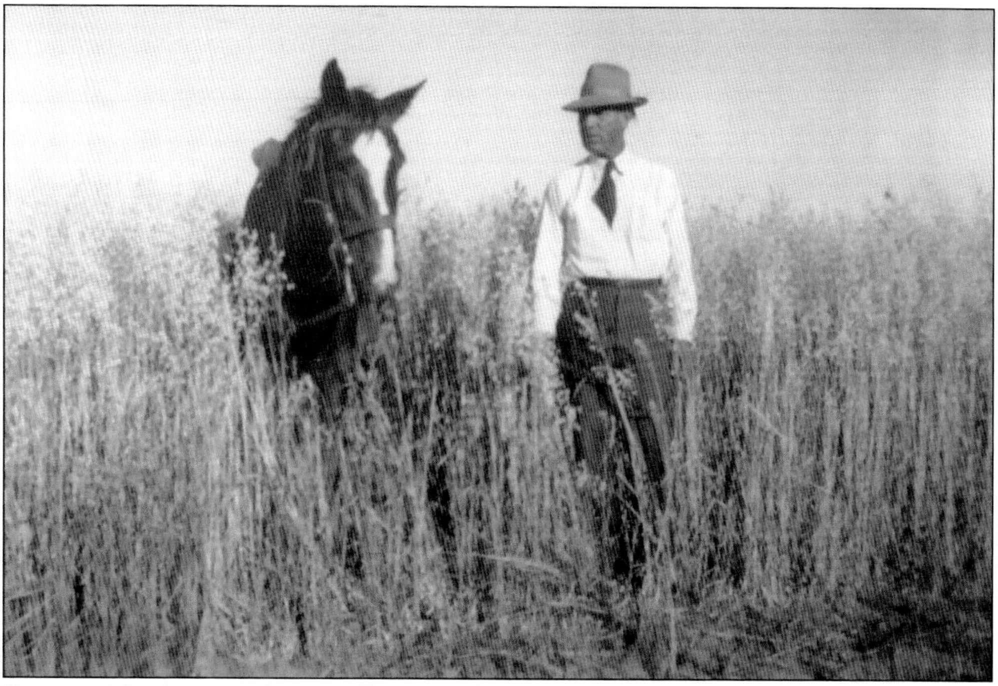

Francisco Mondragon is shown walking with his horse in a field of *cevada* (barley) in Colonias, Colorado, on October 2, 1949. Farmers in the Culebra villages grew grain, oats, barley, and alfalfa. (Courtesy of Pat Trujillo VanZandt.)

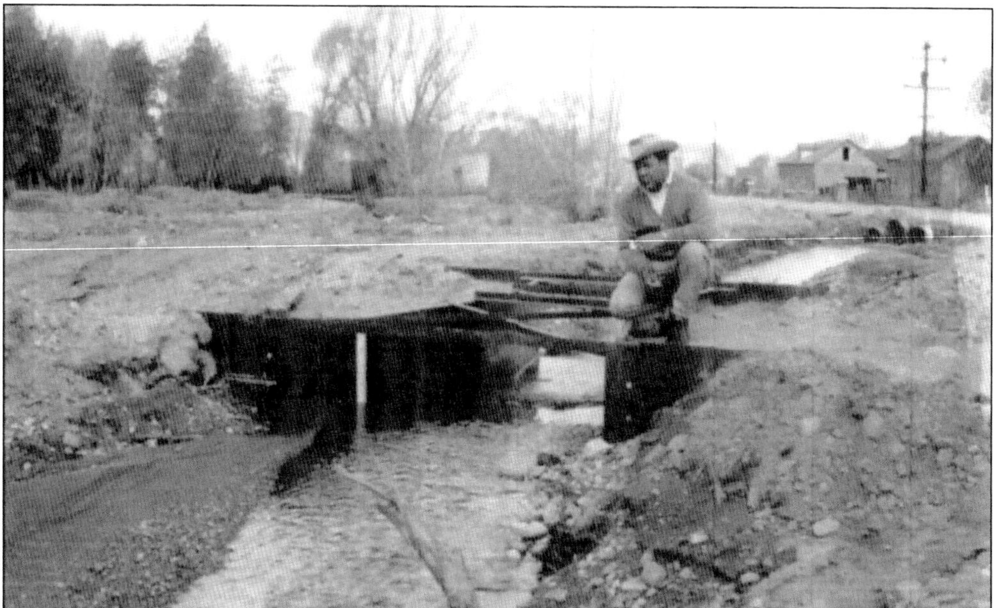

This photograph from the late 1950s or early 1960s shows National Resource Conservation Service employee George Romero checking the culvert structure at the Vallejos Ditch in Los Fuertes, Colorado. Romero is using a weir to measure the water flow as it travels down the acequia to serve the farmers on the ditch. The acequia culture is a system run under democratic values to assure fairness to both large and small landowners. (Courtesy of Diana Cortez.)

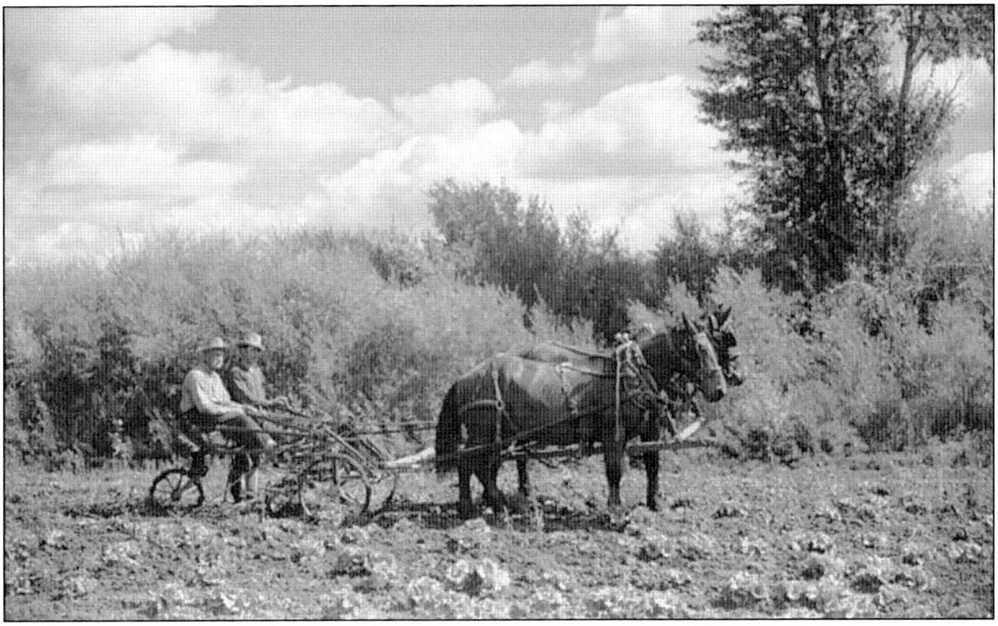

The land that Carlos Beaubien gave the original settlers of the Culebra had some of the finest natural hay and meadows and was some of the best to farm in the region. Shown here are Delfino "Dale" Rael and his grandfather Juan Antonio Rael cultivating the cabbage fields at their San Acacio, Colorado, farm in October 1939. The farmers were participating in the Farm Service Administration's rehabilitation project aimed at helping farmers through the Depression. (Photograph by Arthur Rothstein; courtesy of Farm Service Administration, Library of Congress.)

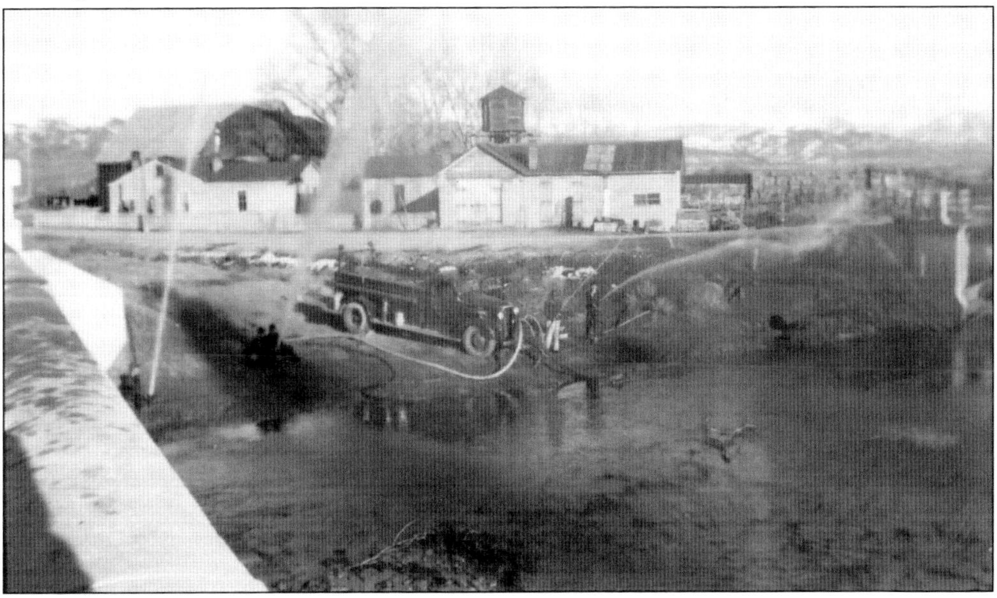

This photograph from the 1920s–1930s shows five men clearing out water hoses before refilling the fire truck's water tank. This task took place at the Culebra River near the bridge south of San Luis. In the background is the San Luis Roller Mill, whose turbine wheels were powered by the forceful waters of the Culebra River. (Courtesy of Cathy Serna-Egana.)

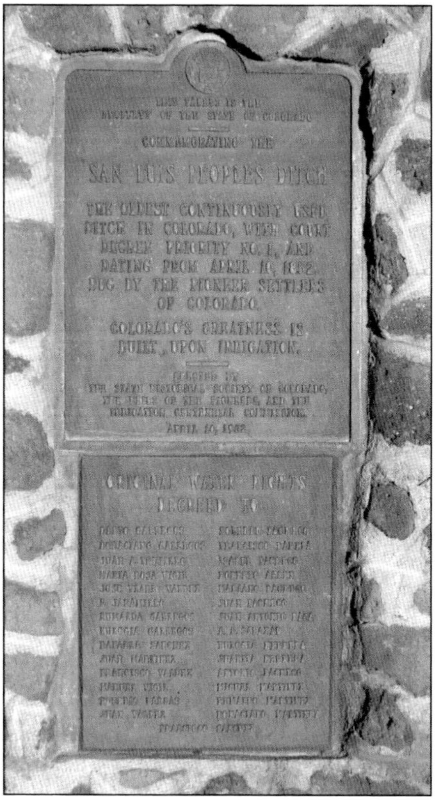

This plaque stands to the south of San Luis to commemorate the San Luis People's Ditch. It reads: "The oldest continuously used ditch in Colorado, with court priority No. 1, and dating from April 10, 1852 dug by the pioneer settlers of Colorado." The acequias, Arabic for "water bearer," are channels of waterways used for irrigation. The farmers of the Culebra use acequia culture for irrigation of crops to sustain their communal way of life. (Courtesy of Huberto Maestas.)

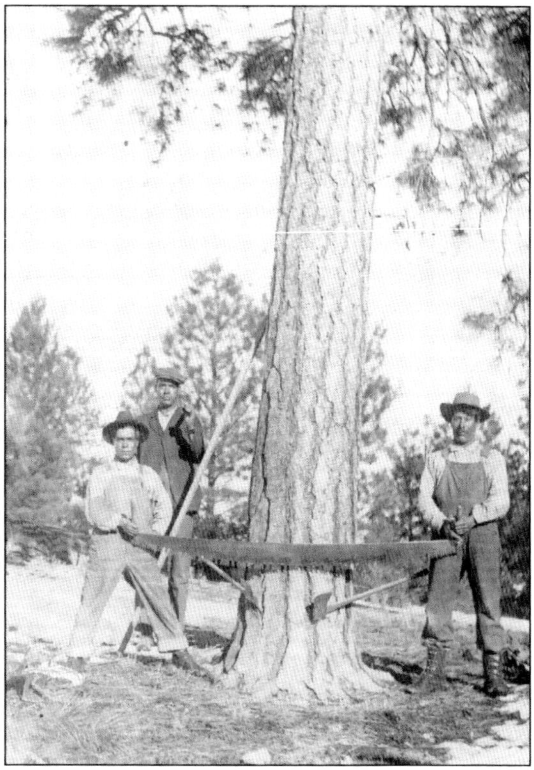

In 1908, from left to right, Tio Filo, unidentified, and Leonardo Chacon use La Sierra, the mountainous communal lands in San Luis, as a source of large and small logs for building homes, cellars, storage sheds, corrals, and fences, as well as for firewood. Chacon used a hand tool to saw logs for delivery to a local mill, where they would be cut for distribution to the valley's residents. (Courtesy of Dora Vialpando.)

In this image from the 1940s, Rufino Gallegos is carrying *brazado de leña*, an armful of firewood. Then as now, the residents of the Culebra villages used the traditional method of heating their homes with firewood and cooking on a wood stove. Rufino and his wife, Rosarito, raised two girls and nine boys. Three of Rufino's sons continued to live in the San Luis area and had successful businesses of their own: two gas stations and a grocery store. (Courtesy of Pat and Lorraine Gallegos.)

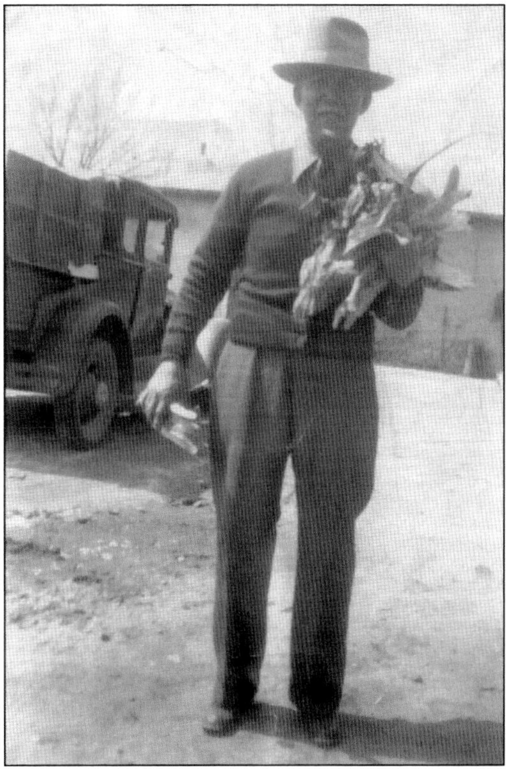

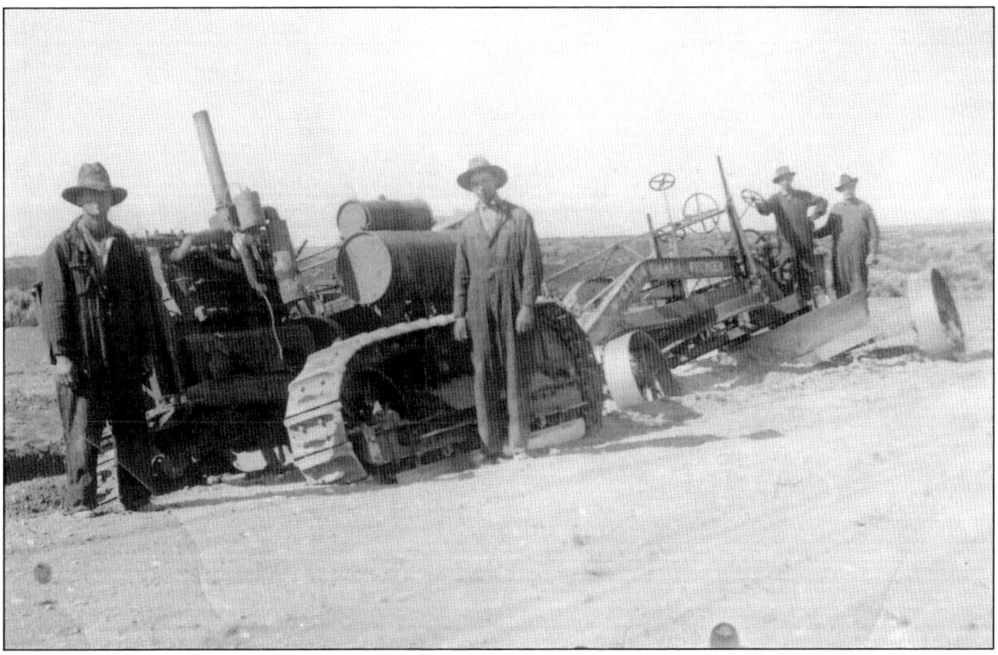

The WPA was founded by President Roosevelt. It created jobs for the building of highways, streets, bridges, and parks. This photograph, taken around 1935, shows Diego Antonio Gallegos (second from right) and three unidentified young men working on a WPA project driving a grader and building roads in the San Luis area. (Courtesy of Hope Gallegos Yost.)

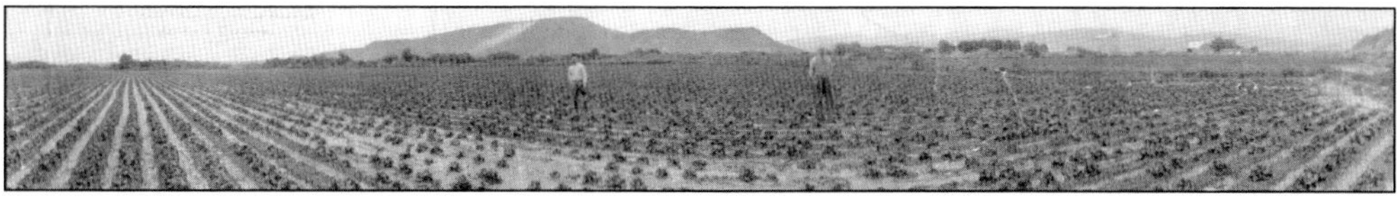

This panoramic photograph, shot from southwest of San Luis, shows Joseph Masahito Sato and his boss William S. Parrish standing in the lettuce fields in the 1920s. Sato migrated to San Luis to marry Emilia Montano, whom he met in Chama, New Mexico. Her family required him to have a job before they could marry. He worked for Parrish Farms as a hired hand for many years. Instead of getting paid a monetary wage, the Parrish family paid him with the land that he farmed. William Parrish was the owner of the San Luis Roller Mill, which can be seen in the background. (Courtesy of Cathy Serna-Egana.)

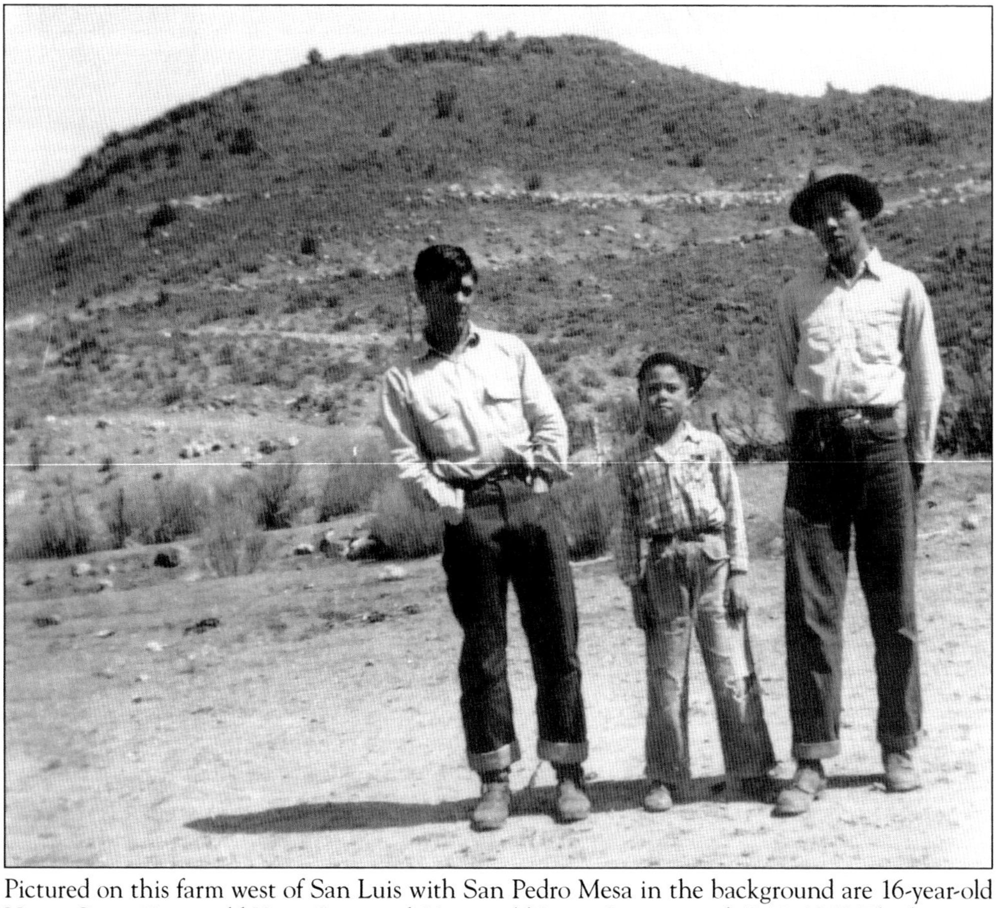

Pictured on this farm west of San Luis with San Pedro Mesa in the background are 16-year-old Henry Sato, 10-year-old Kenji Sato, and 14-year-old Leroy Sato around 1946–1947. The boys are the sons of Japanese farmer Joseph Sato and his wife, Emilia Montano Sato. The Satos had eight children—five girls and three boys. (Courtesy of Cathy Serna-Egana.)

Sheepherding was a primary occupation for many of the settlers of the Culebra villages. They tended the sheep in the Sangre de Cristo Mountains, where they lived during the summer months. These two men are stacking the wool after it has been sheared off the sheep around 1938. Sheep brought in from New Mexico were the churro breed, which had long silky fleece that was ideal for weaving. (Courtesy of History Colorado.)

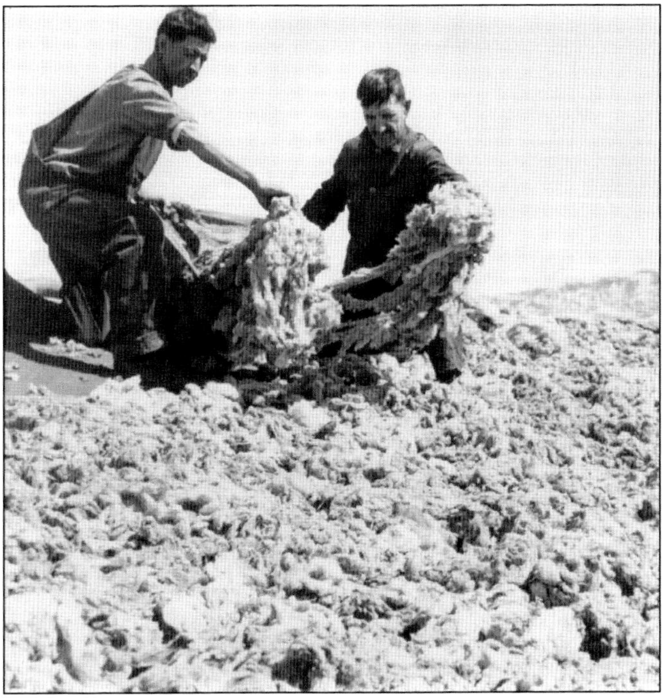

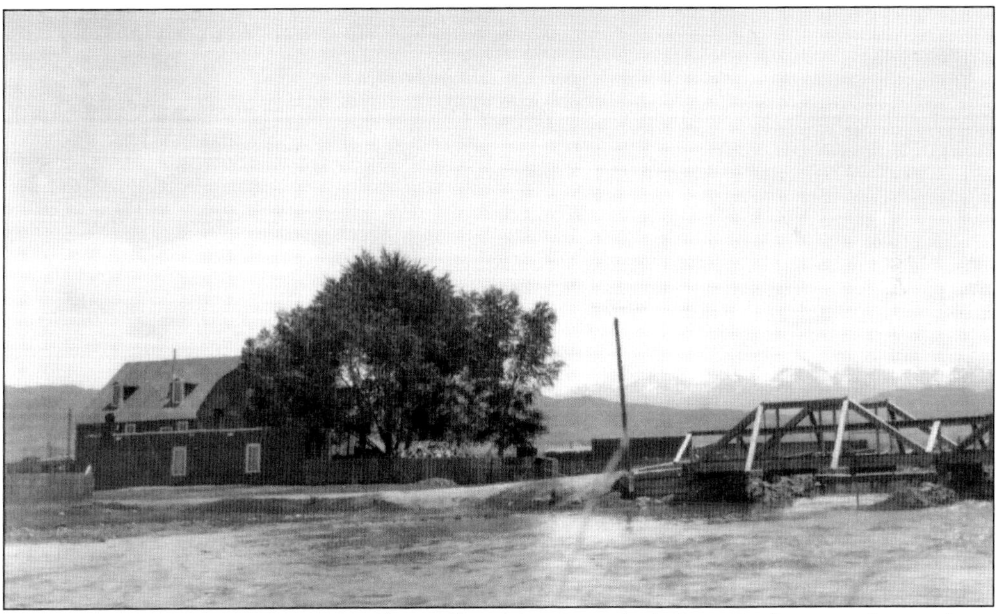

This photograph of the San Luis Roller Mill and San Luis Arch Span Bridge was taken on June 16, 1903. This beautiful San Luis Bridge is significant because it was one of the first concrete open-spandrel arches built in the West. Built in 1911, it was constructed with a unique cement arch design that has a 58-foot span. Most arch block bridges were built with no reinforcement to deal with tensile forces. The San Luis bridge is the oldest of seven remaining examples of this type remaining in the state of Colorado. The bridge is important to the heritage of San Luis because of its use as a river crossing to La Vega. Notice the torrents of water on the Culebra River. (Courtesy of Van Diest Collection, Tutt Library, Colorado College.)

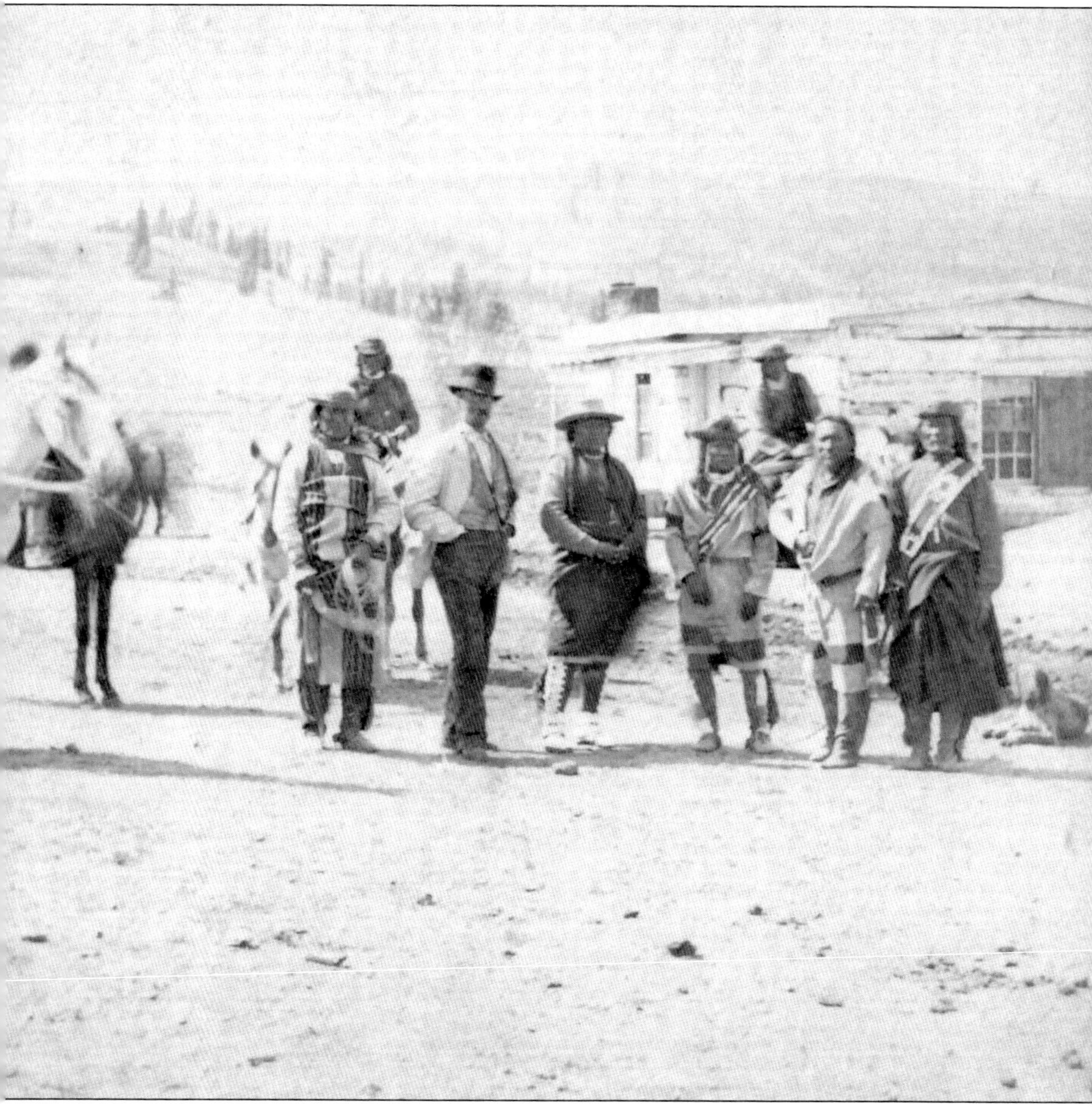

The Ute chiefs at Los Pinos assembled for a photograph in 1873. San Luis history would be incomplete without acknowledging the native peoples' contribution to the cultural identity of the Culebra villages. The Utes held bear dances in the areas of San Acacio and San Luis and had encampments in the El Rito de San Francisco, Colorado, area. For a long time, the Utes discouraged settlements in the area. Stories are told of how the old settlers made agreements with them not to wander past Ute Mountain, and if they grew crops here, they agreed to return home after the harvest. (Photograph by Copelin and Son, negatives by T. Hine; courtesy of Special Collections, Tutt Library, Colorado College.)

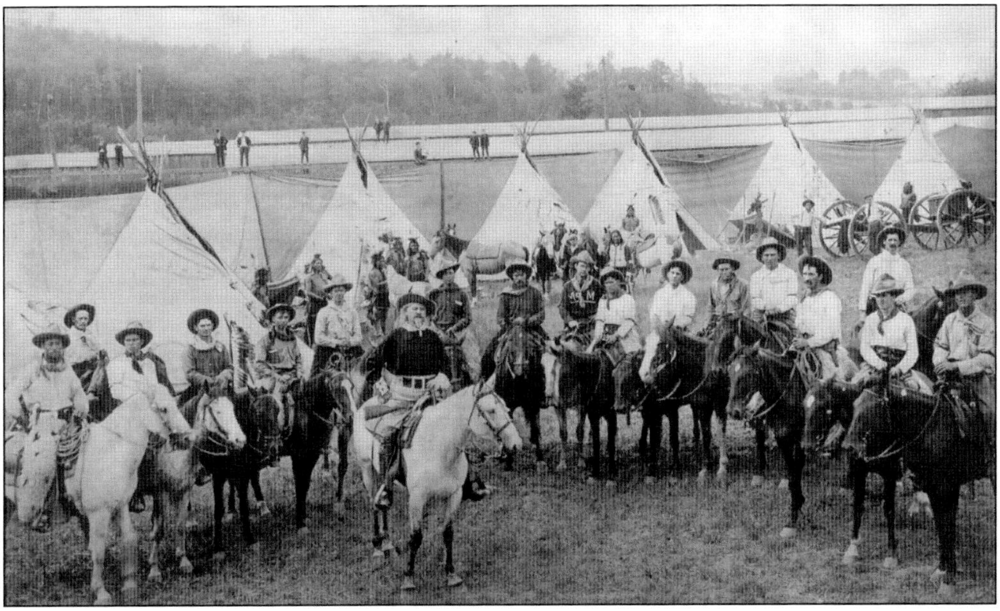

Known by his stage name of "Jake Saunders" from his days of riding with Buffalo Bill Cody, Jacobo "Jake" Sanchez was a local boy from the Culebra settlement of El Rito de San Francisco. Pictured in the center behind Buffalo Bill, Jake and his *compañeros* (companions) pose for this photograph. An excellent horseman and rider, this young man was fortunate to travel the world performing with Buffalo Bill. He even had the privilege of meeting the king of England. On his wedding day in 1908 to his lovely Irene, the photographer insisted he change his clothes, "as no member of Buffalo Bill's troupe should be caught with their chaps down." (Courtesy of Josito Espinoza.)

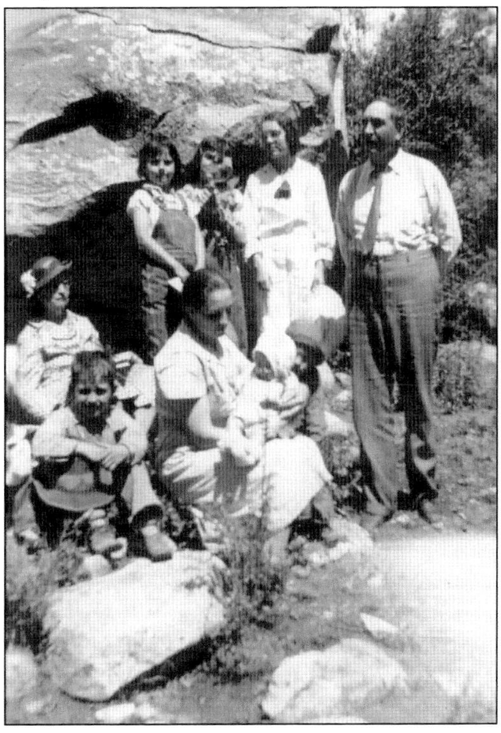

Pictured are Grandma Maria (Mary) Choury, son-in-law Emilio Lobato Sr., and daughter Enriqueta Lobato with their children picnicking at El Poso, in the nearby Sangre de Cristo Mountains on July 4, 1937. The area is a favorite spot for recreation and is part of the original Sangre de Cristo Land Grant. (Courtesy of Henrietta Mascarenas.)

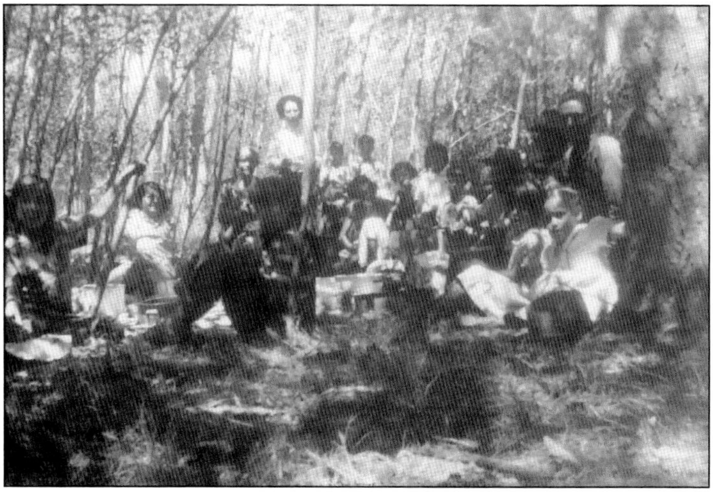

Recreation in La Sierra was something families of the Culebra basin benefited from for generations. The Vigil family of San Luis is shown having a picnic in the mountains. Generations of the Vigil family were sheepherders who spent many months tending their flock in the mountainous terrain. (Courtesy of Olivia Maestas family.)

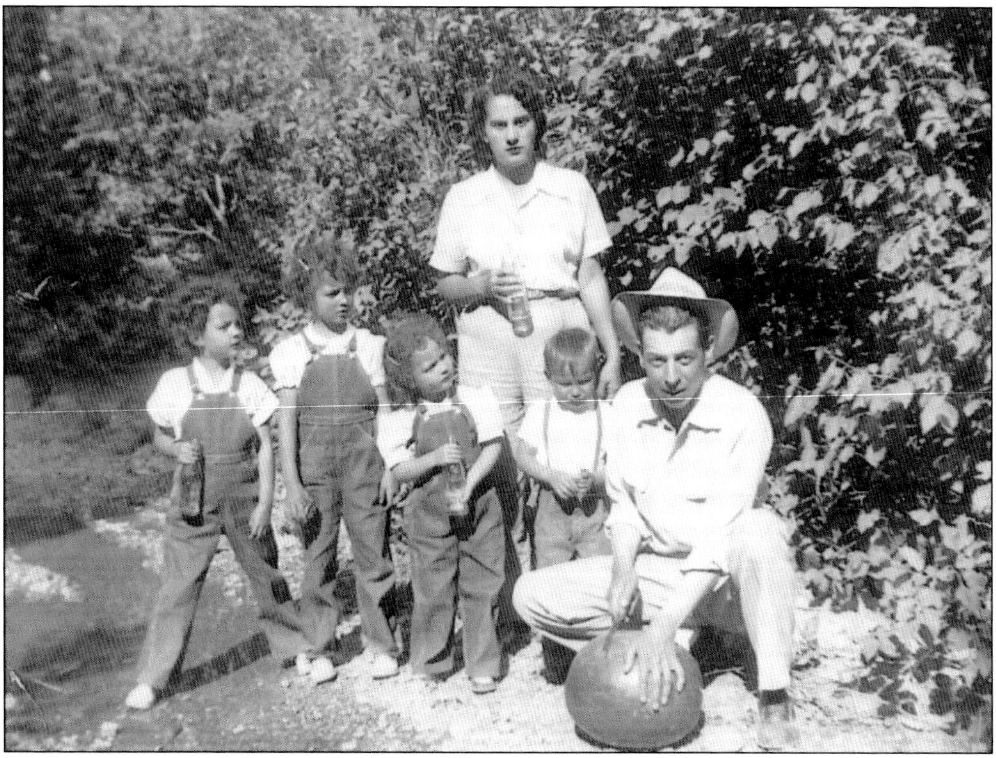

In this c. 1953 photograph, the Jaquez family enjoys a relaxing time in La Sierra in an area just above the meadows called Petramalas. From left to right are Anna Marie, Victoria, Theresa, Estella (back), Jessie, and Henry Jaquez. The picnic area usually opened for local residents for the Fourth of July weekend. Henry Jaquez is shown cutting watermelon for his children. The kids remember lining up several watermelons in the creek to cool them off. (Courtesy of Theresa Medina.)

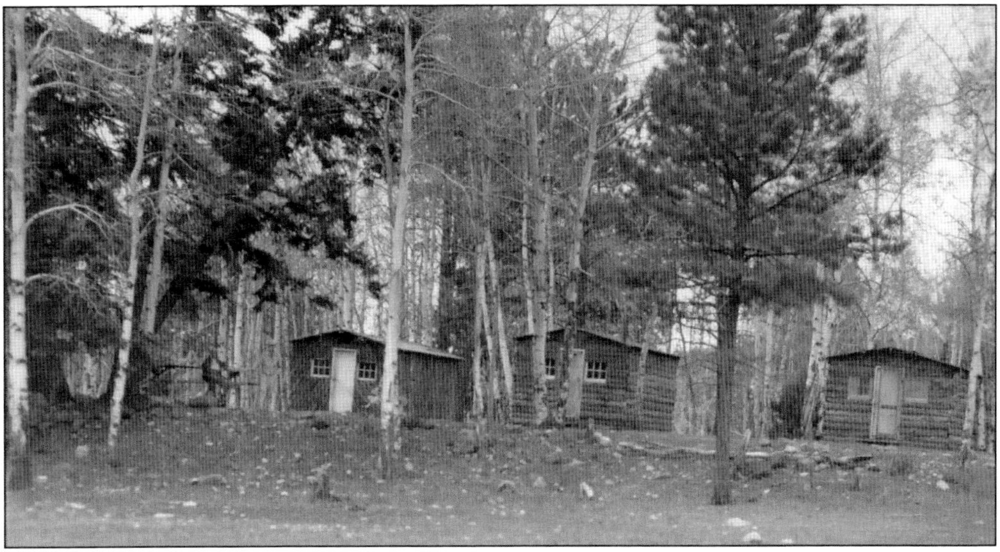

This postcard, labeled "Mountain Cabins, La Valle Ranch, San Luis, Colo.," shows an area above the meadows on La Sierra the locals call Petramalas. Workers from the local water-powered lumber mill used the cabins. The lumber mill was owned by Delfino Salazar, who sold lumber at his hardware store in San Luis. This area, also called Rancho del Valle, was used for picnics, fishing, and hiking. (Courtesy of Olivia Maestas family.)

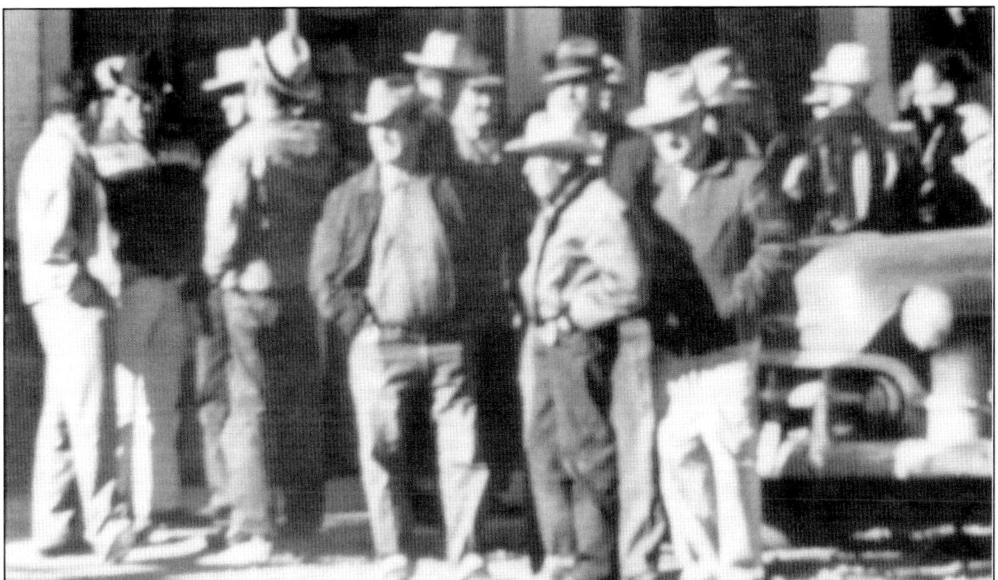

Seen in front of the local hardware store around 1961 is a group of men awaiting news about the beatings of two local men, Lupe and Eddie Medina of El Rito de San Francisco. The community came together to protest the beatings at the hands of Taylor Ranch employees and make sure there was an arrest. In the foreground from left to right are Daniel Sanchez, Ramoncito Sanchez (facing left), Frank A. Vialpando (behind Sanchez), and Rufino Vialpando. The other men are unidentified. Zachary Taylor bought La Sierra and would not comply with the use rights to the mountain guaranteed to the locals by Beaubien through the Sangre de Cristo Land Grant. This was the beginning of the Taylor Ranch Wars. (Courtesy of Brenda Vialpando.)

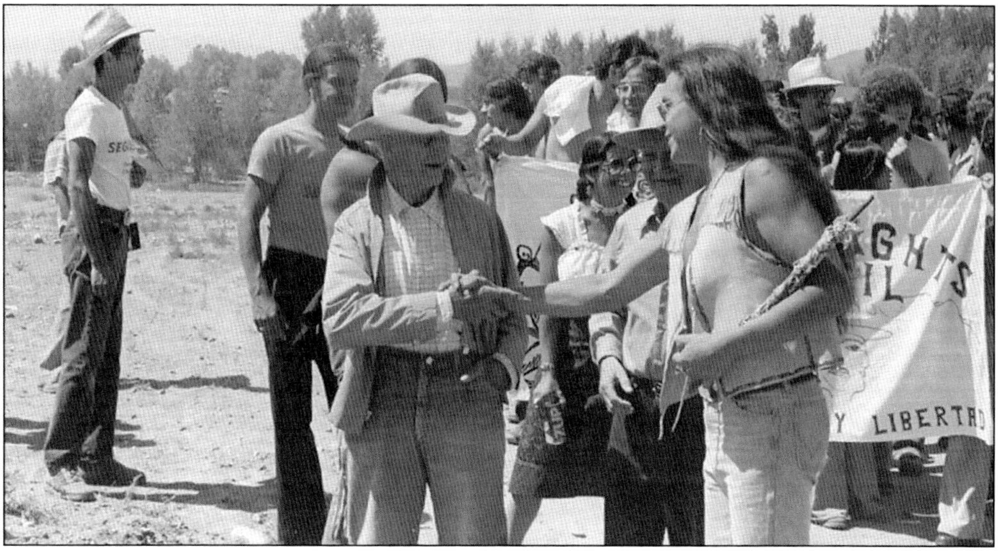

In these historic photographs from around 1978, Apolinar Rael and Juan LaCombe are pictured with community members and activists protesting the lockout by ranch owner Jack Taylor. Farmers Rael and LaCombe were leaders in a movement to regain land use rights to La Sierra. Organized around land grant and environmental issues, the Land Rights Council took on land issues by use of a legal team to regain communal access to La Sierra. After years of legal battles, the Land Rights Council and the descendants of Culebra village's early settlers had a historic opportunity before them. In June 2002, the Colorado Supreme Court ruled for historical communal rights for the people of the Culebra basin. The hard work of the Land Rights Council and bravery of two farmers to stand up and fight for their livelihood and that of their children is commendable beyond words. Currently the Land Rights Council continues to work to develop a use-rights plan that will enable residents of the Culebra River basin to gather wood and graze livestock on La Sierra in a common and ecological way. Apolinar Rael and Juan LaCombe would be proud. (Both, courtesy of Land Rights Council.)

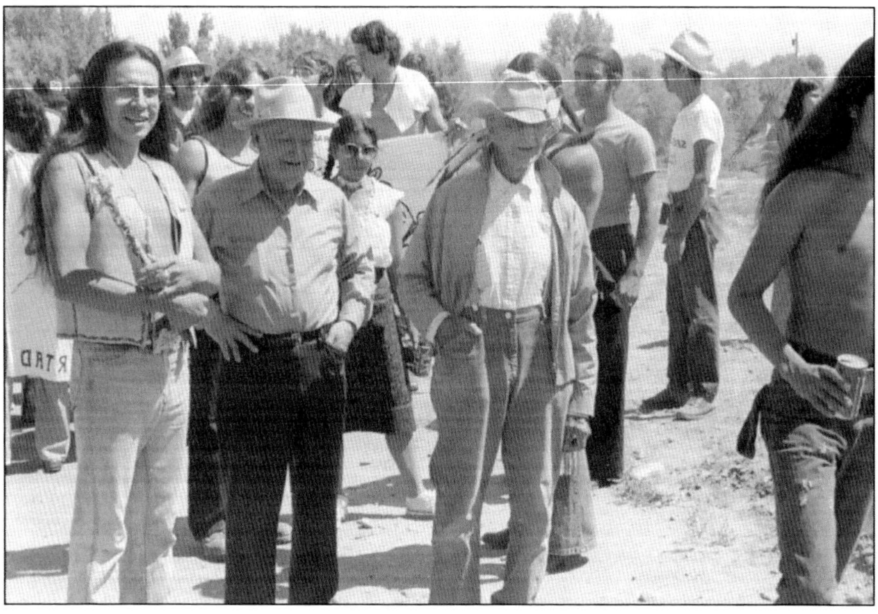

Placida Gallegos Maestas and her husband, Felix Maestas, enjoy an evening of campfire cooking. The Maestas family owned mountain land south of El Rito, Colorado, that was part of the Sangre de Cristo Land Grant. For these campfire meals, Maestas would build a fire pit, creating an underground *horno* (or "oven"), and cook meat, potatoes, and vegetables in a cast-iron cauldron overnight. In the morning, the vegetables were cooked through and the meat tender, and he would prepare a warm stack of tortillas to go with the meal. Felix was the designated cook while the younger men tended to the sheep and cattle. (Courtesy of Olivia Maestas family.)

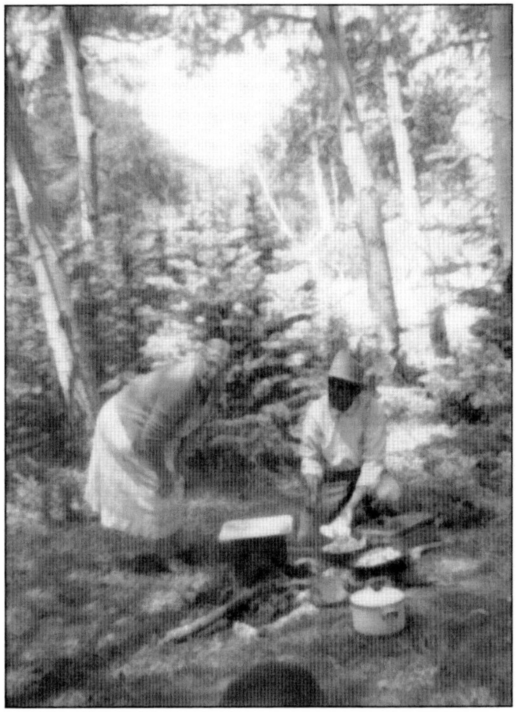

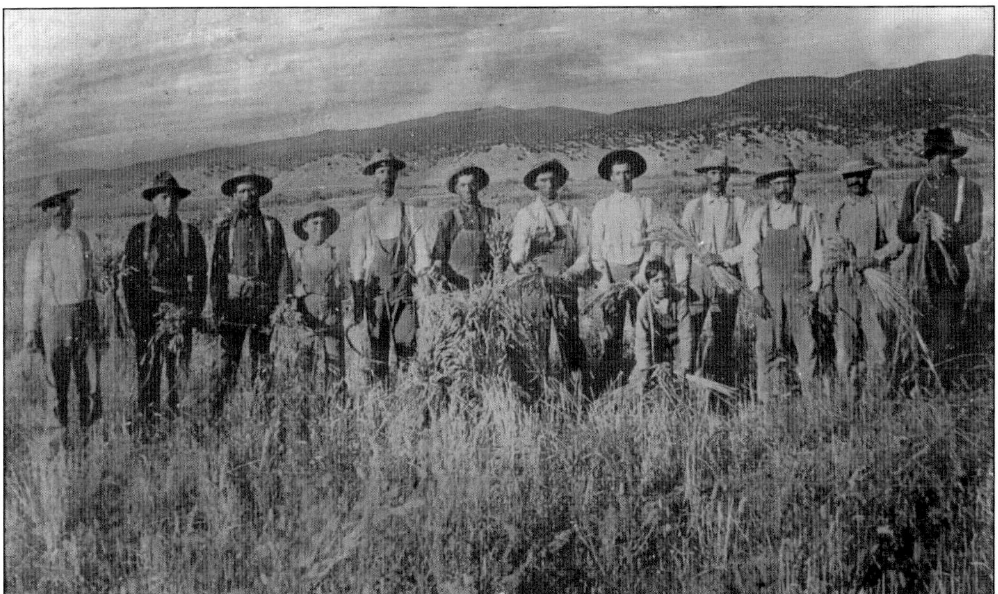

In an area called La Senegitas on a hill going up the Cerro Ditch in Chama, this family takes a break from their work of harvesting and tying wheat to pose for this photograph. Some of the men are wearing black in memoriam of two friends who had recently died when their wagon carrying a load of wheat overturned on the hill behind them. From left to right, they are Marcelino Lopez, Facio Sanchez, Julian Sanchez, Erminio Vialpando (child), Ricardo Vialpando, Lugardo Sanchez, Eutimio Vialpando, Placido de Herrera, Fermin Vialpando (child), Lizardo Sanchez, Gavino Vialpando, Lazaro Sanchez, and Daniel Roybal. (Courtesy of Libby Rivera.)

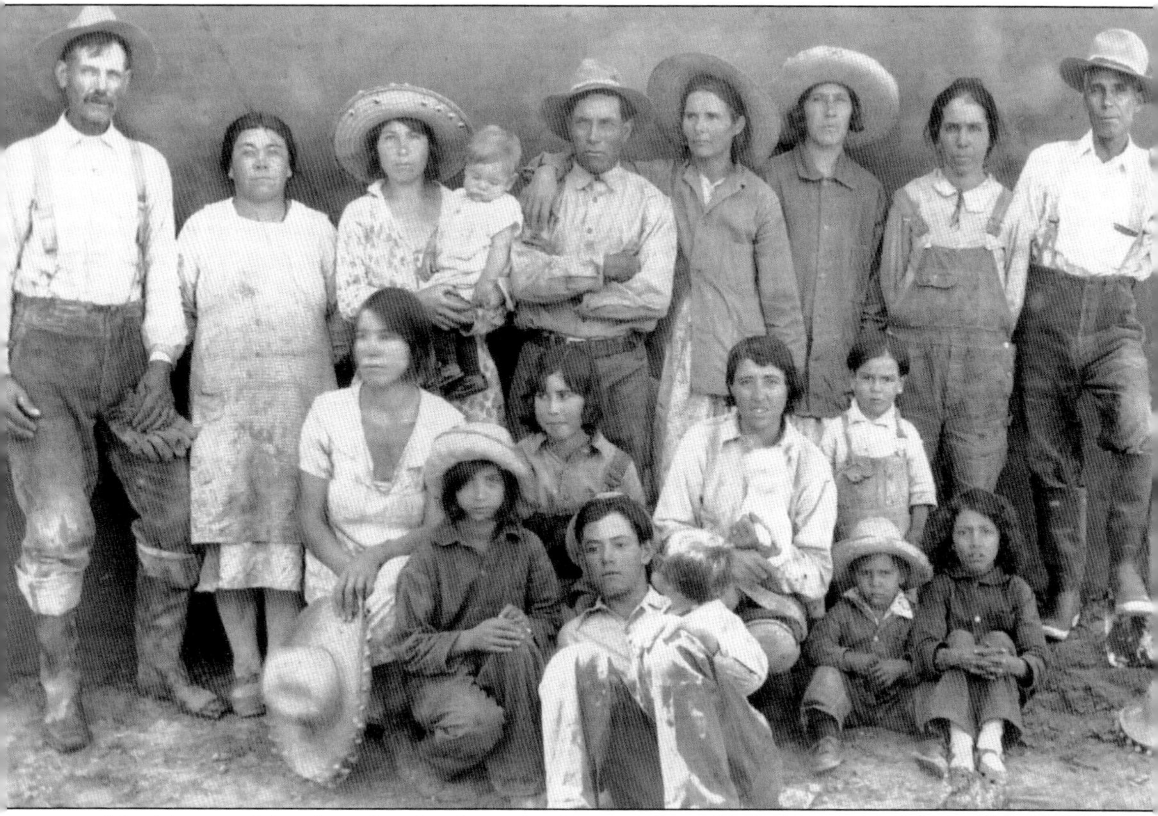

Neighbors and family gather for the annual event of mudding the outside of an adobe home using adobe mortar as a mud plaster. The process is called *embarando* in Spanish. From left to right are (first row) Ursulita Albert Rodriguez, Adelmo Albert, unidentified child looking back, Raymando Vialpando, and Libby Arellano (Rivera); (second row) Frances Rael Vialpando, Casilda Sanchez, Julia Albert, and Tony Herrera; (third row) Antonio Albert, Josephina Sanchez, Aphemia (Lena), baby Estrellita, Gaviano Vialpando, Rebeca Albert Vialpando, Adelida Vialpando Arellano, Ludinda Herrera, and Placido Herrera. Libby Arellano Rivera is 92 years old in 2014. (Courtesy of Libby Rivera.)

Three

Celebrations and Fiestas

Everyone joins in the spirit during the celebrations and fiestas held in the communities of the Culebra River. El Día de Santiago (Feast of St. James the Apostle) on July 25 honors Santiago de Compostela, also known as Santiago Matamoros, the patron saint of Spain. The fiesta begins in Chama with a *procesión de caballería* (procession of equestrians), horse races, or *corridas de gallo. Puestos* or *vendibles* (booths) line the streets as vendors sell ice cream and doilies. The day ends with a *misa cantada* (a sung mass) followed by a potluck and a street dance. El Día de Santa Ana (Feast Day of St. Anne) on July 26 pays reverence to the virtuous mother of Mary. These two events combine to become a two-day celebration in the middle of summer. In San Luis, the fiestas begin by hosting a pageant on Friday evening to select a queen and her court. Young women compete for Fiesta Queen by demonstrating their talent, dress, and speech competence.

A Spanish Catholic tradition honoring the community's patron saints, Las Fiestas de Santiago y Santa Ana, are celebrated through numerous community events and religious processions. The evenings usually end with a dance. Bystanders line the streets as the community and families from far and near come together to partake in the celebrations, a reunion of family, neighbors, and old friends. The traditions surrounding the fiestas were established in the early 20th century and remain part of today's culture.

Devout in their observance of tradition, the people of the San Luis Valley remain connected to an ancestral way of life. The observance of the Fiesta de San Isidro (patron saint of farmers) is a day used to clean the acequias. The traditions of the Fiesta de San Pedro y San Pablo and Fiesta de San Acacio are passed on from great-great-grandparents to the younger generations.

A wedding celebration in the Spanish tradition is a ceremonial affair in which the whole community is involved. The *pedimento* was a custom of asking for the girl's hand in marriage in the form of a letter by the young man's parents. If the girl's parents agreed, arrangements were made for the wedding. If they did not, they would *darle las calabazas*, literally meaning "give him the pumpkins," as a symbol of rejection. A reception and dance traditionally follow the *casorio*, wedding nuptials, where "La Entriega de los Novios," a ballad sung to the couple, speaks of their commitment to each other.

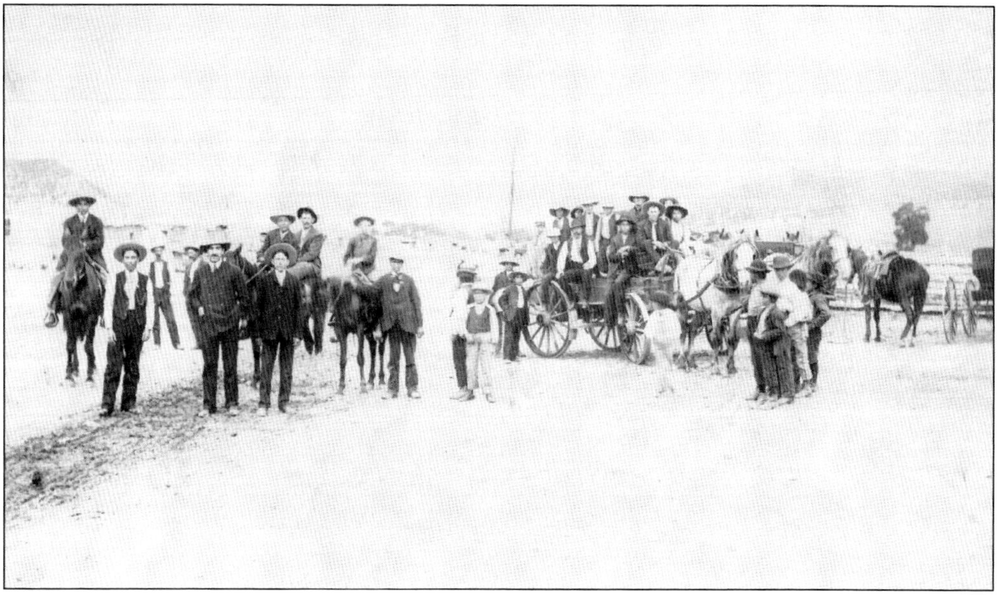

Local residents prepare their horses for the annual El Día de Santiago on July 25, 1908, in Chama. The Feast Days of Saint James and Saint Anne are a two-day religious event whose festivities include a procession, horse racing, foot racing, a rodeo, mass at the local church, and a community potluck. Baseball with the Chama Kitos came later. Second from left standing in the front row is Emilio Lobato Sr., with many unidentified friends. The person on the horse is possibly Adolfo Vialpando, who was always on a horse. (Courtesy of Henrietta Mascarenas.)

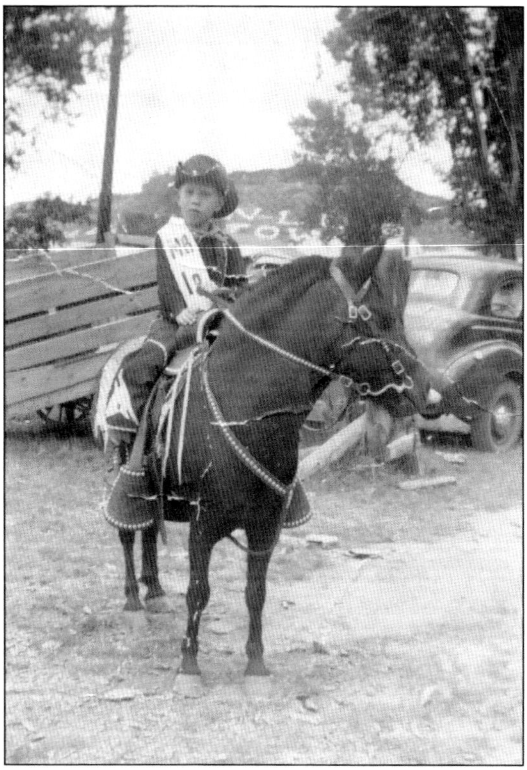

"Mr. 1851" is six-year-old Conrad Garcia, posing on a pony just before the 100th anniversary parade commemorating the establishment of San Luis, the oldest town in Colorado. Little Conrad had the distinct honor of being parade marshal for the centennial celebration held during the annual Santiago–Santa Ana fiestas in 1951. (Courtesy of Conrad and Acela Garcia.)

Six-year-old Conrad Garcia, born in 1945, poses with his elder sister Christine just before the 1951 Santiago–Santa Ana celebrations. The photograph was taken in front of his Aunt Carrie's home on Main Street in San Luis. (Courtesy of Conrad and Acela Garcia.)

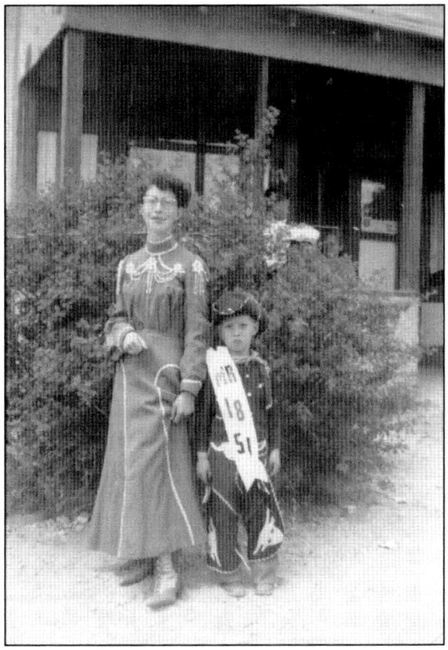

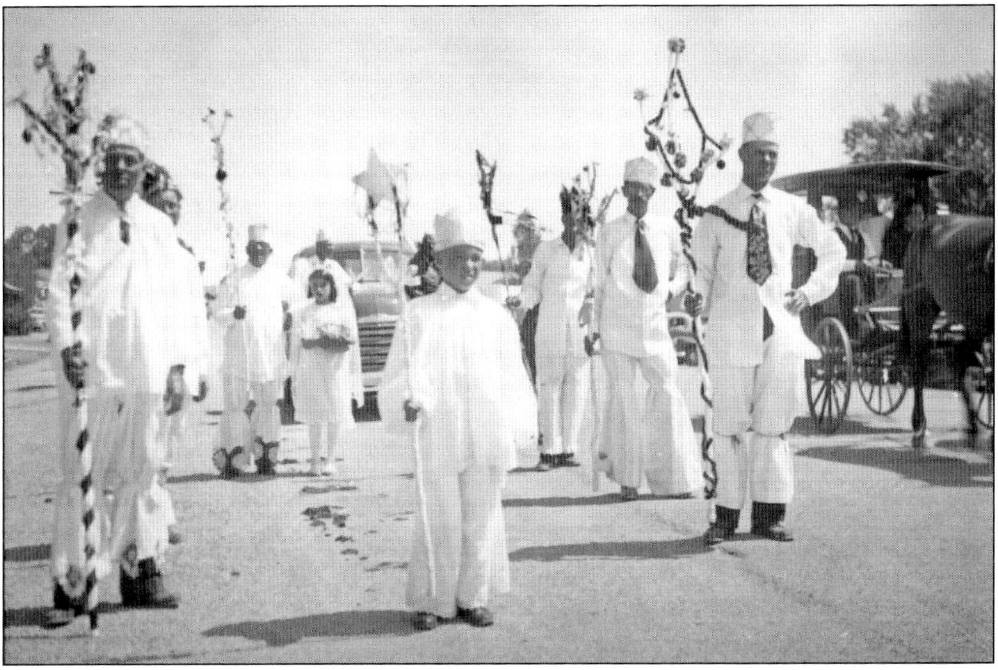

This troupe of actors and community members march in the Santa Ana parade for the town's 100th anniversary in 1951. They are dancers in the old Spanish ritual dance Los Matachines. The dance came about in the midst of the Spanish conquest, and has been performed throughout the Southwest ever since. The play is performed with dance and music as opposed to words. Two groups of dancers representing the Christians and the Moors approach each other from opposite directions. The groups dance toward each other to the same beat. The music and the dance are different for each special feast. In the old version, the little girl bride symbolized virtue and was the bringer of peace. (Courtesy of History Colorado.)

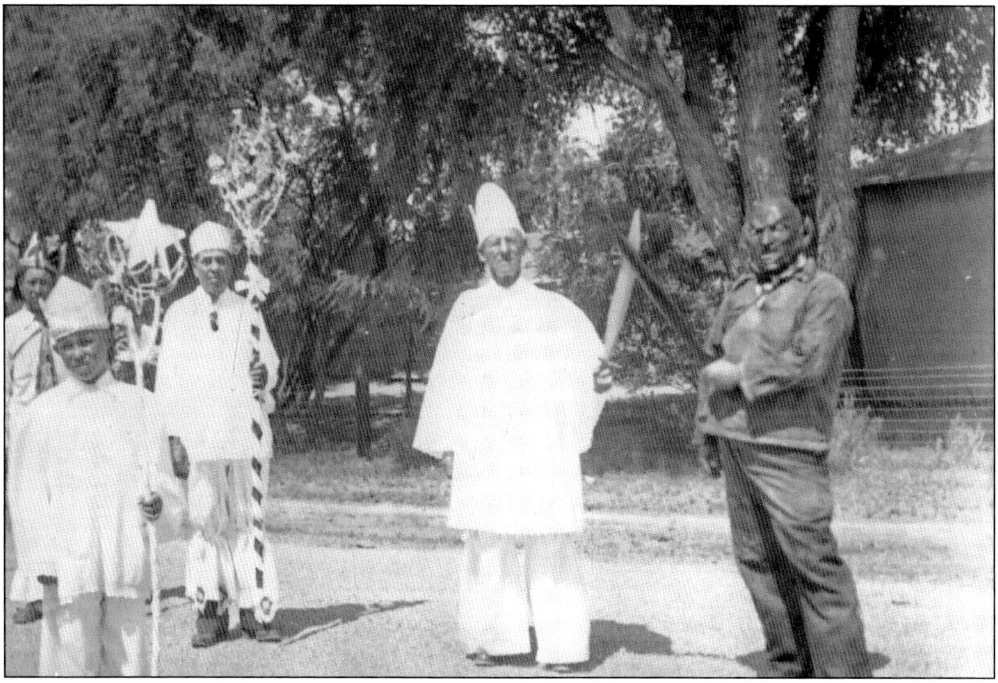

Members of Los Matachines wait for the centennial parade to begin. In this Spanish dance introduced in the 1600s, the Spanish and the Pueblo Indians come together, dancing to the same song, symbolizing their unity. The role of the devil, often called El Abuelo, is to keep the beat and maintain discipline by cracking a whip. He asks the children, "Sabes tus oraciones?" El Matachin, La Malinche, and El Toro are some of the other characters in the dance. (Both, courtesy of History Colorado.)

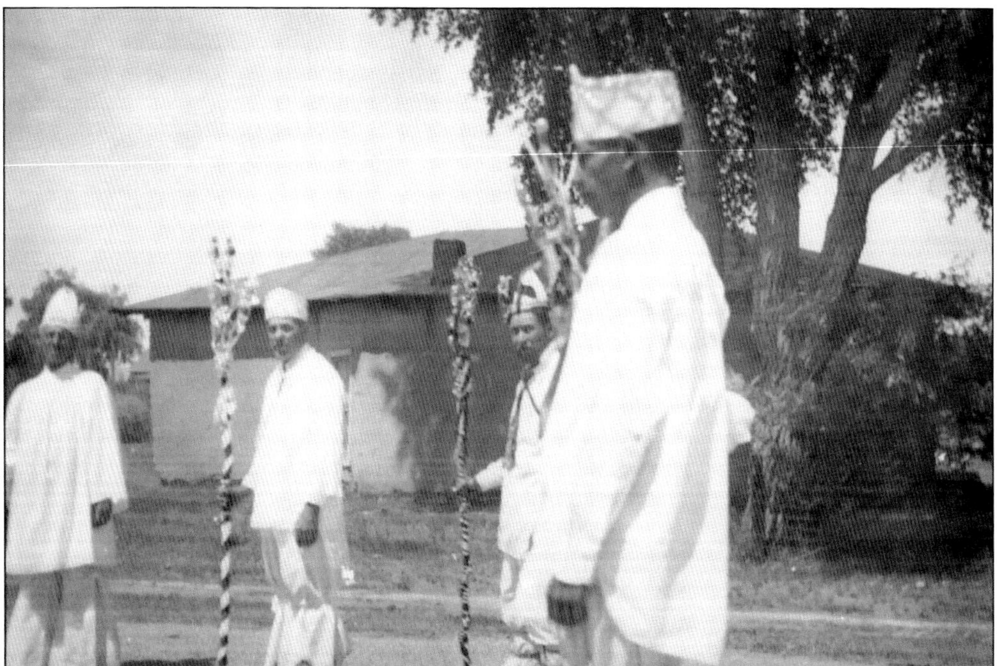

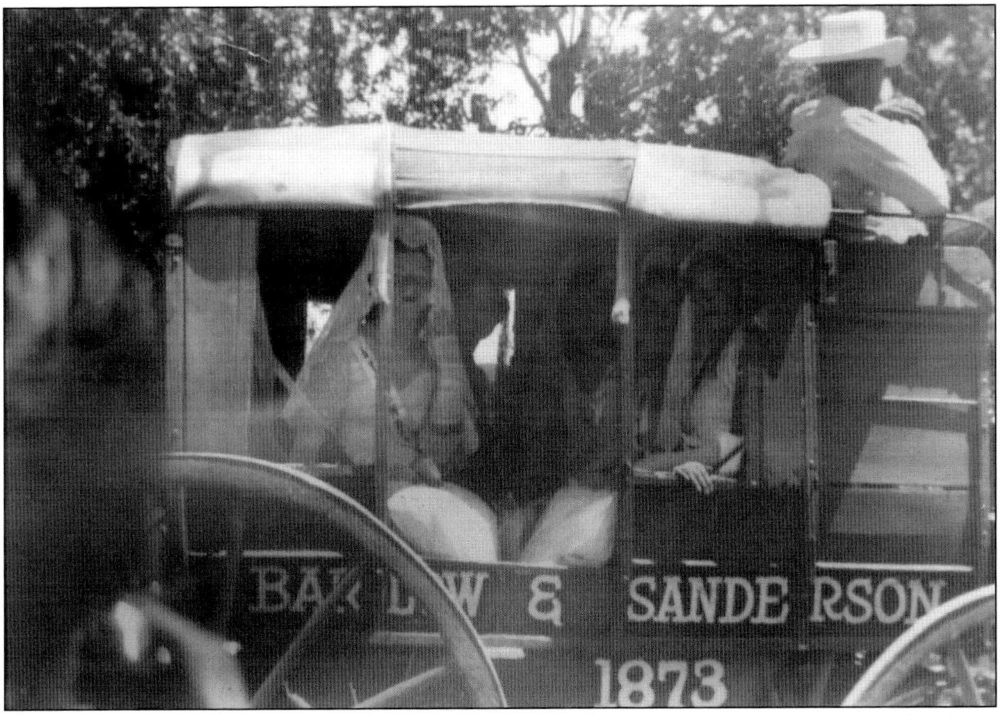

During the 1951 Santiago y Santa Ana fiesta parade, this old-time carriage carried the fiesta queen, Jackie Vigil, and her court—Henrietta Lobato, Ella Martinez, Helen Olivas, and Josephine Maestas. (Courtesy of Henrietta Mascarenas.)

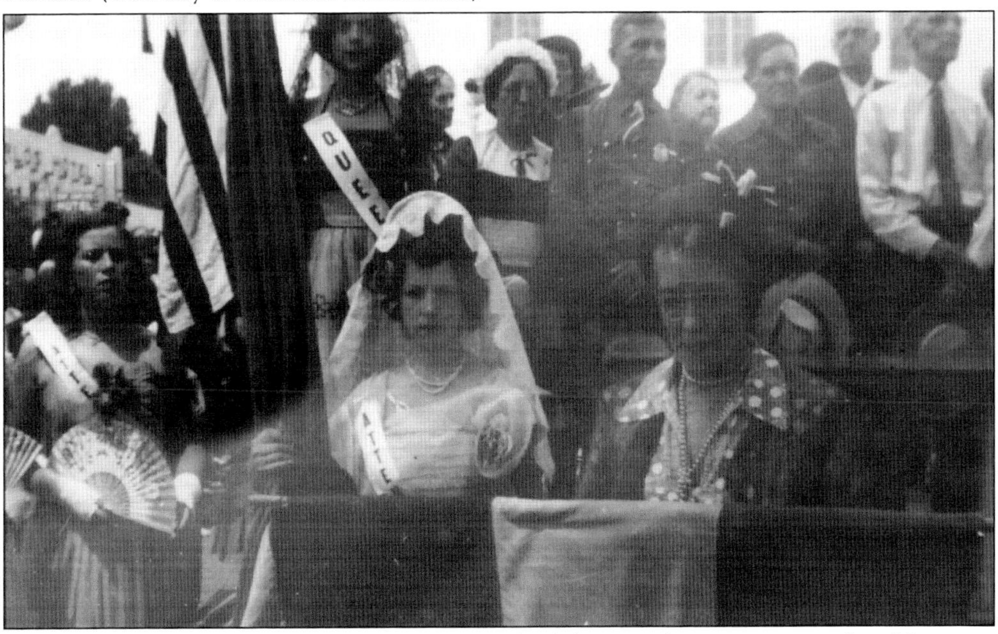

During the 1951 Santiago y Santa Ana centennial celebration, fiesta queen attendant Henrietta Lobato is seated next to her aunt Bertha Hasik, who was a speaker on the history of San Luis. In the background are fiesta queen Jackie Vigil and other dignitaries. The platform is in front of the Costilla County courthouse. (Courtesy of Henrietta Mascarenas.)

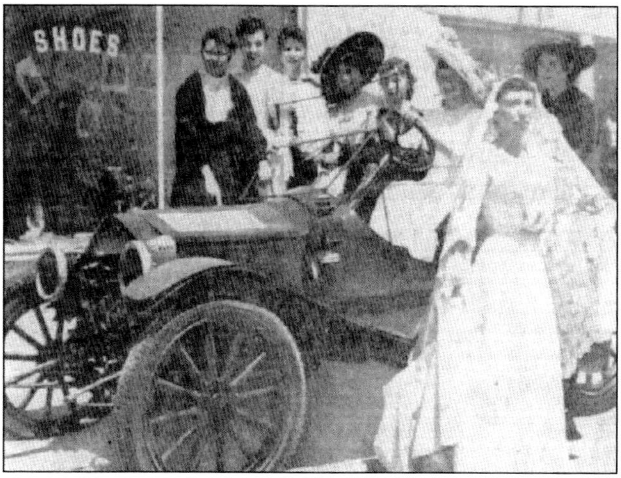

These young women model period costumes to celebrate the 1957 centennial of the Salazar store in San Luis. The original Gallegos Mercantile opened in 1857, nineteen years before Colorado became a state. The girls surround a classic Metz automobile parked in front of the shoe store (presently Mrs. Rios Restaurant). From left to right are Katherine Gallegos, unidentified, Alice Smith, Karen Smith, Elena Gallegos, Louise Smith, Patsy Carpenter, and Kathleen Gallegos (front). (Anonymous.)

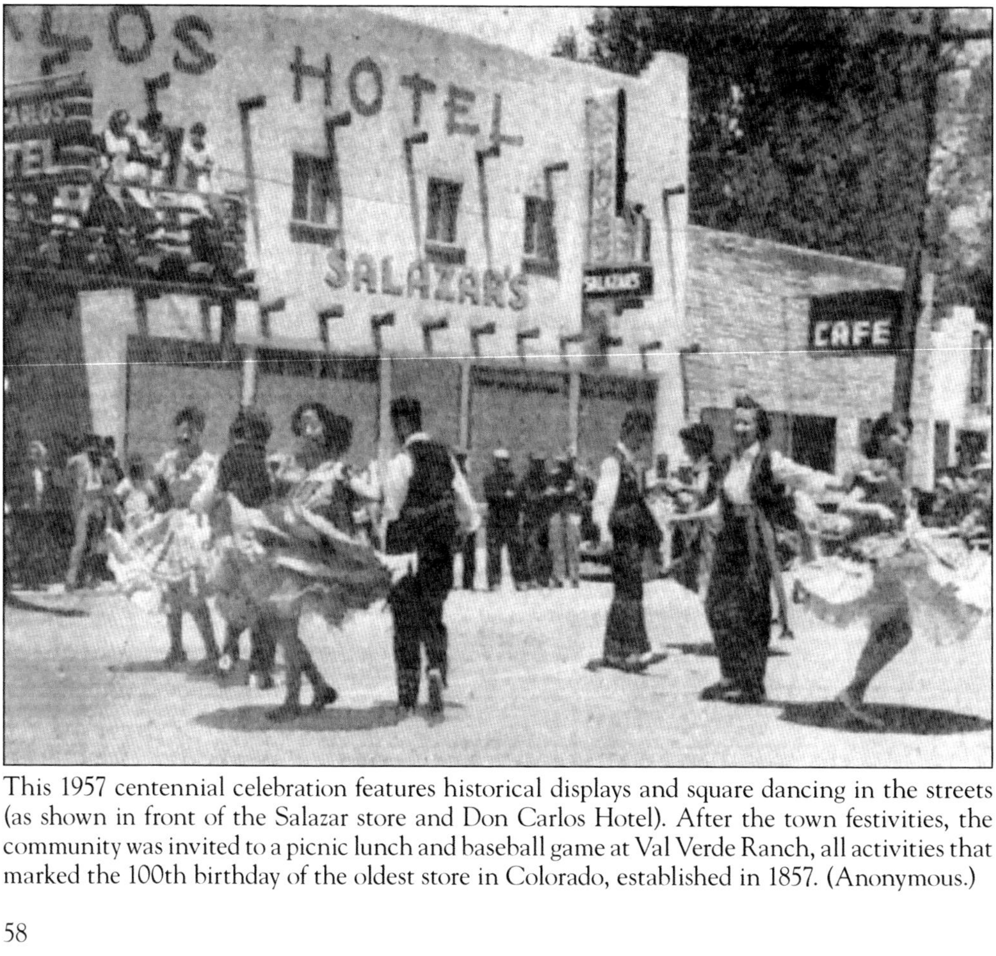

This 1957 centennial celebration features historical displays and square dancing in the streets (as shown in front of the Salazar store and Don Carlos Hotel). After the town festivities, the community was invited to a picnic lunch and baseball game at Val Verde Ranch, all activities that marked the 100th birthday of the oldest store in Colorado, established in 1857. (Anonymous.)

Delino and Sofia Salazar, owners of the Salazar store in San Luis, are pictured with Olivia Vigil during the 1957 commemoration of the store's centennial. An employee of the store, Miss Vigil helped serve hot dogs and drinks to over 500 people at the Val Verde Ranch, also known as the Rancho del Valle. The ranch was owned by Delfino Salazar. (Courtesy of Olivia Maestas family.)

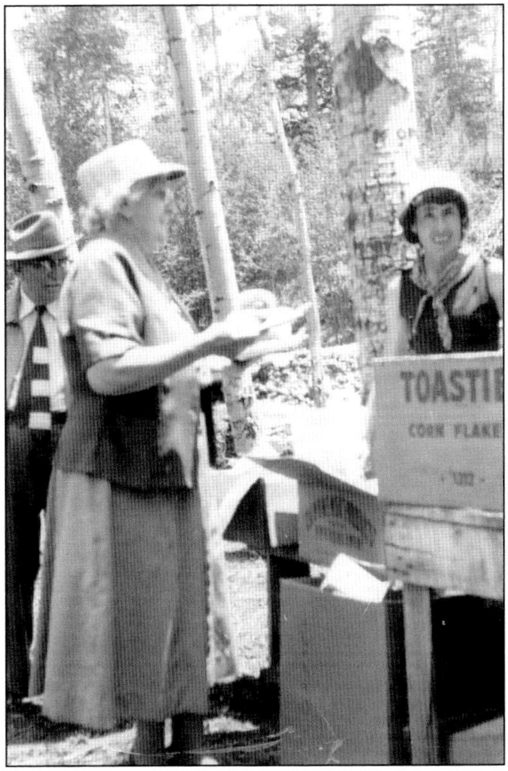

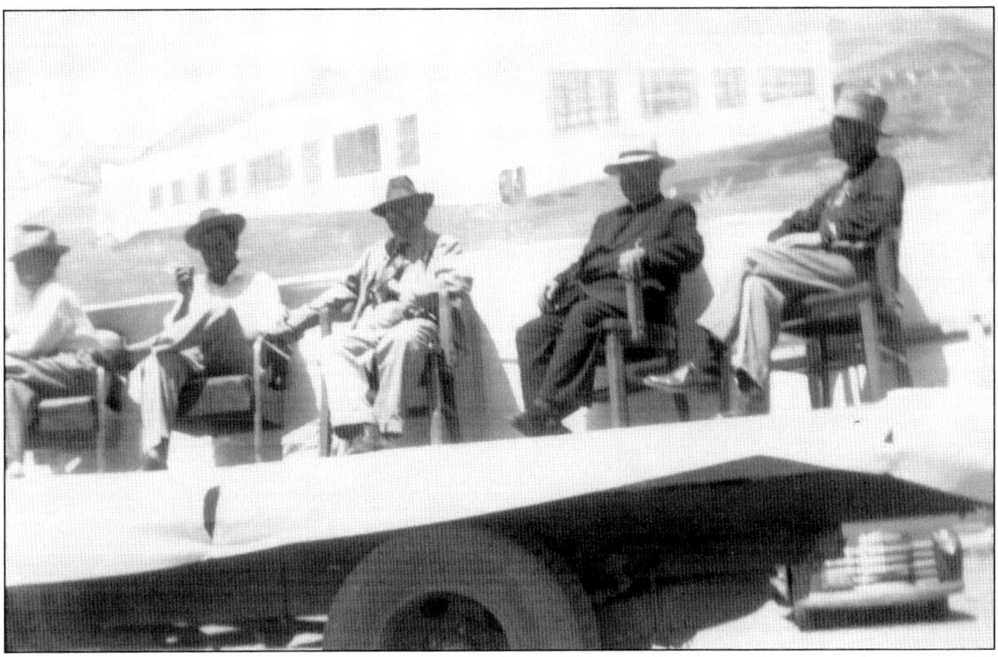

These men are seated on the float for the annual Santa Ana y Santiago fiesta parade. George G. Romero, owner of the oldest continuously family-run business in Colorado, is second from left. Fourth from left is Father Onofrey Mortorell. The other two men are unidentified. (Courtesy of Pat Trujillo VanZandt.)

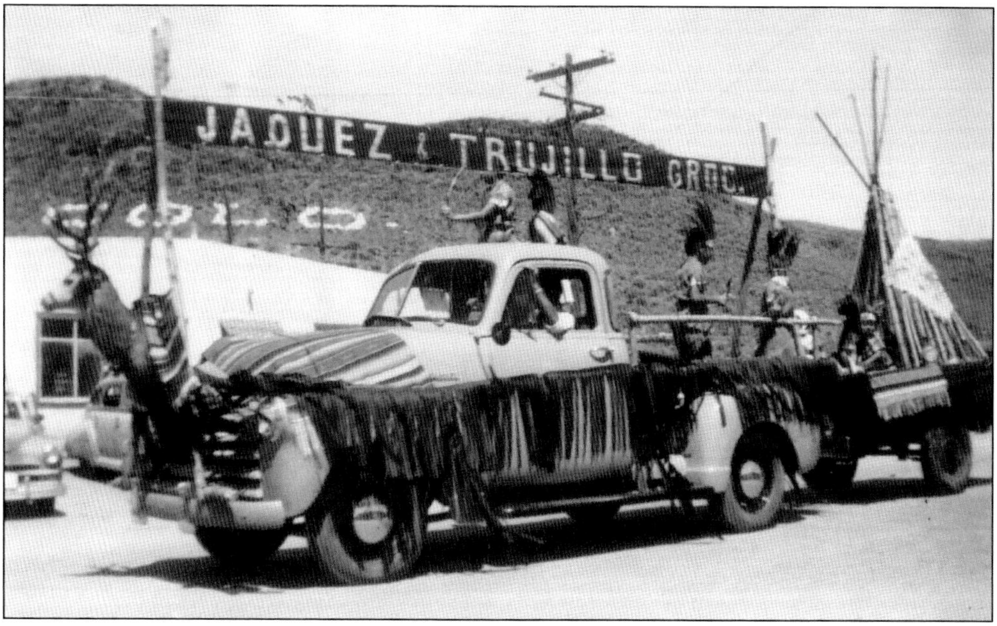

This Native American–themed parade float was sponsored by the Jaquez-Trujillo Grocery Store. An old pickup truck with an elk head mounted in front represented the culture of hunting for food. For the Jaquez children—Charlie, Marie, Jimmy, Freddie, and Lillian, all dressed in native attire—it was a special treat to ride this float during the annual Santiago y Santa Ana fiesta celebrations. (Courtesy of Pat Trujillo VanZandt.)

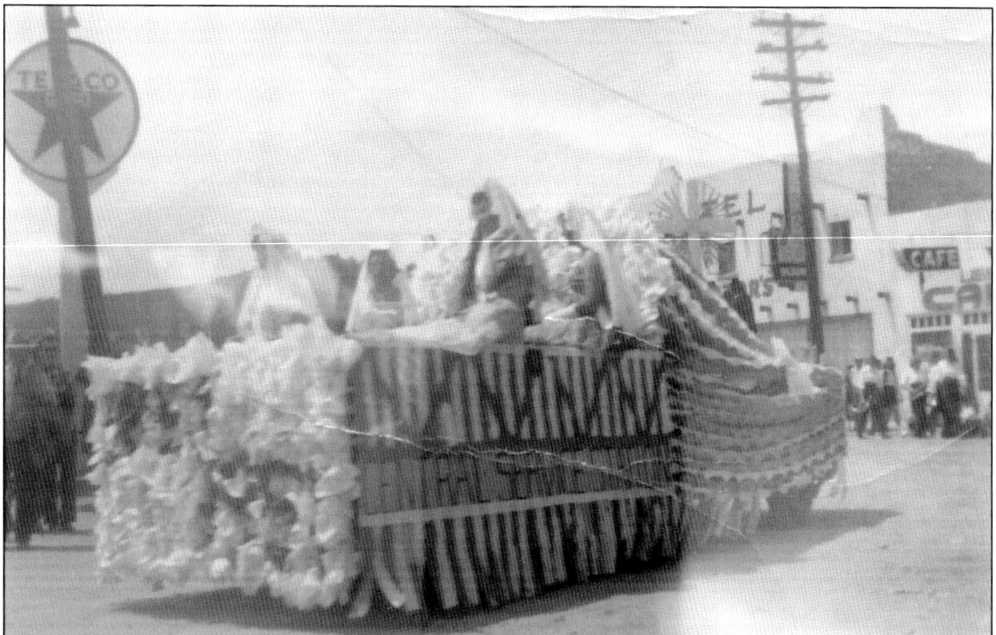

This 1950s Santiago y Santa Ana fiesta parade float carried the fiesta queen and her attendants. The float was sponsored by Central Service Station. As it turns onto Main Street, two prominent businesses, the Texaco Service Station and Liberty Café, can be seen in the background. (Courtesy of Pat Trujillo VanZandt.)

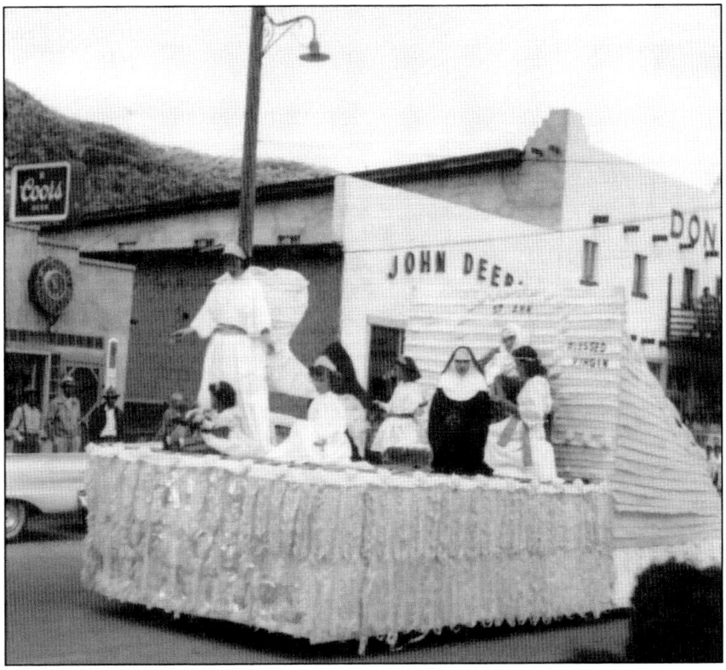

This fancifully decorated parade float represents St. Anne, patron saint of San Luis, and the Blessed Virgin. The children are dressed in religious costumes. In the background is the John Deer hardware store, part of the expansion of the Salazar store in the 1950s. (Courtesy of Richard Olivas y Cordova.)

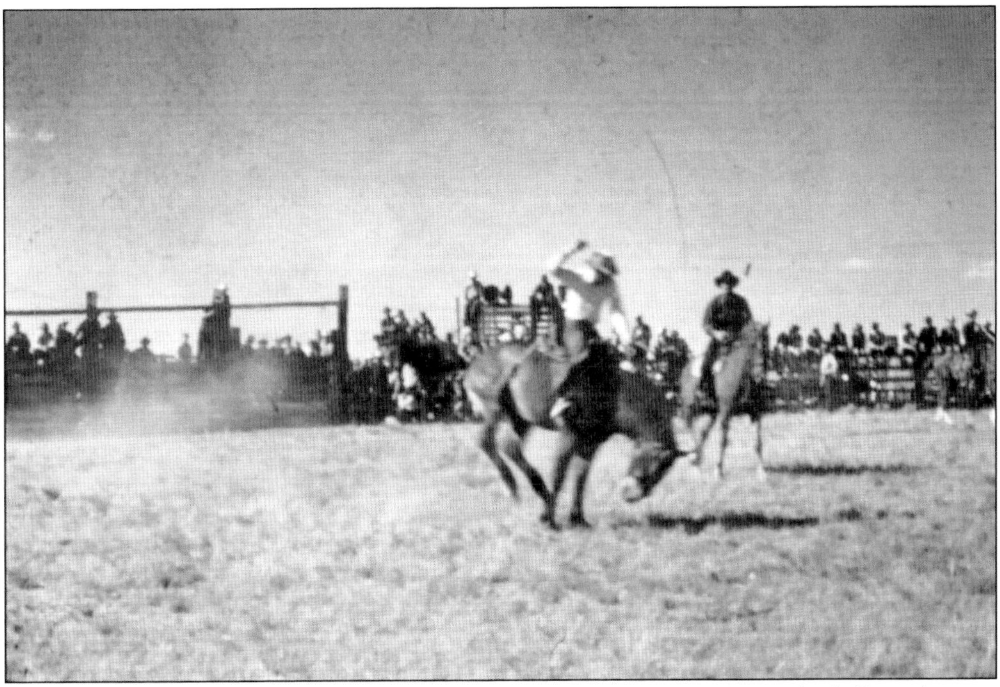

The fiestas of the Culebra basin would not be the same without a rodeo and *caballeros* showing their skill at riding horses. Pictured is an unidentified young man trying to remain on a bucking horse at the local rodeo grounds. Rodeos and horse races were a favorite pastime of the settlers, and the fiestas were the best time for cowboys to show off their talents. (Courtesy of Richard Olivas y Cordova.)

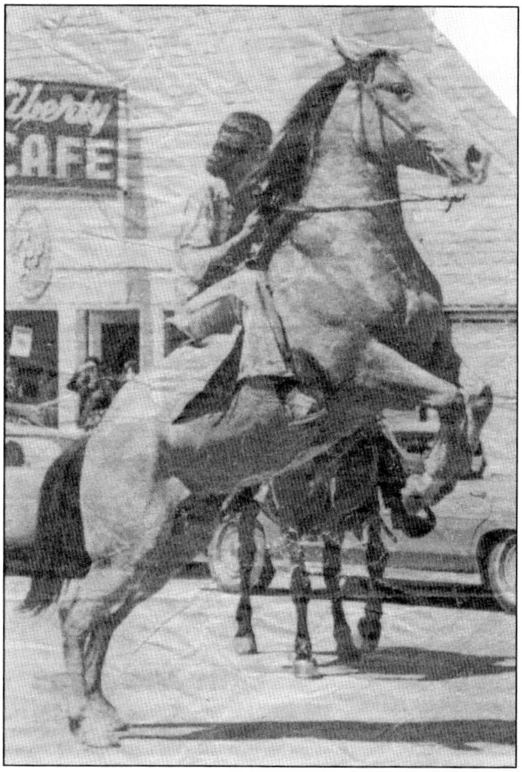

Pictured on a rearing horse is Clarence Vigil on July 26, 1980. The photograph was taken during the annual Santiago–Santa Ana parade in celebration of the town's patron saint. The Vigil family continues to ride in the annual parade, garnering attention and applause for their expert horsemanship. (Courtesy of Clarence and Casilda Vigil.)

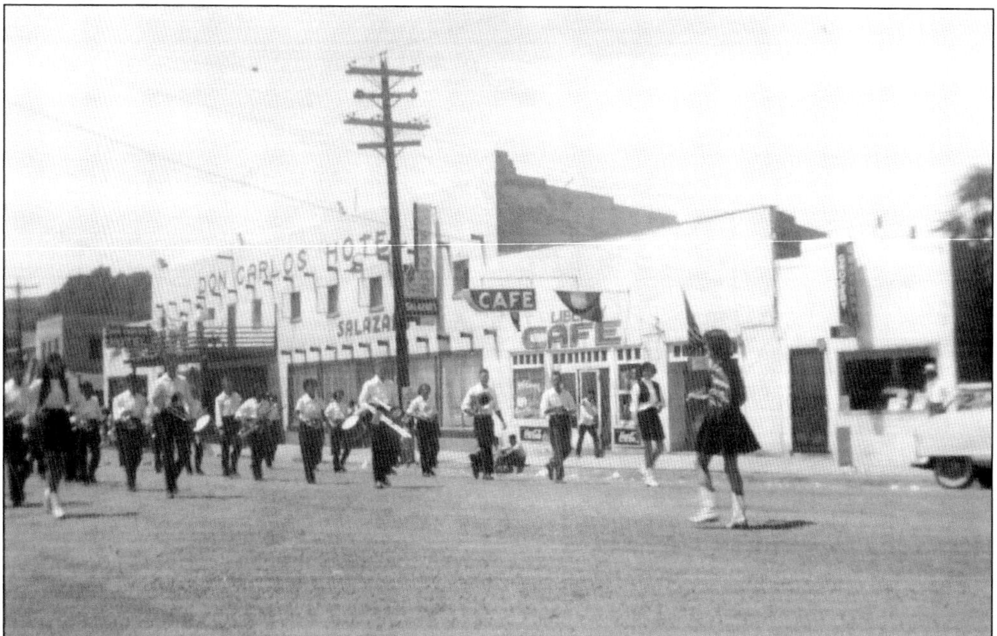

In this c. 1950s photograph, the school marching band is led by an unidentified drum major, and two majorettes perform in front of the Don Carlos Hotel, Salazar store, Liberty Café, and bus depot. The fiesta parades were always led by the commanding sound of a marching band. (Courtesy of Pat Trujillo VanZandt.)

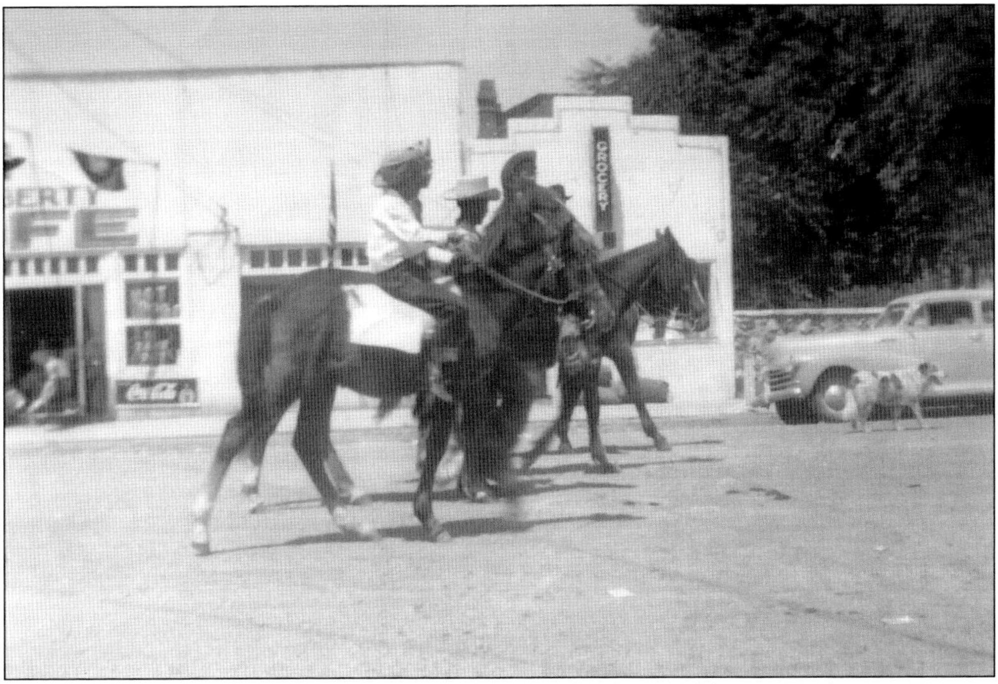

Veteran riders have always been a traditional part of the fiesta celebrations. These young men brought out their horses for the annual fiesta parade and rode up and down Main Street, just as was done years ago. (Courtesy of Pat Trujillo VanZandt.)

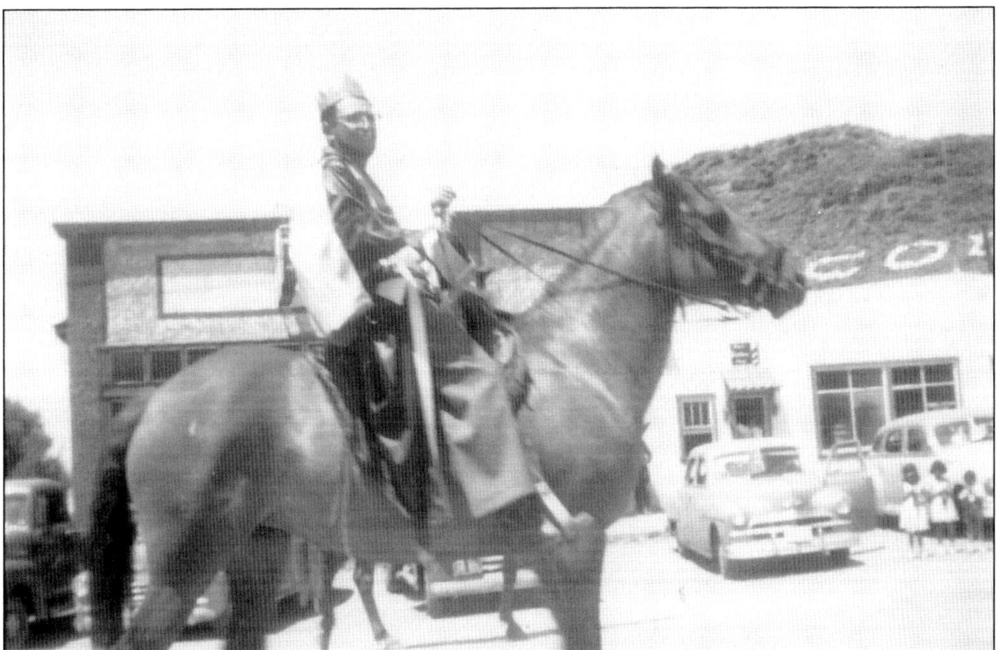

This unidentified rider is dressed as a king during the 1951 Santiago y Santa Ana parade. He could have been one of the many characters who performed in plays during the fiestas. Three children watch in front of the barbershop. (Courtesy of Pat Trujillo VanZandt.)

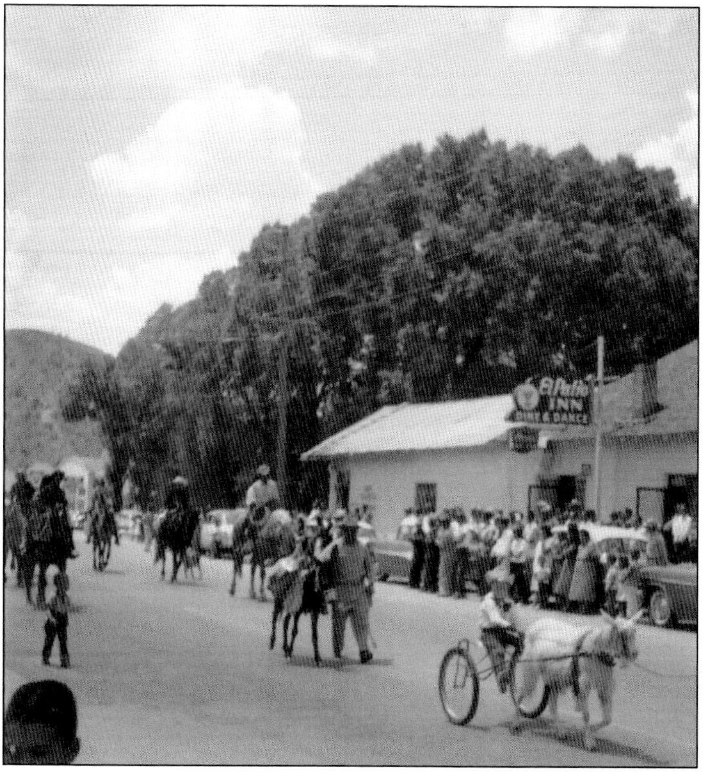

Spectators line the streets to watch the caballeros and riders parade on Main Street in San Luis during the Santiago–Santa Ana fiesta parade in the 1950s. Before the riders are a man walking a donkey and a youngster with a cowboy hat riding a small metal carriage pulled by a goat. The infamous Emma's Hacienda "Food of the Southwest" and El Patio Bar are in the background. (Courtesy of Richard Olivas y Cordova.)

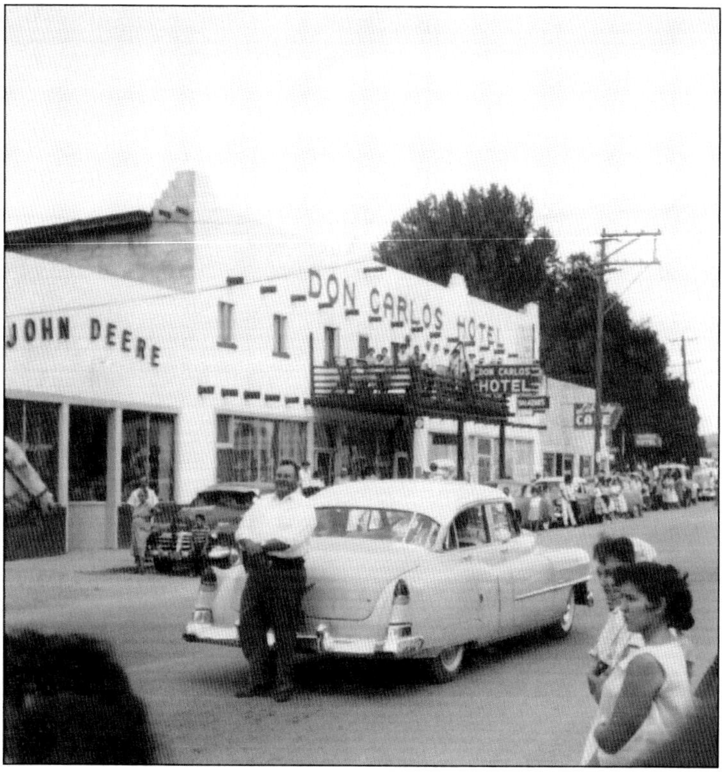

Posing for a photograph before the 1950 fiesta parade begins is Sheriff Ruben Navarro. Navarro was a forthright man who took his job seriously. He was gifted a half Alaskan huskie and half German shepherd seven-month-old puppy from the Pueblo Police Department. The dog, named King, was a perfect protector for his master. He was instrumental in keeping the peace during the Taylor Ranch Wars. (Courtesy of Richard Olivas y Cordova.)

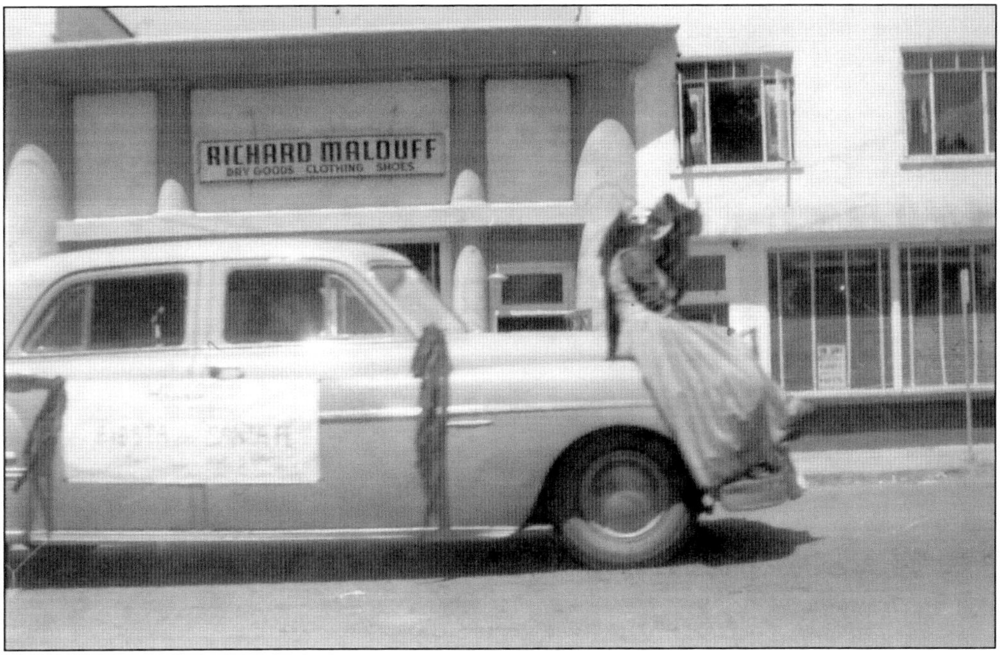

Two young women sit on a car hood with *ristras* hanging off the side windows. They are representing the city of Santa Fe for the annual Santiago–Santa Ana parade in the 1950s. In the background is the Richard Malouff store, serving the community with dry goods, clothing, and shoes. The store also sold many household items. (Courtesy of Olivia Maestas family.)

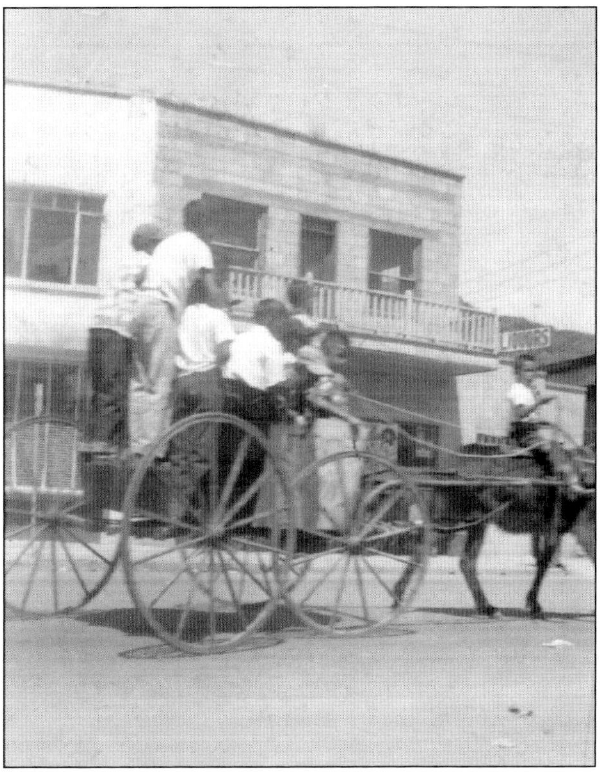

A little boy riding a horse pulls this fiesta float entry of an old wooden wagon with several children riding in it. The fiestas are a fun time for families, especially children. (Courtesy of Oliva Maestas family.)

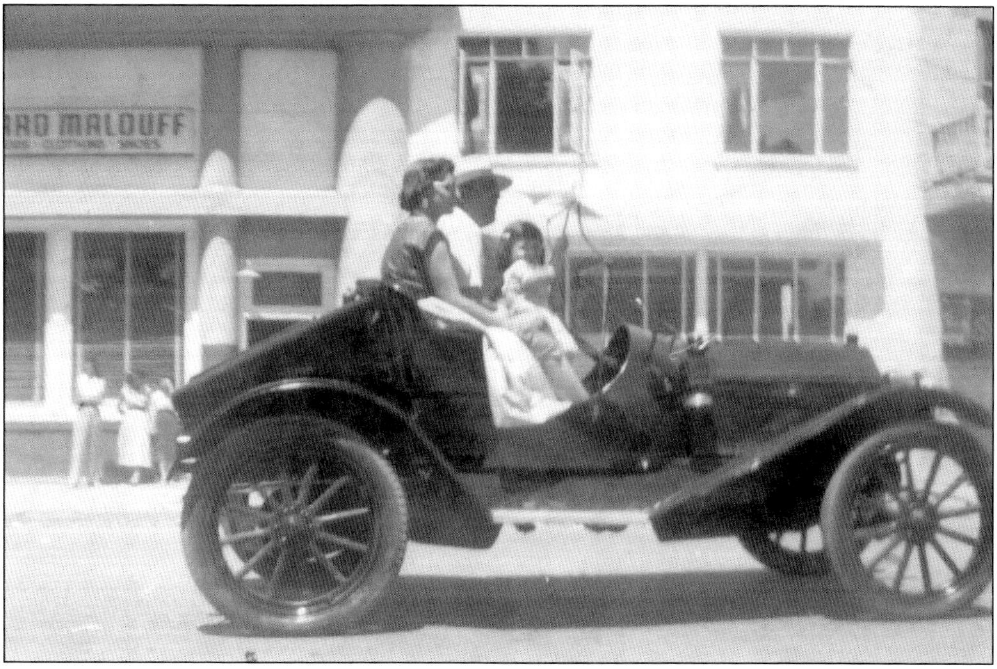

Riding in this black 1911 Metz are Charles Mondragon Sr. and his wife, Katherine (Nigro) Mondragon. The Mondragons were proprietors of the San Luis Company, a business serving the community with various types of hardware and paints. The San Luis Company was also a propane company. Their two-year-old daughter Maria rides along with them, holding an umbrella to block the sun. The fiestas are held in July, when the San Luis Valley lives up to its name of "Land of Cool Sunshine." (Courtesy of Olivia Maestas family.)

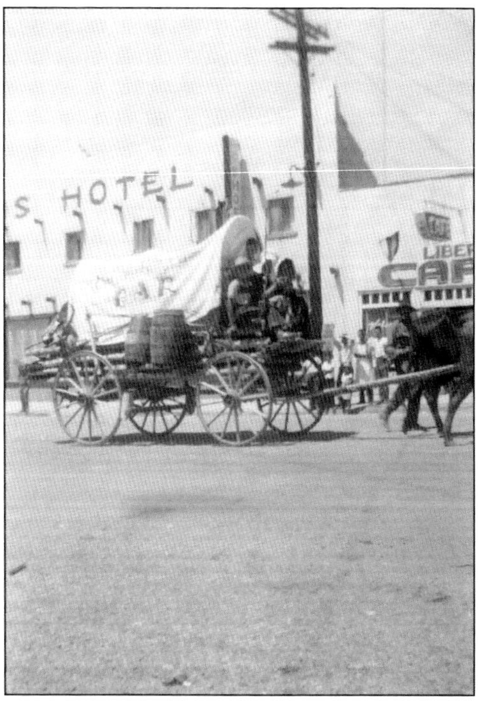

An old-fashioned covered wagon pulled by horses is the fitting ride for the Covered Wagon Bar and Restaurant, owned by Rose and Sam Medina. The business entry is pictured in front of the Salazar store and Don Carlos Hotel as it moves along in the parade during the Santiago and Santa Ana fiestas. (Courtesy of Pat Trujillo VanZandt.)

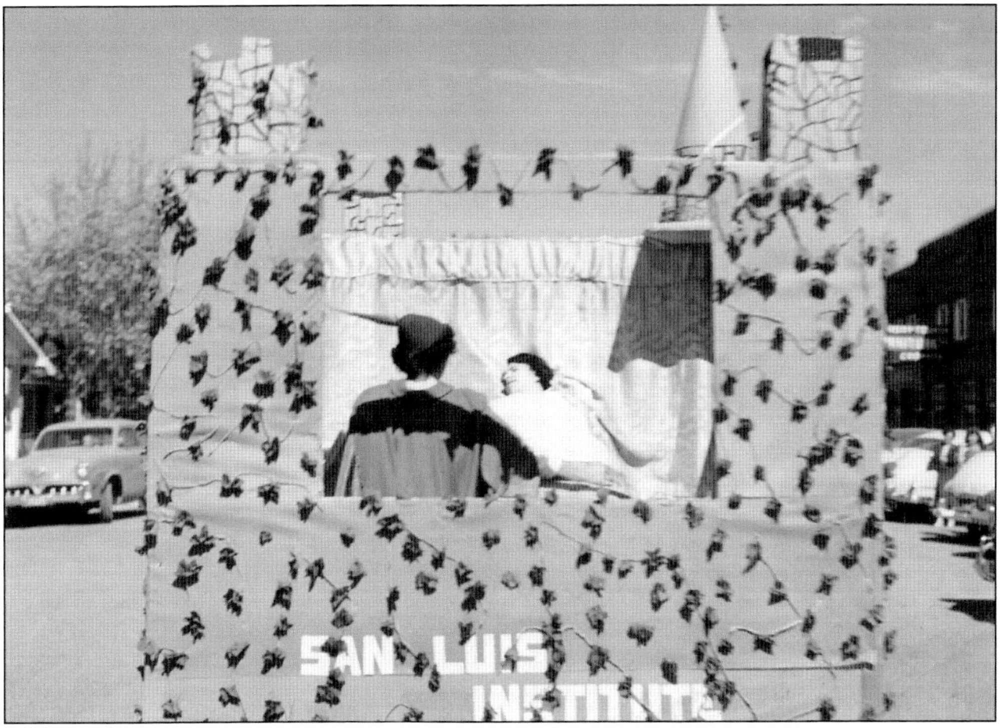

Students Sally Trujillo Chavez and Henrietta Lobato Mascarenas represent the San Luis Institute of Arts and Crafts (San Luis Museum and Cultural Center) with the themed float Sleeping Beauty. The float was part of Adams State Teachers College Homecoming Parade in Alamosa, Colorado, in 1952. (Courtesy of Henrietta Mascarenas.)

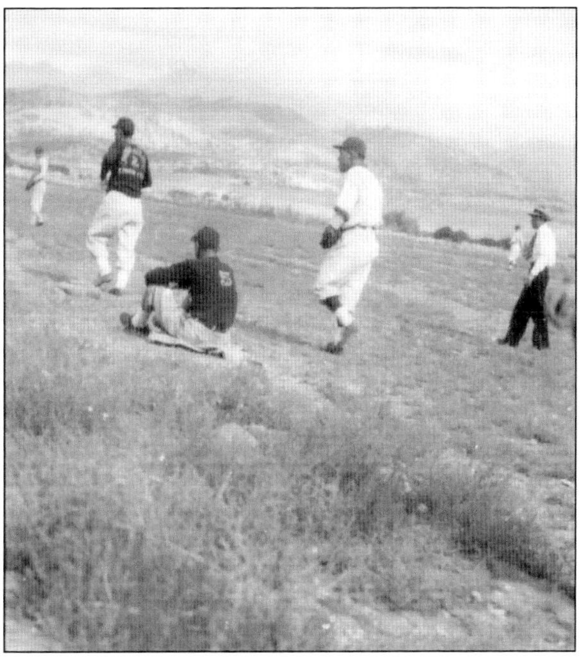

Sports have always been a way to unite a community. This 1930s photograph shows Chama's infamous baseball team the Chama Kitos. The team's humble beginnings were due to the neighborhood's need to repair a church roof. The team was organized to help raise money, and at last, the roof was repaired. As it happened, the team rarely lost a game. Families packed picnic lunches and enjoyed a Sunday afternoon watching their hometown baseball team. Some of the known early players on the team were Roberto Sanchez, Carpio Sanchez Jr., James Mascarenas, catchers Alfirio Sanchez and Solestiano Martinez, and infielders Dan Jaquez and Margarito Sanchez. (Courtesy of Richard Olivas y Cordova.)

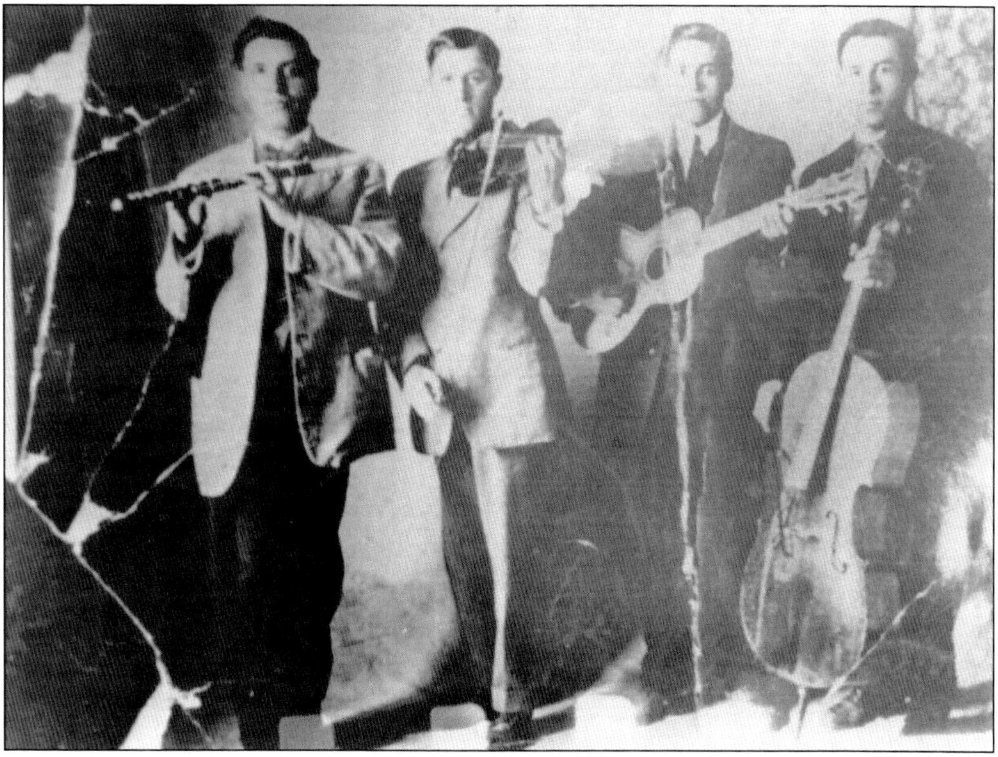

In dance halls and homes across northern New Mexico and southern Colorado, the performance of music has been a mainstay since the settlement of the Culebra villages. Taken in 1929, this photograph of the local band the Bluebirds features, from left to right, flute player José Cardenas, violinist Celestino Valdez, guitarist Jesús Garcia, and cellist Juan Espinosa. (Courtesy of Eugene and Josie Lobato.)

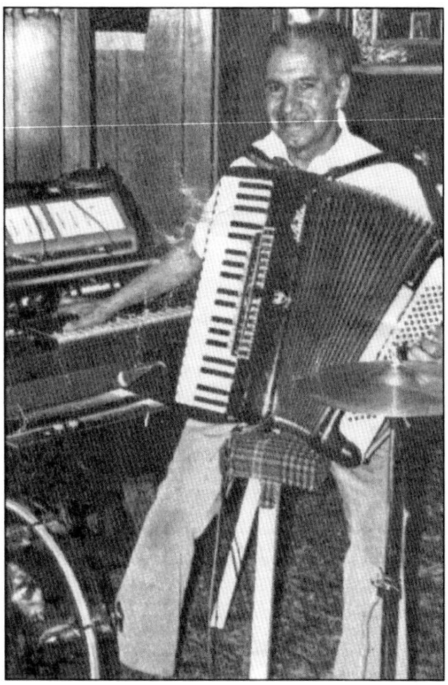

This photograph of Juan Chacon on organ, drums, and accordion shows why he was a popular one-man band who was always in demand. Chacon taught music lessons in Trinidad, Colorado, in 1928. After moving to the San Luis area, he played for weddings, dances, birthday parties, and any celebration that called for a musician. He continued to play his music, entertaining the people of San Luis, Chama, San Pablo, El Rito, and San Acacio. He is fondly remembered for a lifetime of musical talent and performances. (Courtesy of Dora Vialpando.)

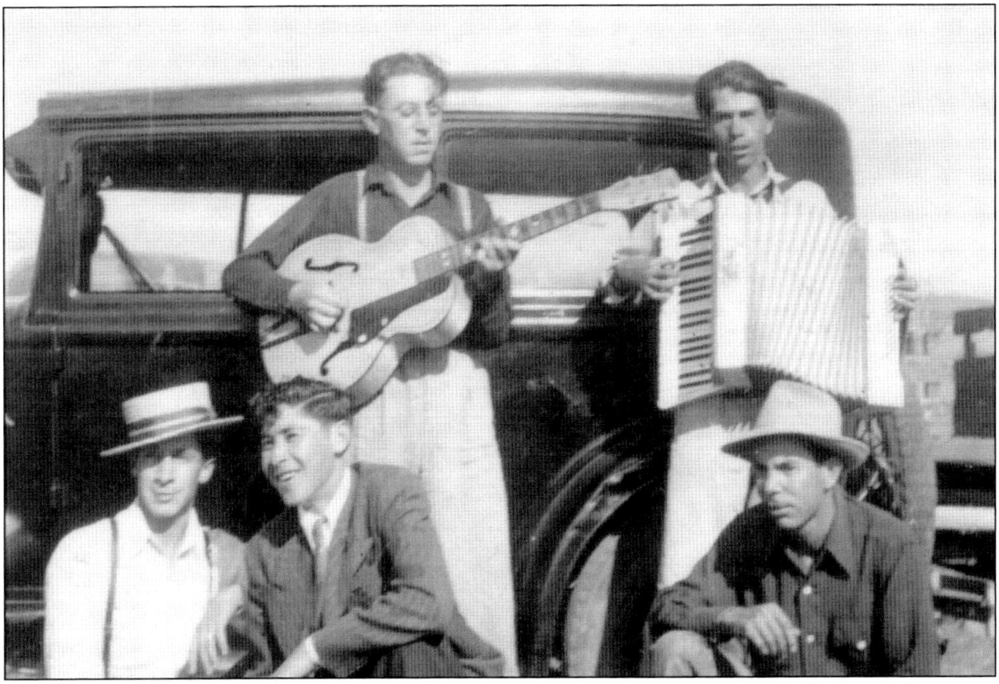

Pictured around 1939 are Anselmo DeHerrera on guitar and Margarito "Mague" Espinoza (also known as "Doc Johnson") with the accordion, along with (kneeling, from left to right) Fred Vialpando, Nestor Martinez, and Armando Valdez, in San Pedro. Musicians were a large influence on the community's social life. They turned a home into a place of entertainment. (Courtesy of Richard Olivas y Cordova.)

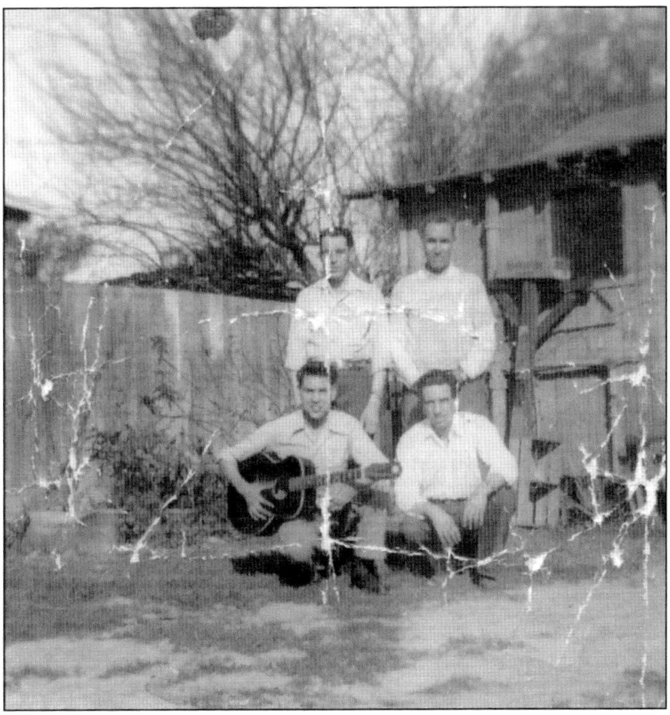

This group of young men enjoyed playing and singing together near Cañon de Chama. The man with the guitar is Orlando Atencio or Estevan Atencio; the other two are unidentified. Families gathered at a designated home after a hard day of work to tell stories, listen to music, and dance. *Músicos* (musicians) played the violin and guitar as a way to entertain and socialize with their friends and families. (Courtesy of Clarence and Casilda Vigil.)

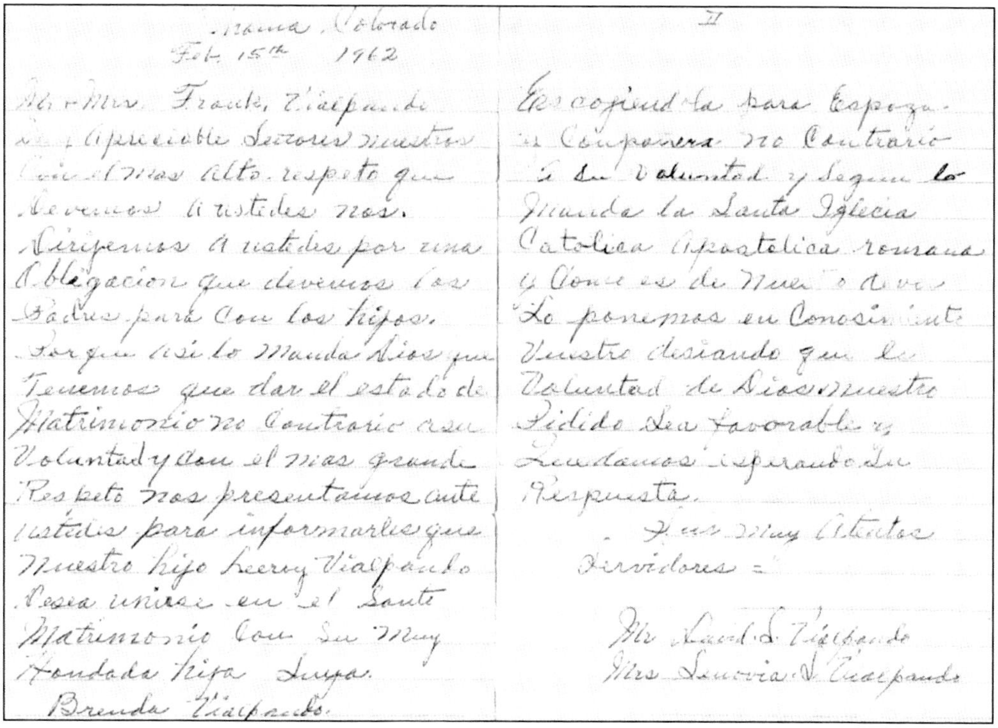

Nama, Colorado
Feb 15th 1962

Mr + Mrs. Frank, Vialpando
muy Apreciable Señores nuestros
Con el mas Alto respeto que
devemos a ustedes nos
Dirijemos A ustedes por una
Obligacion que devemos los
Padres para Con los hijos.
Porque asi lo Manda Dios que
Tenemos que dar el estado de
Matrimonio no Contrario a su
Voluntad y con el mas grande
Respeto nos presentamos ante
ustedes para informarles que
Nuestro hijo Leroy Vialpando
Desea unirse en el Santo
Matrimonio Con Su Muy
Honrada hija Suya.
Brenda Vialpando.

II

Escojiendola para Esposa
y Compañera no Contrario
a Su Voluntad y Segun lo
Manda la Santa Iglecia
Catolica Apostolica romana
y Como es de Nuestro deber
Lo ponemos en Conosimiento
Vuestro desiando que la
Voluntad de Dios nuestro
Pidido Sea favorable y
Quedamos esperando Su
Respuesta.
Sus Muy Atentos
Servidores =

Mr David S. Vialpando
Mrs Senovia S. Vialpando

Written in Spanish, this pedimento is from February 15, 1962. David Vialpando and Senovia Vialpando requested the hand of Brenda Vialpando in marriage to their son LeRoy Vialpando. The letter is addressed to Frank and Isabelita Vialpando. A pedimento was the custom of asking for a girl's hand in marriage in the form of a letter. Brenda and LeRoy Vialpando have been happily married for 52 years. They raised two children and have five grandchildren. (Courtesy of Brenda Vialpando.)

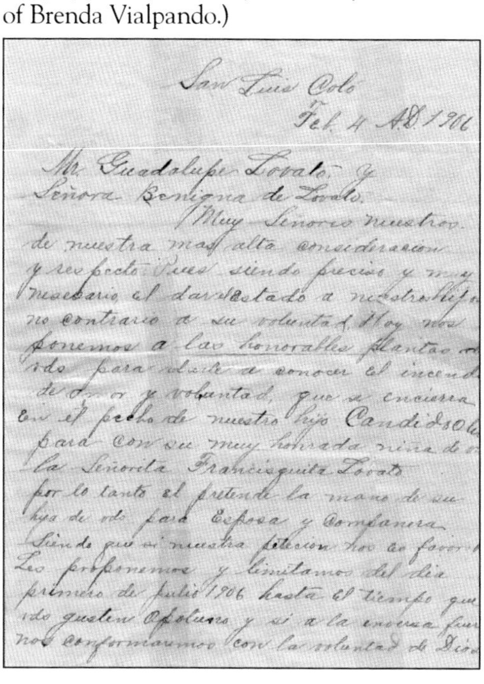

San Luis Colo
Feb. 4 AD 1906

Mr. Guadalupe Lovato y
Señora Benigna de Lovato.
Muy Señores nuestros
de nuestra mas alta consideracion
y respecto. Pues siendo preciso y muy
necesario el dar estado a nuestros hijos
no contrario a su voluntad Hoy nos
ponemos a las honorables plantas de
uds para darle a conocer el incendio
de amor y voluntad, que se encierra
en el pecho de nuestro hijo Candido Ol
para con su muy honrada niña de
la Señorita Francisquita Lovato
por lo tanto el pretende la mano de su
hija de uds para Esposa y Compañera
Siendo que si nuestra peticion hoy es favor
Les proponemos y limitamos del dia
primero de Julio 1906 hasta el tiempo que
uds gusten Ofoluro y si a la inversa fuer
nos conformaremos con la voluntad de Dios

This pedimento is from Maria de Ignicita Olivas to Benigna and Guadalupe Lovato, asking for their daughter Francisquita's hand in marriage. It is dated February 4, 1906. The woman's parents had seven days to respond with a no or ten days to respond with a yes. Asking for a woman's hand in marriage is a custom dating back to medieval Spain. The *prendorio*, a meeting to formally introduce the bride and groom to their respective families, would took place one week or one day before the wedding. (Courtesy of Candido Olivas Sr. family.)

This lovely picture shows newlyweds 27-year-old Maria Odila Lobato and 28-year-old Diego Antonio Gallegos. They were married at Most Precious Blood Catholic Church on July 12, 1926, in San Luis. In 1929, they built a family home three miles west of San Luis. (Courtesy of Hope Gallegos Yost.)

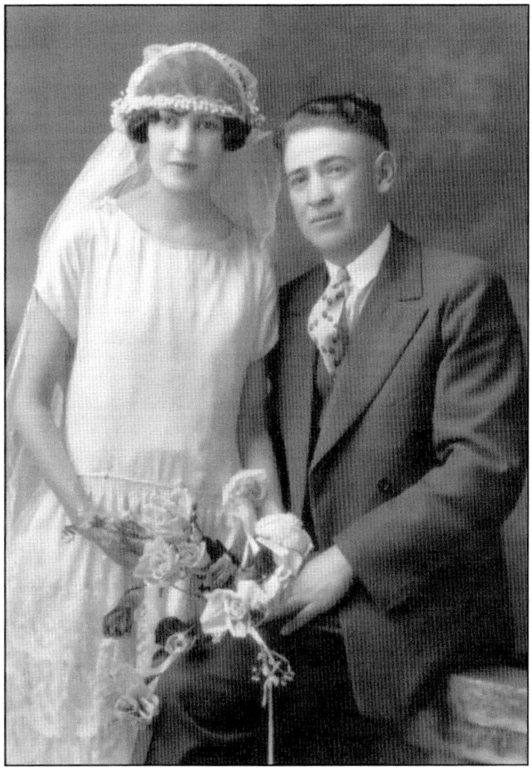

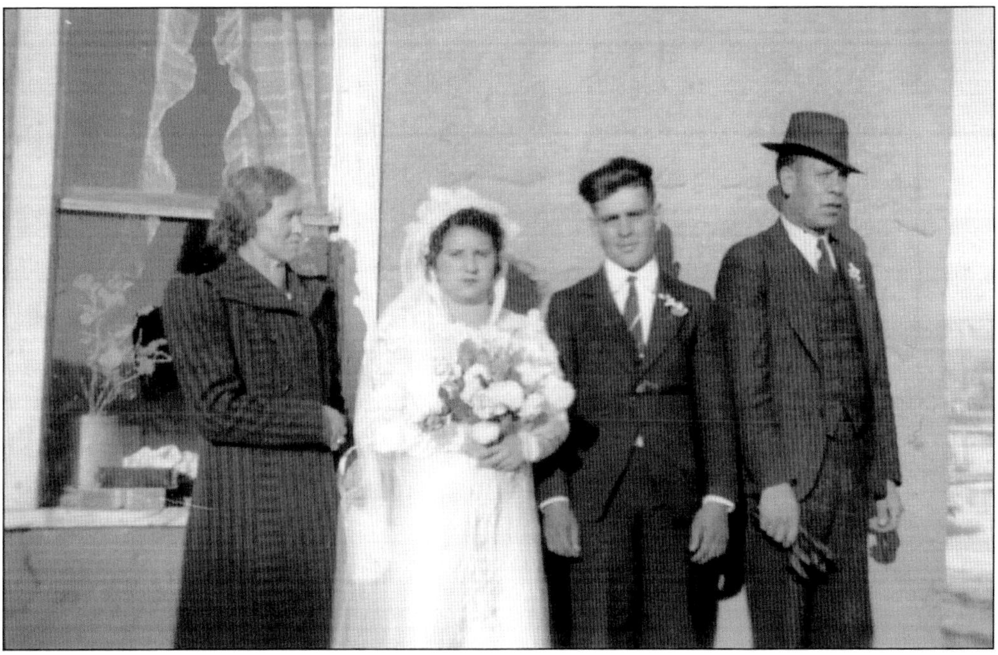

This newlywed couple poses in front of their family's adobe home on November 25, 1940. From left to right are Leonarda Mondragon, affectionately called "Mamita;" bride Ciria Taylor Sandoval; groom Federico Sandoval; and, looking off into the distance wearing what appears to be a fedora, Francisco (Kiko) Mondragon. (Courtesy of Pat Trujillo VanZandt.)

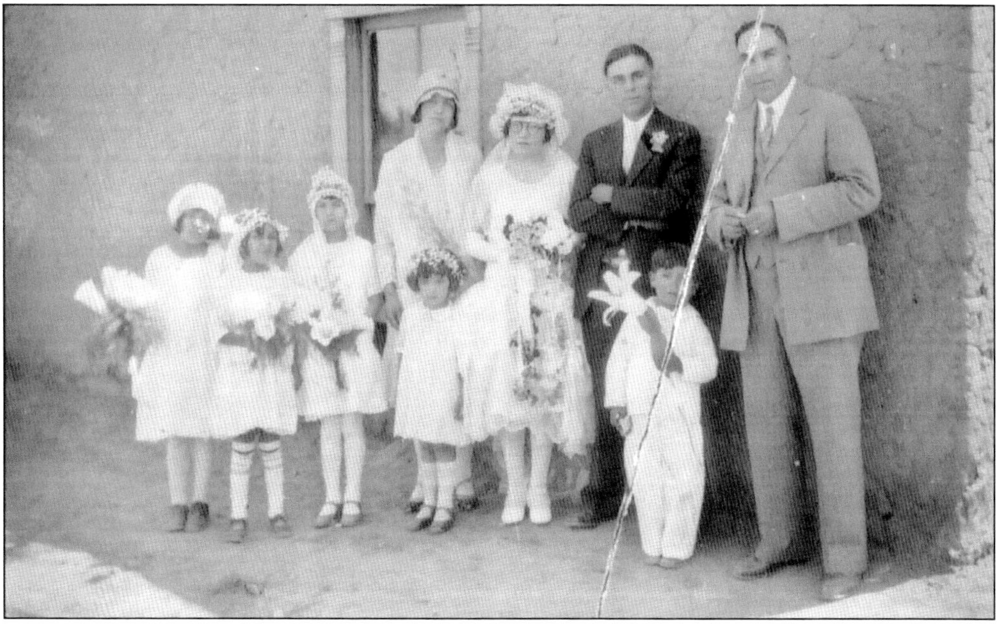

This c. 1928 photograph shows the marriage celebration of Felix Vialpando and Josefita Valdez. The wedding party includes children of family members. The *padrinos* (maid of honor and best man) are Enriqueta Choury Lobato and Emilio Lobato Sr. Felix is the Lobatos' nephew. (Courtesy of Henrietta Mascarenas.)

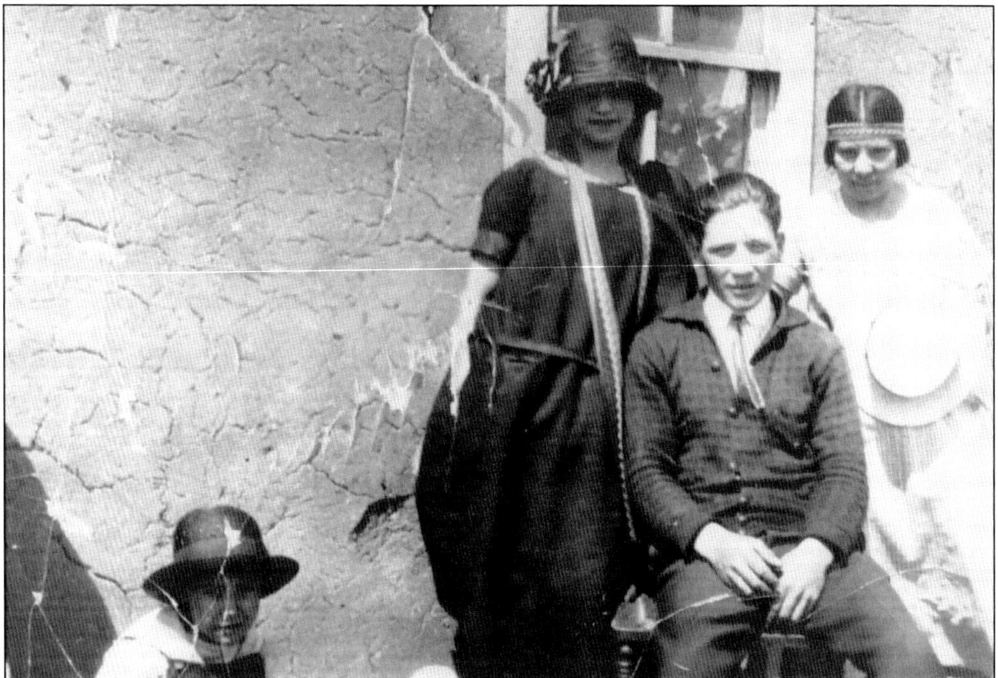

Pictured in the 1920s is newly married couple Julian Lucero and Charlotte Cardenas Lucero, with Clorinda Aragon, who later married Ernest Cardenas. The little boy kneeling is Clorinda's younger brother Felipe Aragon. (Courtesy of Eugene and Josie Lobato.)

This wedding portrait was taken on November 24, 1917, in San Luis. The bride is Lucinda Gallegos, who was born on May 15, 1894, and the groom is Manuel Pacheco, who was born on December 18, 1894. Mrs. Gallegos Pacheco taught school for many years in a small town around La Veta Pass, Colorado. (Courtesy of Hope Gallegos Yost.)

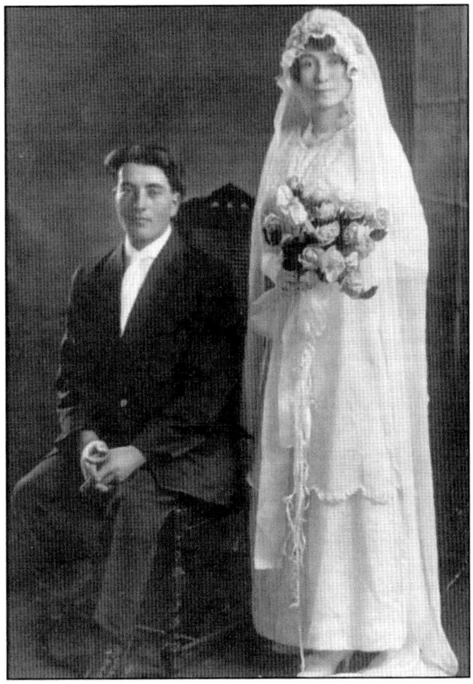

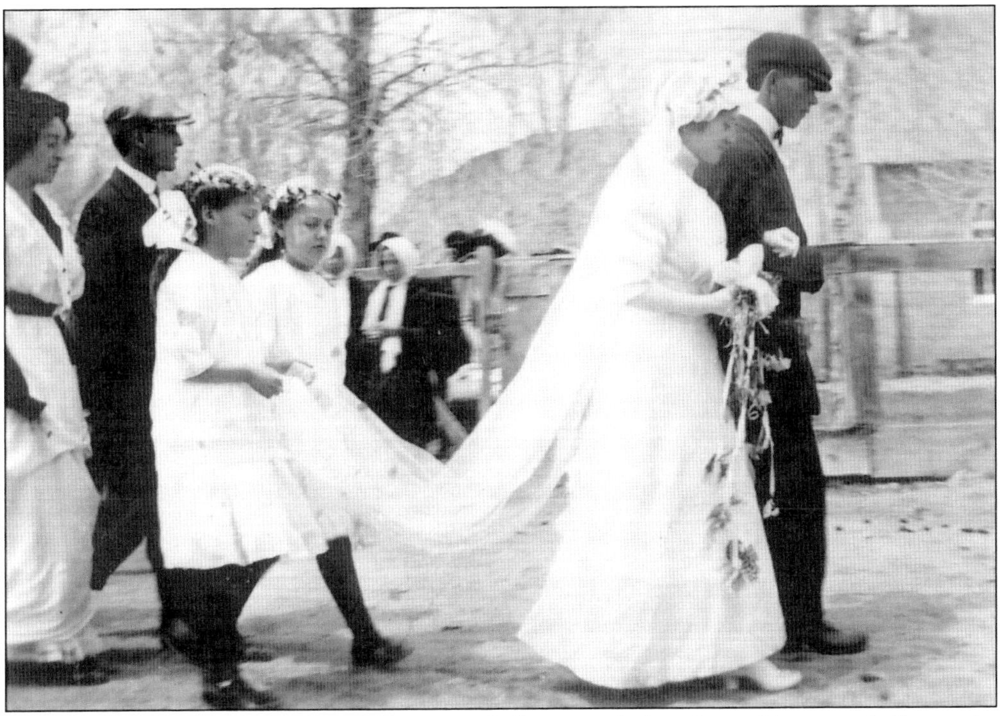

Newlyweds Timoteo Martinez and Genoveva Gallegos are led in the wedding march (*la marcha de los novios*) as their attendants and guests follow in a procession to the reception area. The Sangre de Cristo Church, formerly Most Precious Blood Parish, is in the background. Timoteo and his wife ran a grocery store, Timotes, in Cuba, the residential area of San Luis, for many years. (Courtesy of Diana Cortez.)

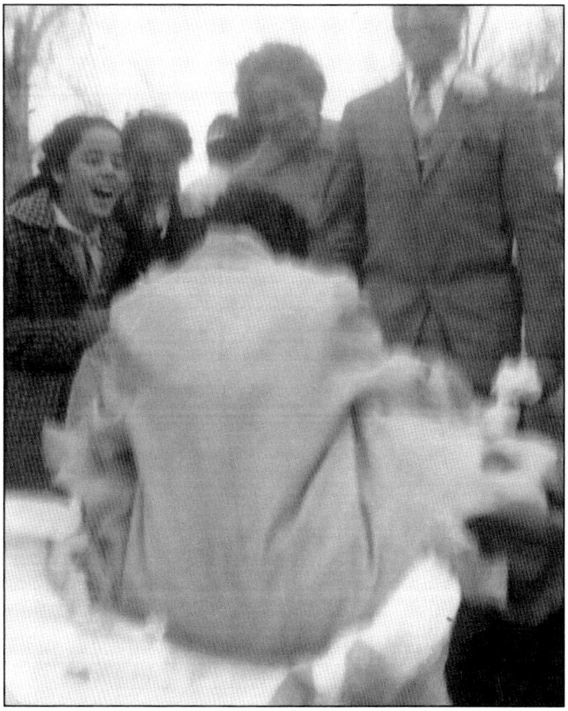

Donald Maestas and family happily look on as bride Olivia Vigil Maestas positions herself on a wheelbarrow to be carried through the wedding procession, or la marcha, from the church to the reception hall. The wheelbarrow was used in many processions, and has become a Maestas family tradition. The wedding party, family, and the community all joined in the festivities of April 1958. (Courtesy of Olivas Maestas family.)

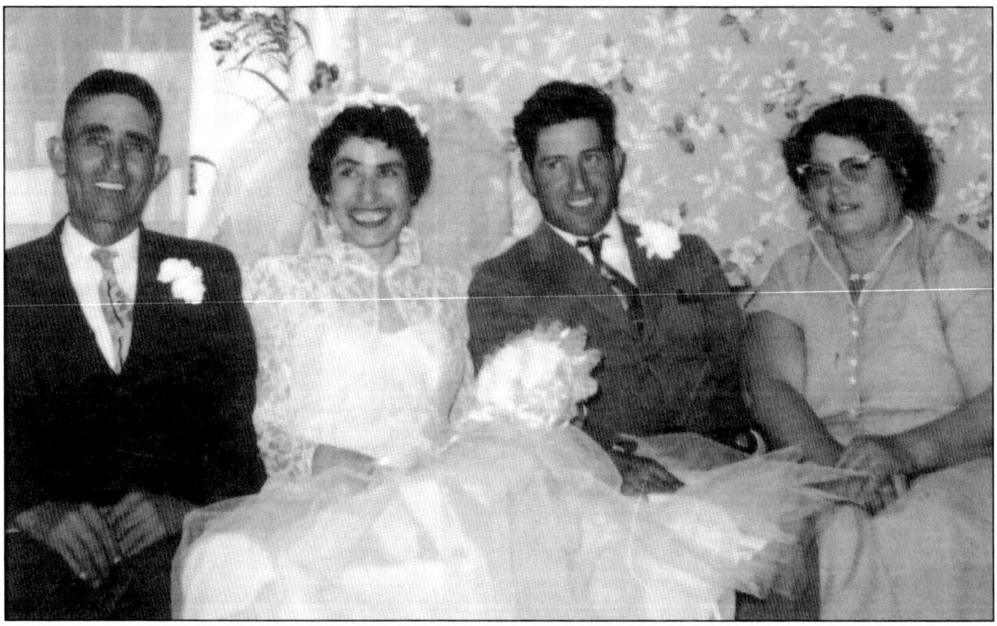

Seated in the family living room on Olivia and Donald Maestas's wedding day in April 1958 are, from left to right, the bride's father, Demostenes Vigil; the bride, Olivia Vigil Maestas; the groom, Donald Maestas; and the bride's mother, Aranita Jaramillo Vigil. The couple raised two sons, Huberto and Patrick, in San Pablo, Colorado. Donald was a farmer and rancher who loved his animals and the land. Olivia was the Centennial High School librarian and spent her summers working the farm. She had a green thumb and could grow the most fruitful organic gardens in the region. (Courtesy of Olivia Maestas family.)

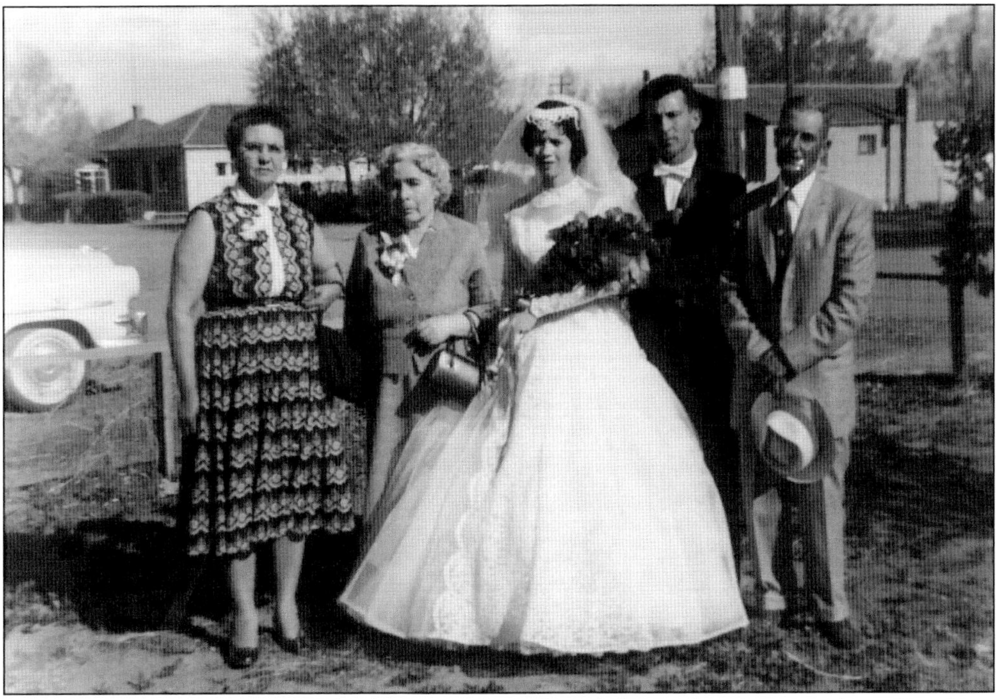

Posing for a wedding photo in the family yard are, from left to right, the groom's mother, Lucy Vialpando Valdez; the bride's mother, Magdelena Arellano; the bride, Louisa Arellano Valdez; the groom, Evan Valdez; and the groom's father, Anastascio José (Joe) Valdez. The couple was married on May 17, 1958, in Alamosa. They lived in San Luis and raised six children: Dana, Roland, Mathew, Bernadette, Maria, and Evan Jr. Evan was a teacher and principal for the Centennial school district who loved farming and ranching. Louisa was a schoolteacher who, before marrying, taught school in Flagler and Pueblo, Colorado. She was a beloved teacher who cared deeply for her students, especially her first graders in the Chama schools and then those at Centennial Elementary School in San Luis. (Courtesy of Evan A. Valdez.)

Francisco Mondragon and his wife, Leonarda Padilla Mondragon, pose with an unknown bride and groom around 1920. Leaning against the bare adobe building with exposed *vigas* (roof beams) are onlookers, children, and a woman wearing a *tápalo* (shawl). (Courtesy of Pat Trujillo VanZandt.)

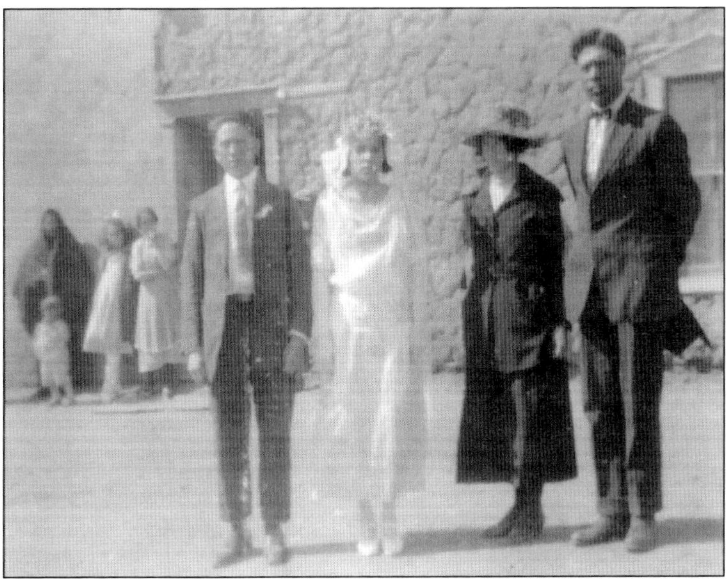

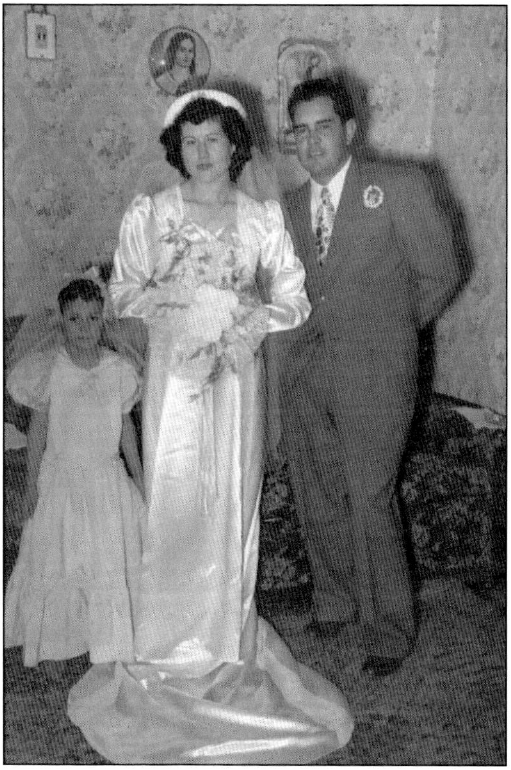

This 1951 wedding photo of Celina Martinez and Leo Cordova was taken at the San Acacio home of the bride's parents, Aniceto and Eufrasia Martinez. The room contains typical Spanish décor, with the *santos* (saints) in the background. Visible are the Sacred Heart of Jesus, St. Terese of the Little Flower, and St. Joseph and the Virgin Mary with baby Jesus, with dry palms from Palm Sunday mass placed on the picture frame. (Courtesy of Wanda Vigil.)

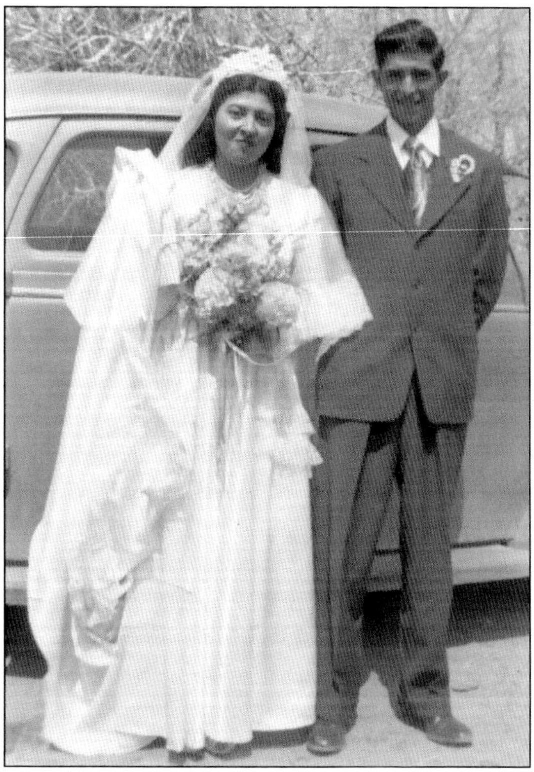

This wedding photo of Alfonso Rael and Theresa Martinez was taken in San Acacio in 1951. Alfonso farmed in San Pablo for his father, Apolinar Rael, and later worked for Robinson Brick and Tile in Denver. Theresa was a homemaker. Together they raised eight children: Sandra, Teddy, Jerry, Gene, Wanda, Debbie, Alan, and Rick. (Courtesy of Wanda Vigil.)

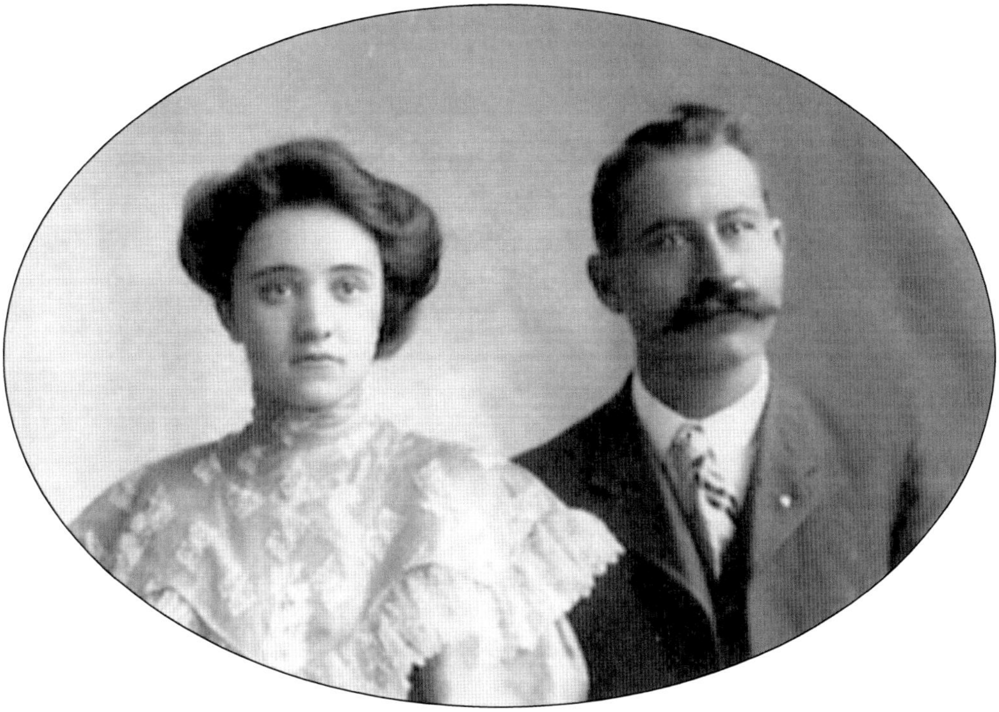

The newlyweds in this beautiful portrait are Beatriz Valdes Olguín, born in 1887, and James M. Olguín, aka Jesús Maria Olguín, born in 1871. The couple was married on September 17, 1906, at Most Precious Blood Parish in San Luis. The presider was the Rev. Samuel J. Garcia, and the witnesses were Miquel Martinez and Fidelia G. Martinez. The Olguíns owned and operated the Olguín Mercantile in San Luis. (Courtesy of Monica and Carmen Olguín.)

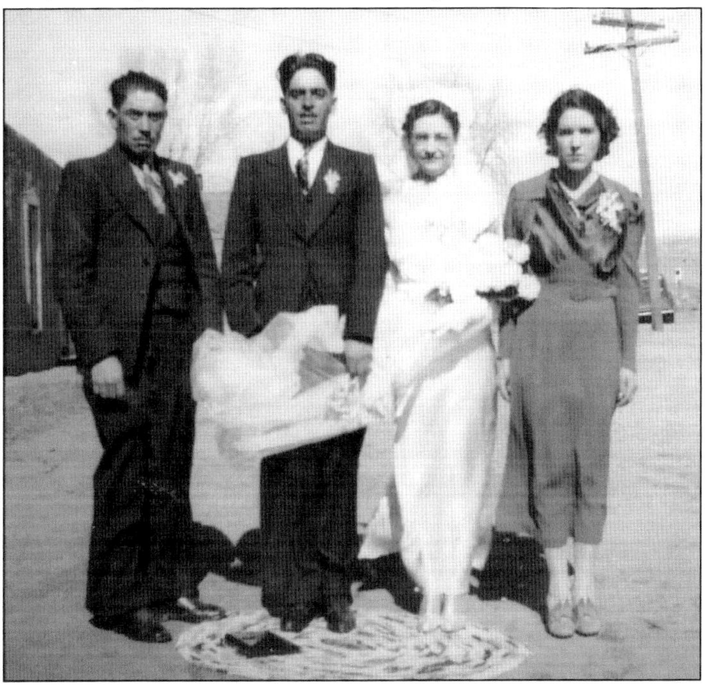

Best man Eduardo Taylor and matron of honor Eufelia Taylor pose with groom Rosendo Mondragon and bride Frances Esquibel Mondragon on their wedding day in 1938, near El Rito de San Francisco (Also known as La Valley). (Courtesy of Pat Trujillo VanZandt.)

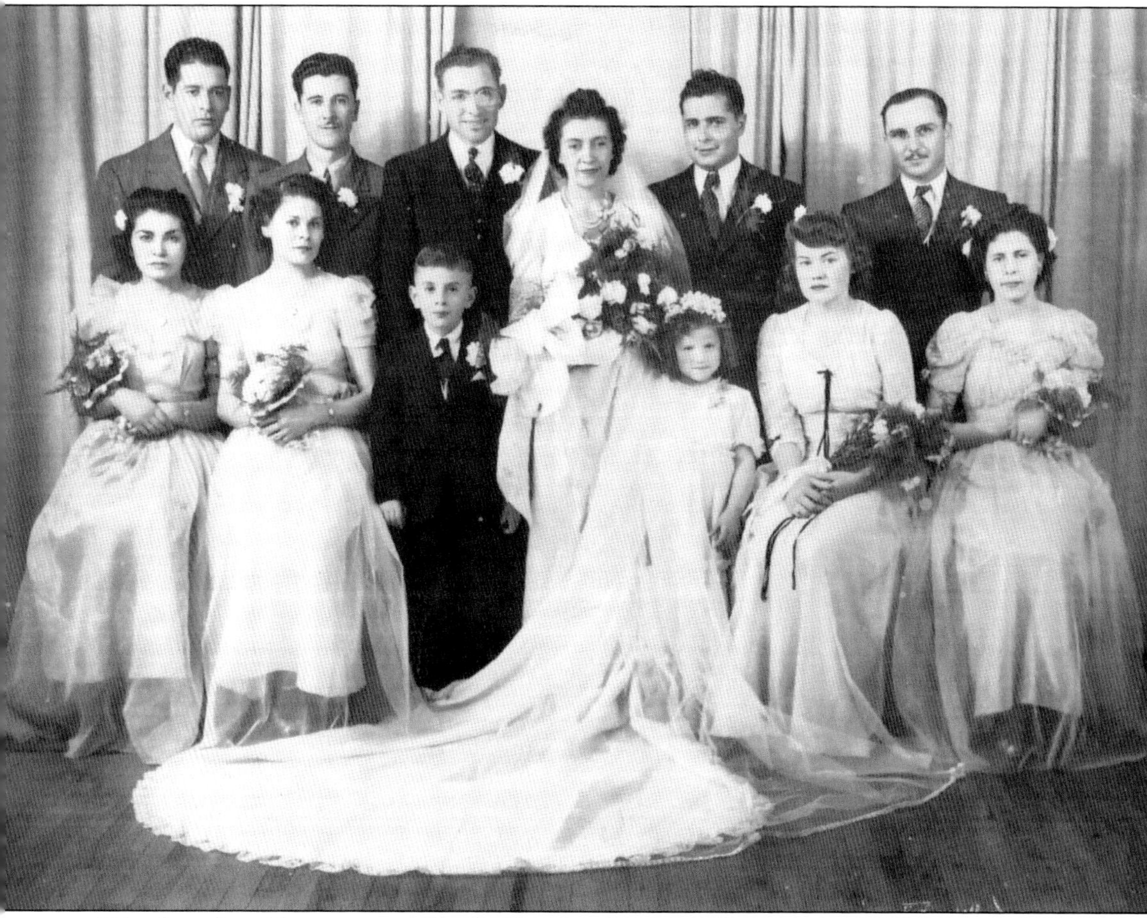

This formal wedding portrait of bride Elva Trujillo and groom Charlie Jaquez Sr. was taken on October 29, 1945, in San Luis. From left to right are (first row, seated) Cordy Cordova, Rose Maes, one of the Gold children, unidentified little girl, Celina Mondragon, and sister of the bride Beatrice Trujillo; (second row, standing) Gilberto Maes, Frank Chacon, groom Charlie Jaquez Sr., bride Elva Trujillo Jaquez, bride's brother Alonzo Trujillo, and Alfirio Sanchez. (Courtesy of Pat Trujillo VanZandt.)

Four

Religion, Art, and Architecture

The missions of San Luis and its surrounding communities offer a touch of peace and spirituality. The Capilla Viejo San Acacio (Old San Acacio Chapel), built in the 1850s, is the oldest standing religious structure in Colorado. It is constructed of 36-inch-thick adobe walls that maintain a pitched wooden roof. Many of the adobe buildings are representative of adobe vernacular design. The Sangre de Cristo Parish, built in 1886, continues to build and maintain adobe mission chapels.

Central to the culture is faith. Soon after the establishment of San Luis de la Culebra, a religious worship space was built. The first chapels constructed were built using the jacal method (log and mud construction). The chapel in San Luis was 200 yards from the present-day church, and housed the traveling priests who came up from Taos, New Mexico. In between these visits, church devotions were practiced by the Hermandad Penitente (Penitent Brotherhood). The Penitente society was a functioning part of the settlement, keeping it organized by administering to the sick, burying the dead, and addressing the spiritual needs of the people.

In San Luis, as in other Southwest villages, the church is the heart of the community, and the art within church walls creates an aura of mystery. The isolation of the area led the settlers to create sacramental images for their churches. *Retablos* and *bultos* are religious folk arts that are crafted from inferior tools and materials of the 18th and 19th centuries. The collection of devotional items serve as a symbol of faith.

Before the opening of the Santa Fe Trail in 1821, the Spanish brought in the treadle loom and sheep, the source of the fiber (wool) used to make homespun clothing, *sarapes* (blankets), *jergas* (rugs), and *colchas* (loosely-stitched tapestries). Colcha refers to a specific embroidery stitch and is also called a bed coverlet.

The early settlers constructed the plazas, individual rooms joined together with a common wall and a flat roof. The use of adobe covered by adobe mortar and mud plaster on walls was a primary means of construction. The affluent settlers lived in *plazuelas* (interconnected L- or U-shaped family compounds). Ranchers and farmers lived in *corrilleras* (corridor of houses). There is a spirit that persists in the land, a clear expression of the sacredness of San Luis de la Culebra.

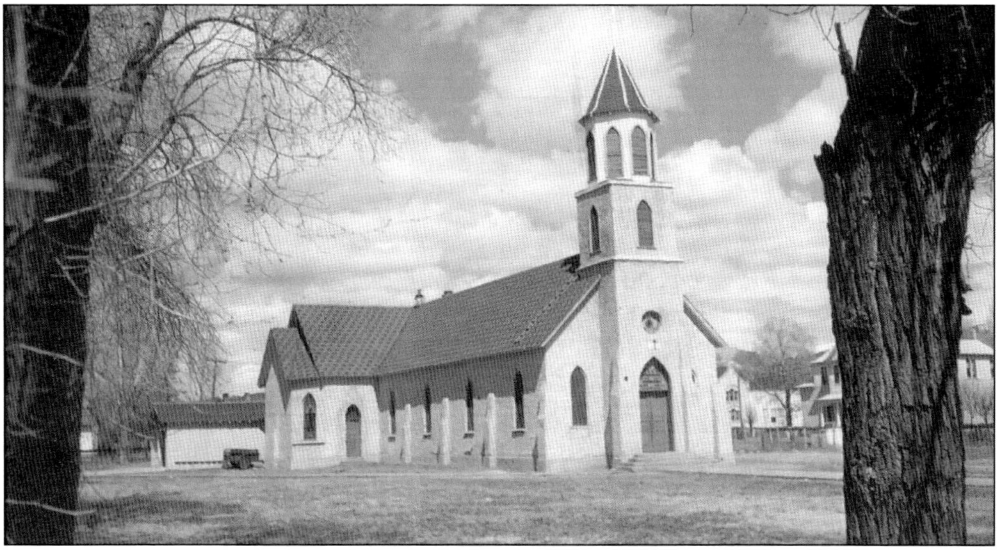

San Luis was made a parish and given the name Sangre de Cristo after 30 years of being a mission. The new church was completed in 1886 under the tenure of Father J.B. Pitaval, who later became the archbishop of Santa Fe. The Sangre de Cristo Parish continues to serve the spiritual needs of the community. Generations have been baptized, wed, and buried in the Catholic church, which remains the hub of the community. Before the church was built, priests from New Mexico journeyed to the mountainous settlement to say mass and administer sacraments in private homes and *oratorios* (small chapels). (Courtesy of Nielsen Library, Adams State University.)

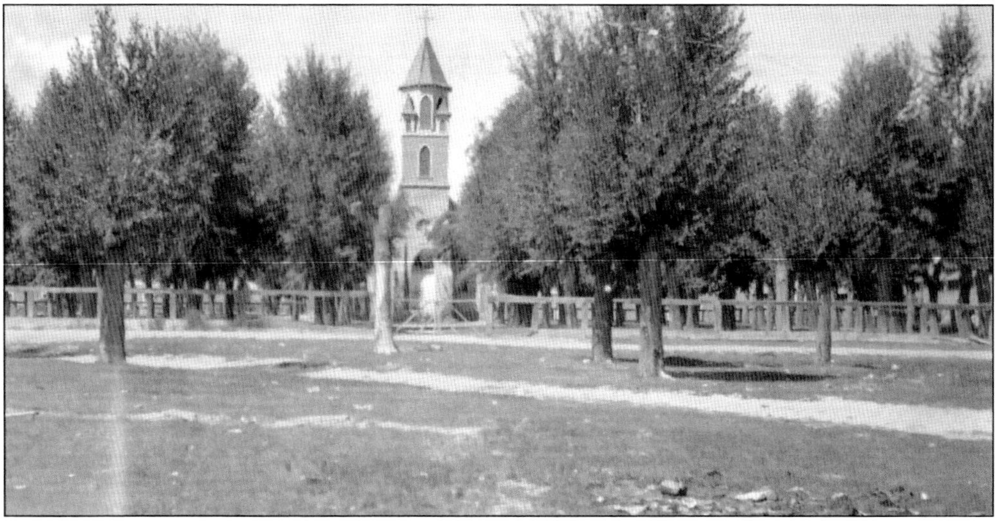

This postcard of the Most Precious Blood Church in San Luis shows the completed church built in 1886. The church had a humble wooden fence around it and was built of adobe. Above a middle entry tower was a modest belfry. A zealous and enterprising priest by the name of Joseph S. Garcia was appointed to the parish. He soon worked to enlarge the church and build a small rectory, chapels in the different missions, a school, and a convent. Nearly 60 years later, a priest by the name of Patrick Valdez did the same by restoring what his predecessors began. It was Bishop Arthur Tafoya of the Archdiocese of Pueblo who decreed to Reverend Valdez that the name of Most Precious Blood be changed to its new name of Sangre de Cristo Catholic Church. (Courtesy of Richard de Olivas y Cordova.)

The San Acacio Mission Church lies in the center of the village of Viejo San Acacio, formerly Culebra Abajo. The church was built as a promise to San Acacio for answering the townspeople's prayers that a raid by the Utes in 1854 be miraculously averted. It is told that as the attackers approached the placita, an image of a soldier mounted on a horse appeared in the sky, guarding the village. When the Utes saw the image, they fled and never attacked again. This adobe church is the oldest church structure in Colorado. (Courtesy of Huberto Maestas.)

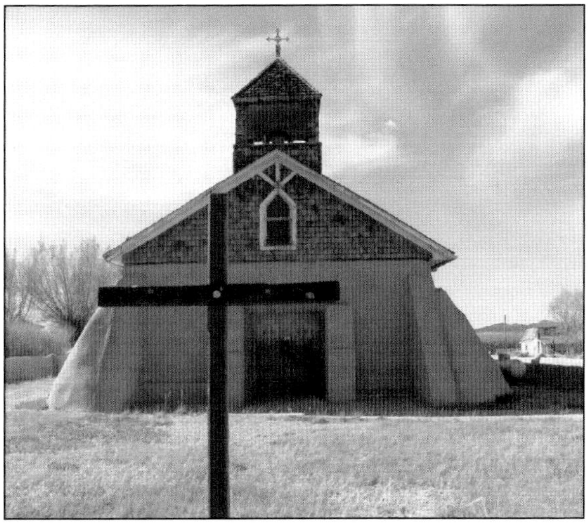

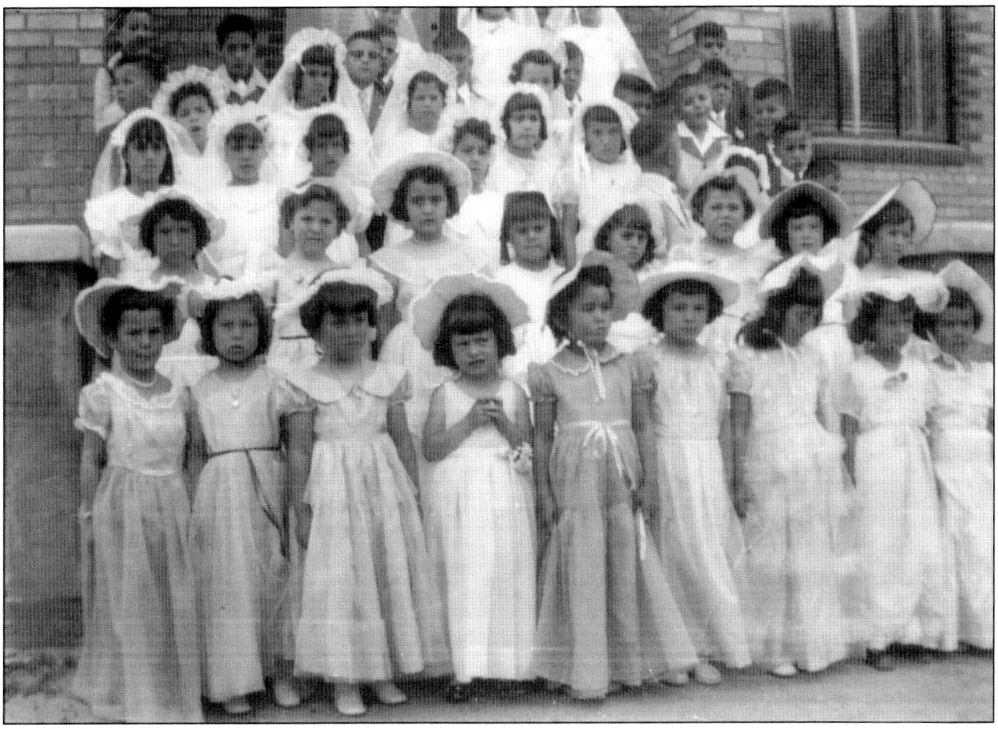

The First Holy Communion class of 1954 poses in front of the Most Precious Blood Catholic Church rectory steps. The lovely attendants escorted the class as they made their communion vows. Pictured in the first row, far left, is Kathy Sanchez, and in the first row, third from the left, is five-year-old Patricia Trujillo. (Courtesy of Pat Trujillo VanZandt.)

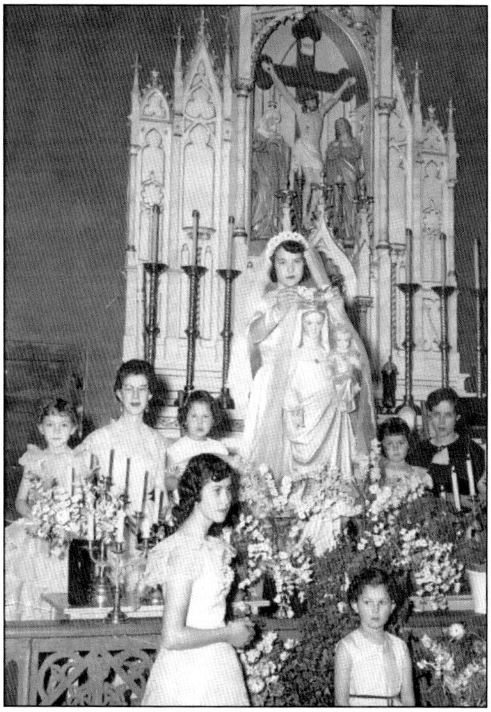

The Mercy High School Sodality Chapter voted high school senior 18-year-old Josephine "Josie" Lucero as their sodality prefect for the 1954 May crowning ceremony. Prom queen and May queen were elected by the school's senior class. From left to right are (front) Priscilla Meyer and Iva Valdez; (back) unidentified, Christine Garcia, unidentified, Josephine Lucero, unidentified, and Josephine Lobato. (Courtesy of Eugene and Josie Lobato.)

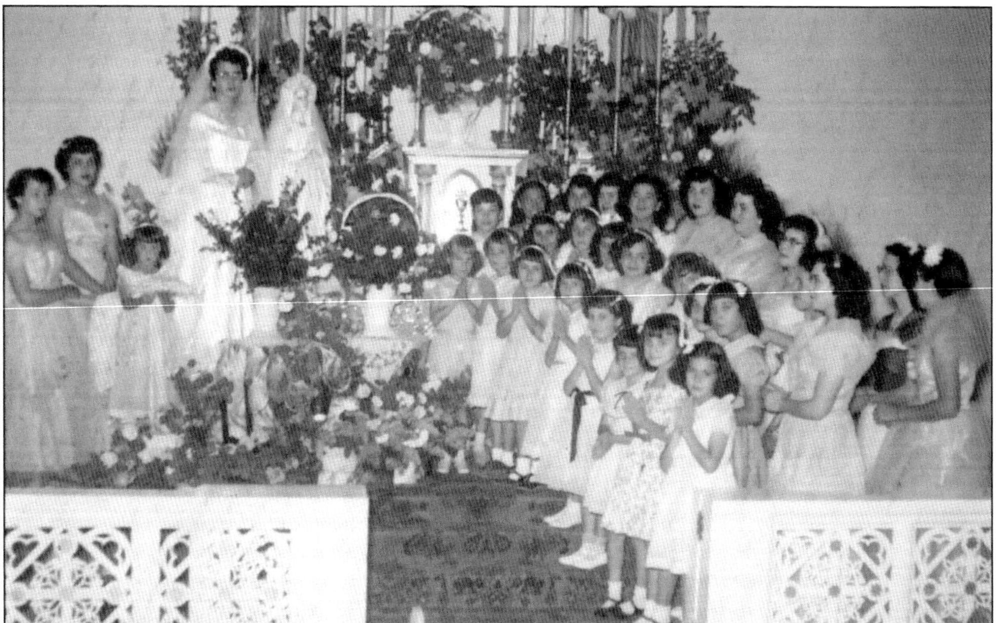

A religious tradition, the annual celebration of May crowning is usually held on Mother's Day. This 1953 May crowning at Immaculate Conception Church in Chama features high school senior Rosita Rodriquez (Quintero) as the May queen. Dressed in formal attire, all the attendants to the queen would follow in a procession to the altar to crown the statue of the Blessed Mother in the crowning ceremony, held in the evening. A local bride would donate her wedding veil to crown the statue. (Courtesy of Henrietta Mascarenas.)

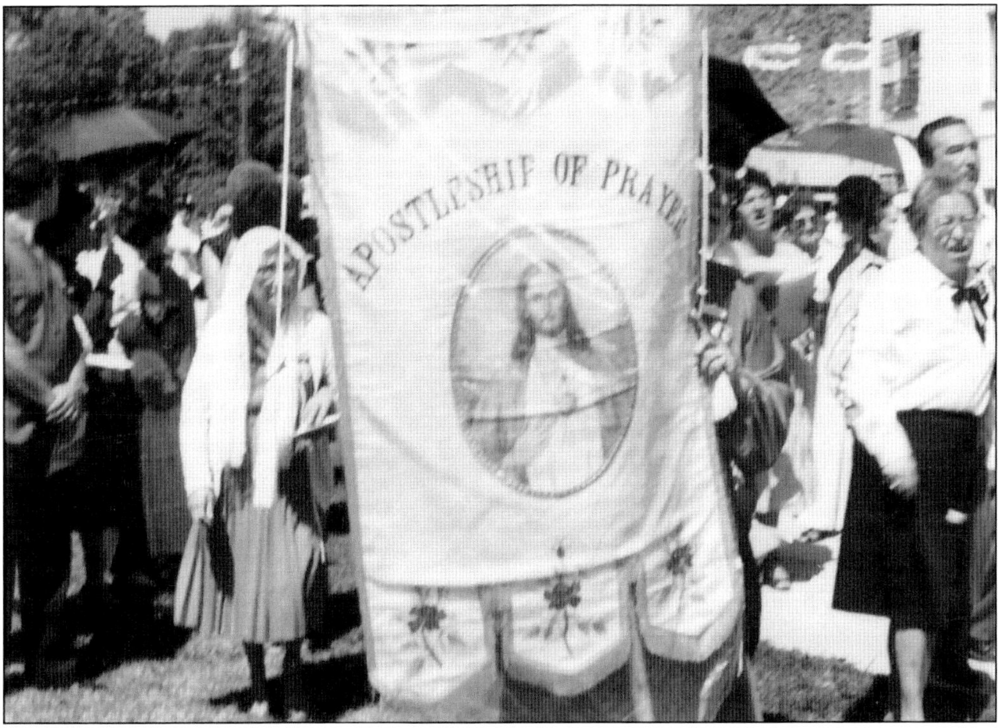

Many traditions of the Culebra villages continue today just as they did 100 years ago. Elder Emma Maes considers it an honor to hold the banner of the Sacred Heart Society, a religious organization within the church. This religious celebration involves children as well as adults in honoring the oldest religious statue of the Blessed Mother in the community. Sangre de Cristo celebrated the honor of having the statue, *La Conquistadora* (Our Lady of Conquering Love)—the country's oldest Madonna, dating to 1625—in their parish. Many times the caballeros would lead the religious procession in the town. In 1694, the Spanish colonists began an annual thanksgiving observance by taking *La Conquistadora* from the shrine to the encampment sites, where they prayed for victory. (Both, courtesy of Theresa Vigil.)

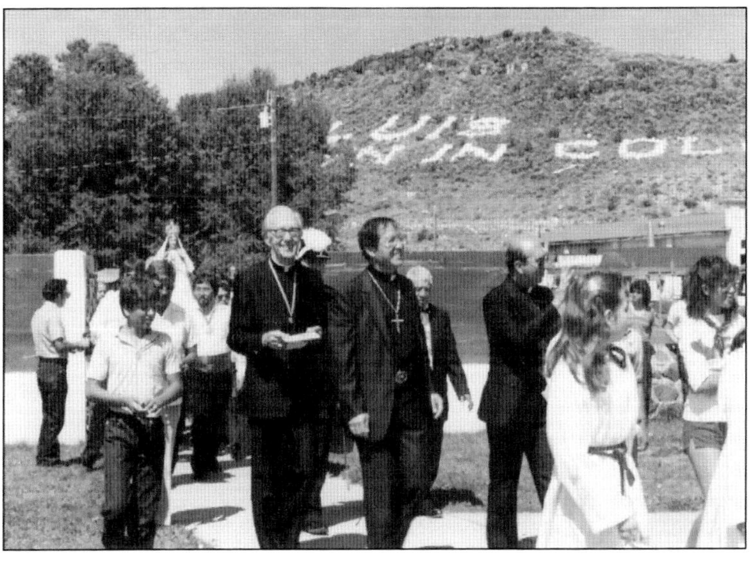

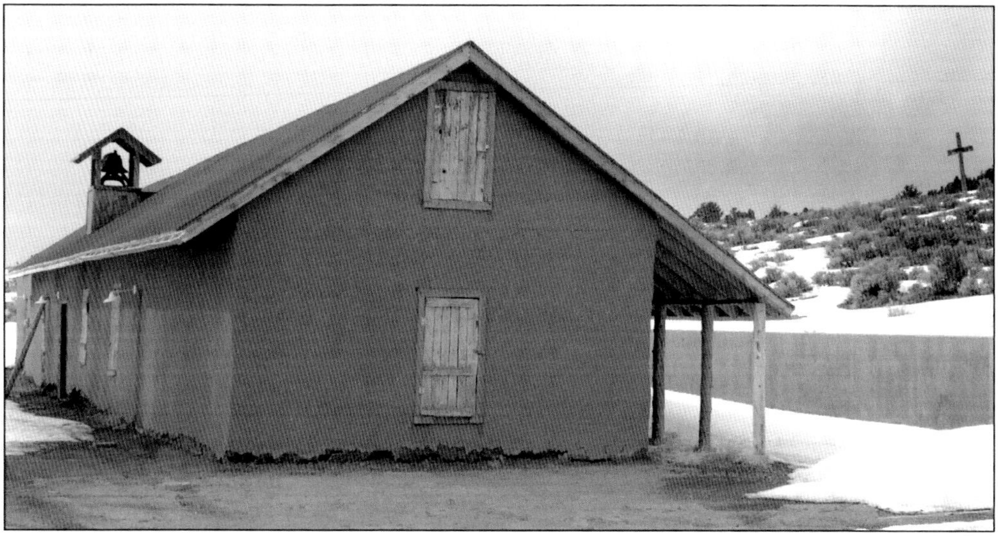

The history of La Hermandad, or penitential society, began in the New World in 1692 with Don Diego de Vargas. These photographs are of the San Francisco Morada in El Rito de San Francisco, built between 1880 and 1908. It is the only traditional historically designated adobe morada in Colorado. The lettering on the cross stands for Fraternidad Piadosa de Nuestro Padre Jesus Nazareno, also known as the Penitente Brotherhood. The morada is their meeting house and chapel. Because the villages were isolated, the primary source of strength and support was the penitente brotherhood. The Hermanos played a vital role in providing spiritual nourishment for the settlers and their families. The Hermanos provided food and clothing to widows and orphans. They helped take care of the sick, bury the dead, baptize newborns, and sometimes united couples in marriage until a priest could come. In the past, the Hermanos gathered in secret to pray and participated in penitential rites including self-flagellation. The whip used is called a *disciplina*. It was a deep honor to be chosen for such a task. Today, the Hermanos gather to pray the Stations of the Cross and rosary every Friday during the Lenten season. During Holy Week, they spend three days at the morada praying, and the community gathers to feed them. (Both, photograph by and courtesy of Dana EchoHawk.)

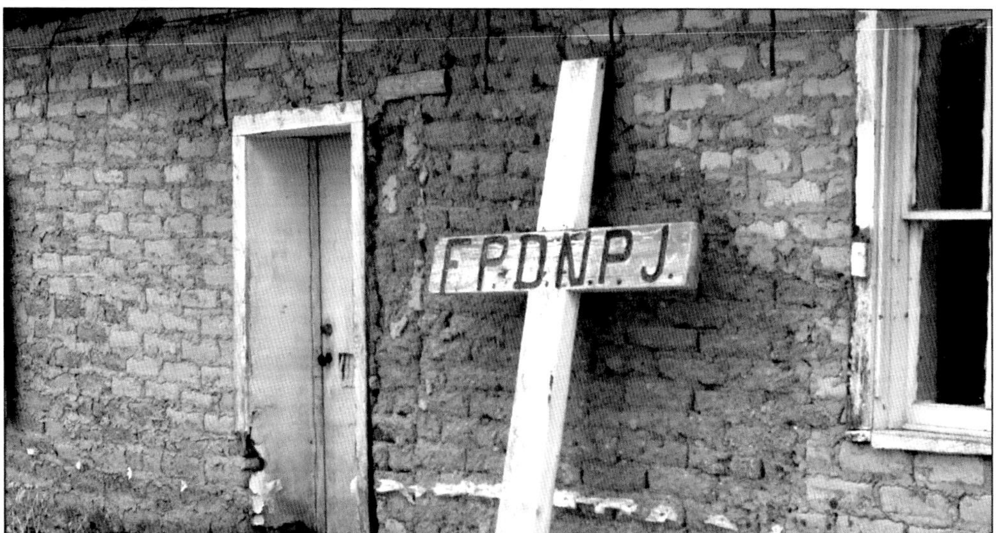

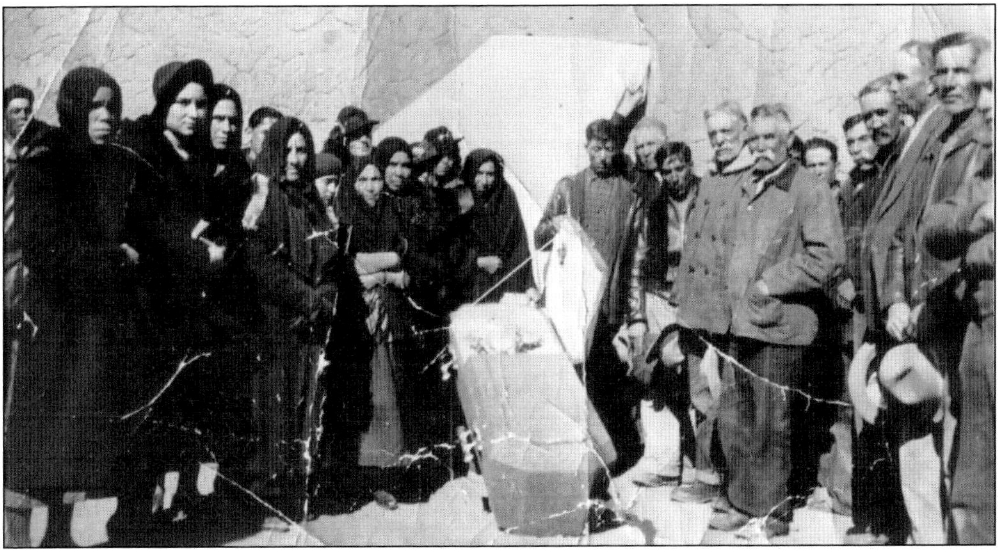

In the cold winter month of February 1937, just before the mass and burial of 11-year-old Gilberto Mascarenas, his family and friends pose in front of the morada in Chama. The youngster was one of many children who died of influenza. From left to right are David C. Vialpando, Julianita Vialpando (Lopez), Criselda Sanchez, Rosanita, Emilia Herrera Maestas, Cora Mascarenas, Severa Montoya, Libradita Herrera, Lucinda Herrera, Josephina and Clorinda Mascarenas, Dona Francesqita Mascarenas, Don Fred Mascarenas, Carmelito Martinez, Eutimio Vialpando, Jose Francisco Lobato, Carlos Lopez, Daniel Sanchez, Juan de Dios Vialpando, Florencio Atencio, Celestino Atencio, Don Ricardo Vialpando, and Leandro Montoya. (Courtesy of Henrietta Mascarenas and Brenda Vialpando.)

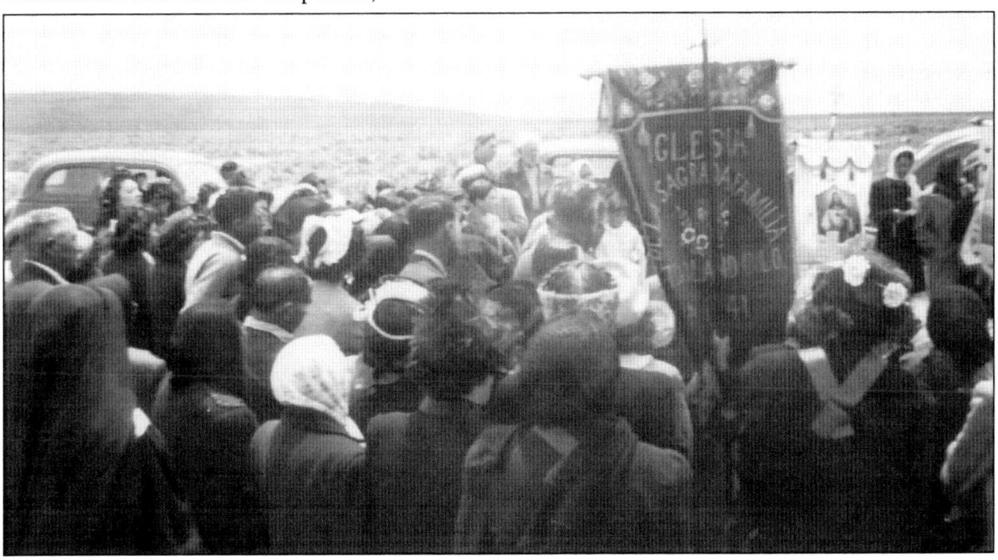

Family members and friends gather for the solemn occasion of a loved one's passing during burial services in San Acacio in the 1940s. Shown are the *estandartes*, the standards or banners of the different church Sodality organizations or church missions. One custom is that the mourners wore black, and another is that no one would leave the cemetery until the body was buried. Everyone took a handful of dirt and tossed it into the grave. Symbolically this means that the dead are leaving all possessions behind. (Courtesy of Cathy Serna-Egana.)

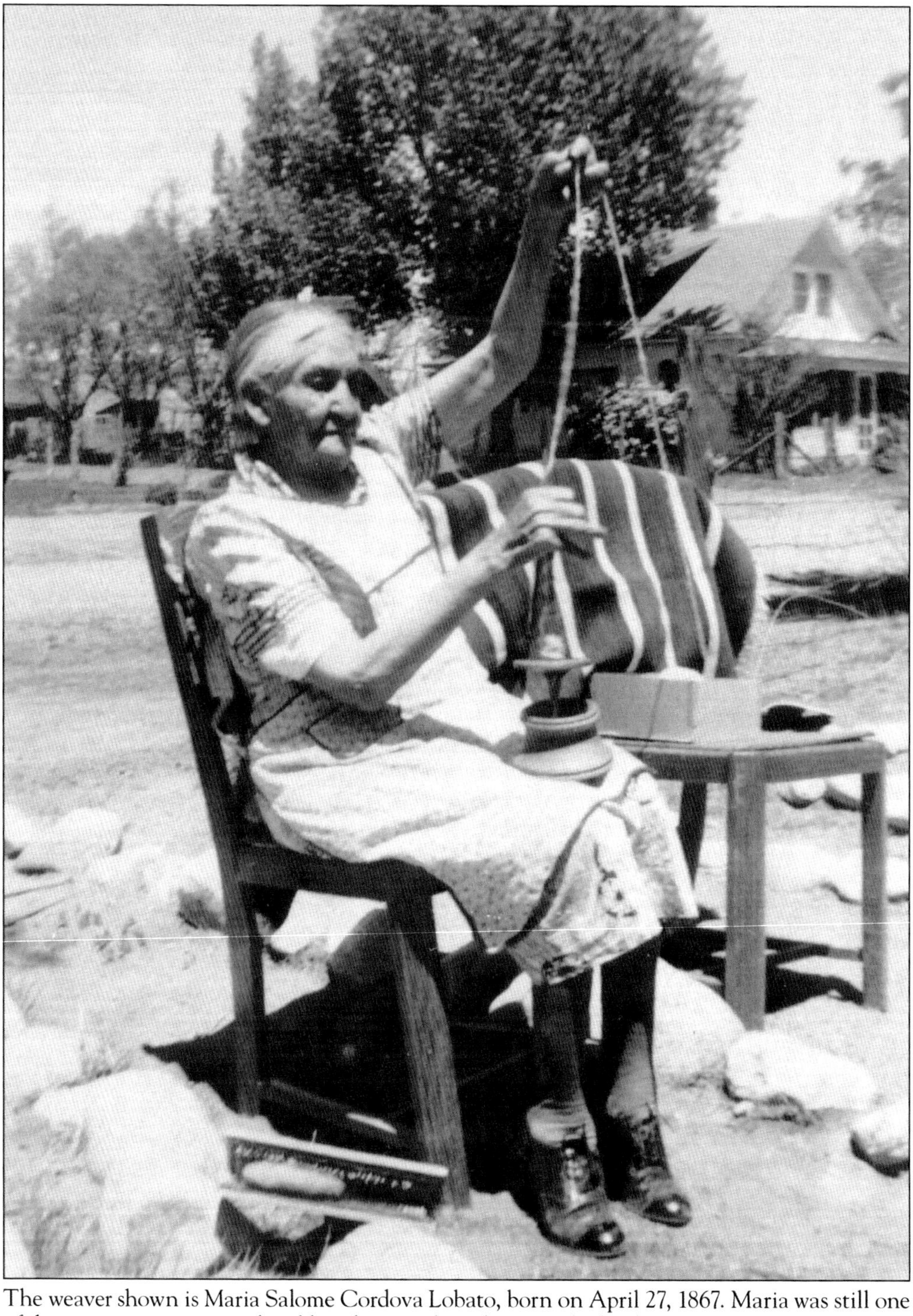

The weaver shown is Maria Salome Cordova Lobato, born on April 27, 1867. Maria was still one of the weavers continuing the old traditions when she was asked to be a consultant to the WPA's weaving project in San Luis in 1935. The spindle was placed on the bowl as she spun the wool to form and twist the yarn. She is shown here spinning wool with a spindle and bowl made by her son Alberto Lobato. (Courtesy of Hope Gallegos Yost.)

These two women are cleaning the wool fibers, a process called carding. In 1938, there remained a few weavers continuing the old traditions. Some of the weaving students participating in the project were Julian Lucero, Luz Lucero, Demostenes Vigil, Norberto Vigil, Domatila Cordova, and Dan Fishert. (Courtesy of History Colorado.)

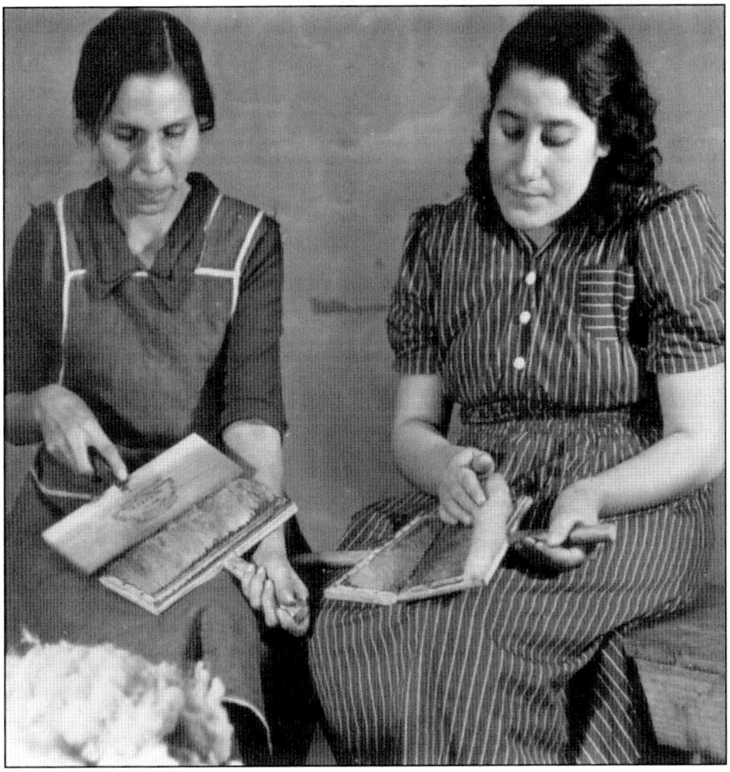

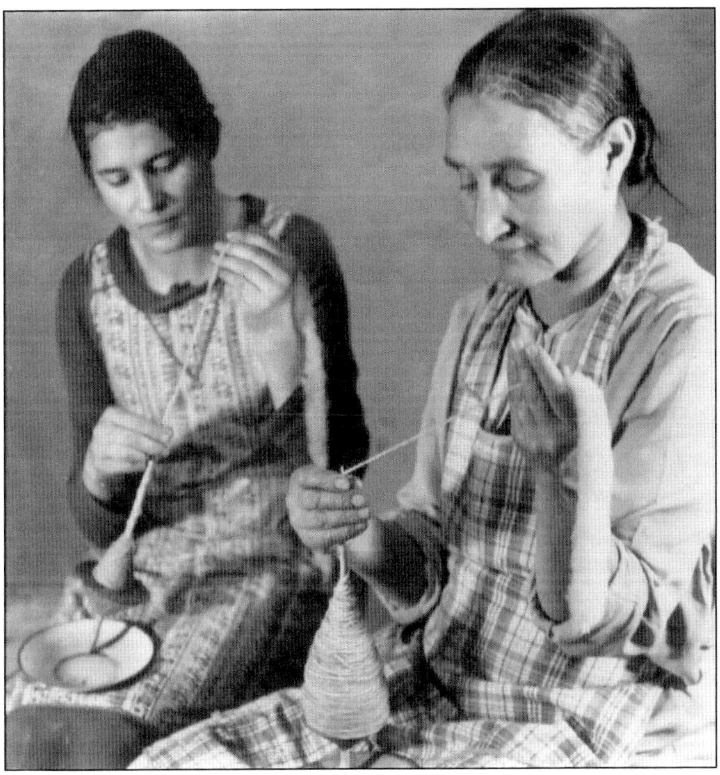

These two women are demonstrating the use of stick spindles, *malacates*, to spin the wool. The spindle was rolled against the thigh or twirled in midair, as shown here. Yarn for warp was given an S twist. (Courtesy of History Colorado.)

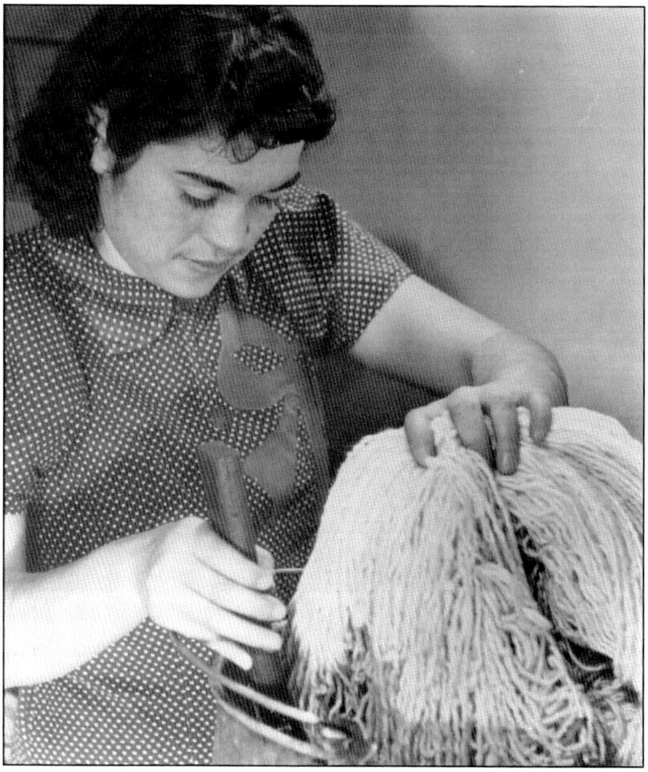

The weaving project from 1935 to 1938 included learning the entire process of preparing the wool. Shown here is a woman dying the yarn. Originally, the colors of yarn were natural colors of wool like off-white, gray, tan, and dark brown. The hues were colors derived from roots, leaves, berries, bark, and flowers. A few dyes came in from New Mexico with the settlers. Dying the yarn was a labor-intensive task usually done by the women and children. (Courtesy of History Colorado.)

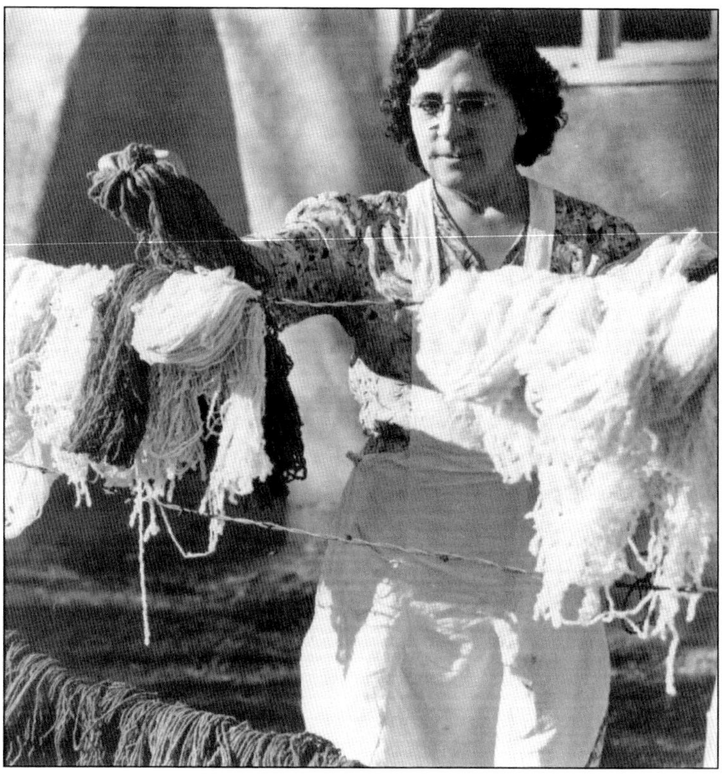

This woman is hanging the natural and dyed wool up to dry. Before any dying took place, the yarn was washed with soap and water to remove the dirt and lanolin. This process also shrinks the yarn and mats the fibers. (Courtesy of History Colorado.)

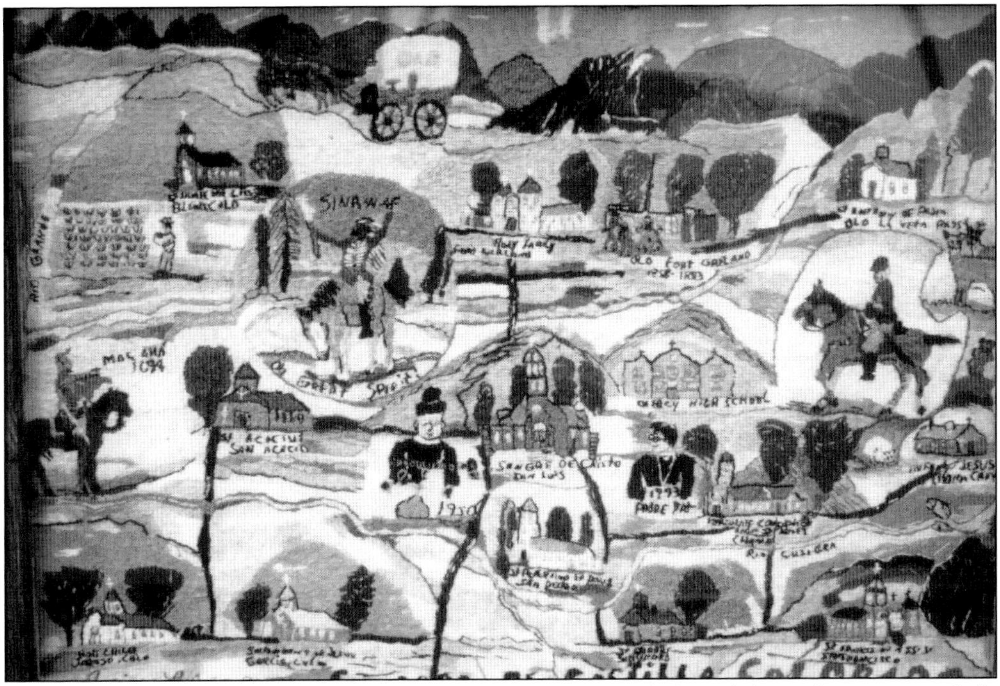

This colcha by Josephine Lobato tells the story of San Luis de la Culebra. The scenes include several mission churches, the Great Spirit, Mercy High School, Father Mortorell, a sheepherder's wagon, and Father Patrick Valdez. (Courtesy of Eugene and Josie Lobato.)

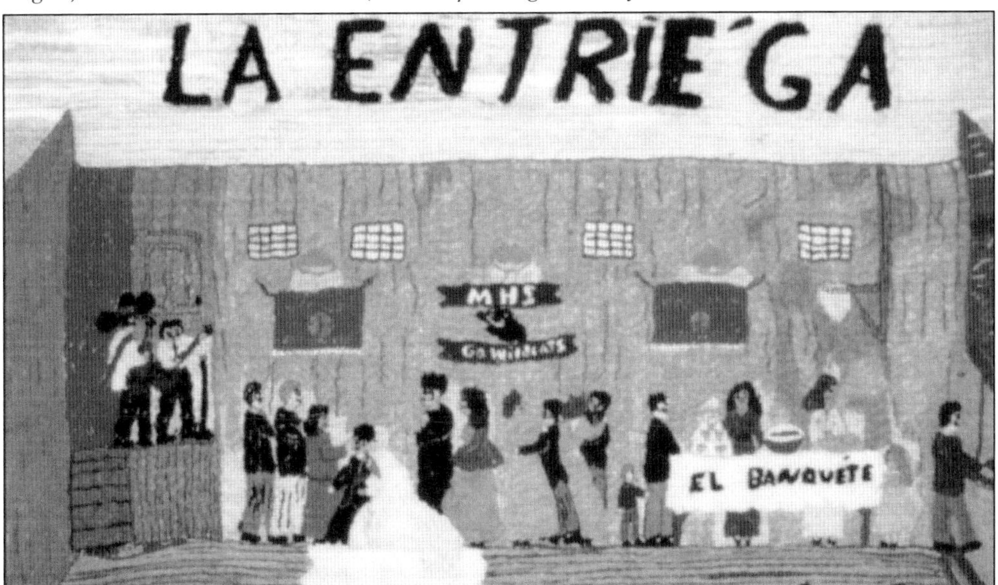

The "Entriega de Los Novios" is one of the oldest wedding traditions. It is sung to a couple on the day of their wedding. It is a giving of the couple to each other and to the community. It explains marriage and the duties of being a parent. Josie Lobato's colcha is set at the Riverside Dance Hall, which served as the Mercy High School gym. The *banquete* (banquet) is stitched in also. You can't have a wedding without *bizcochitos* (crisp, anise- and cinnamon-flavored cookies). (Courtesy of Eugene and Josie Lobato.)

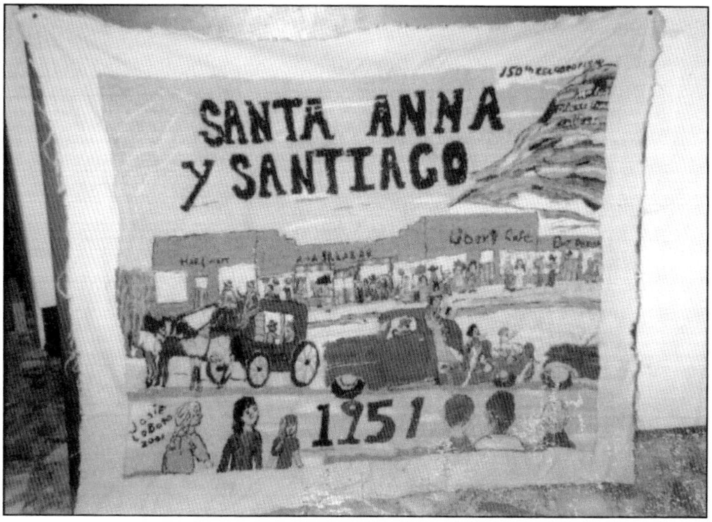

This colcha is the work of Josephine Lobato. It represents the 1951 centennial celebration of the town of San Luis and the 150th anniversary celebration in 2001. Parish priest Father Patrick Valdez loved the crowds in town, indicative of the people who return every year to spend time with family and friends. (Courtesy of Eugene and Josie Lobato.)

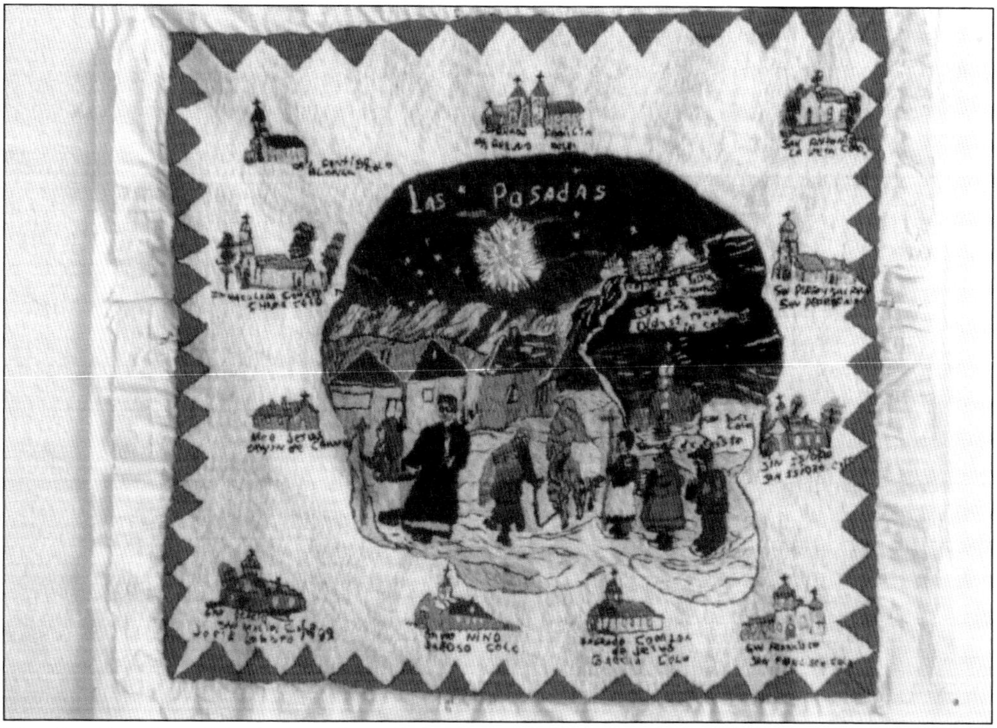

This Las Posadas colcha by Josephine Lobato was crafted in the 1990s. Eleven mission churches are stitched along the center image of Mary and Joseph on a donkey looking for a place to rest. Las Posadas is an annual procession reenacting the search for shelter in Bethlehem. This takes place in the nine villages in the nine days before Christmas, usually December 16 to December 24. Each mission church hosts an evening of people opening up their homes to weary travelers. A procession with singing and supper is held each night. (Courtesy of Eugene and Josie Lobato.)

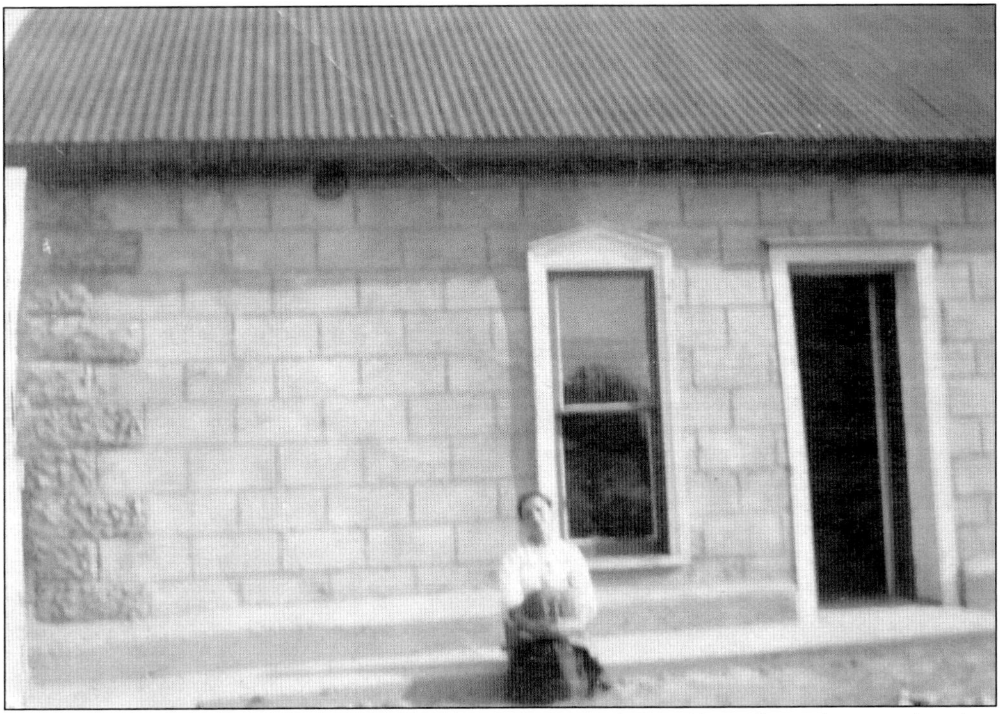

Seventeen-year-old Enriqueta Choury Lobato is posing in front of her Chama home in her first year of marriage in 1911. The home was built as a gift to the young bride. She raised 13 children in this adobe building, plastered with whitewash and made to look like stone bricks. (Courtesy of Henrietta Mascarenas.)

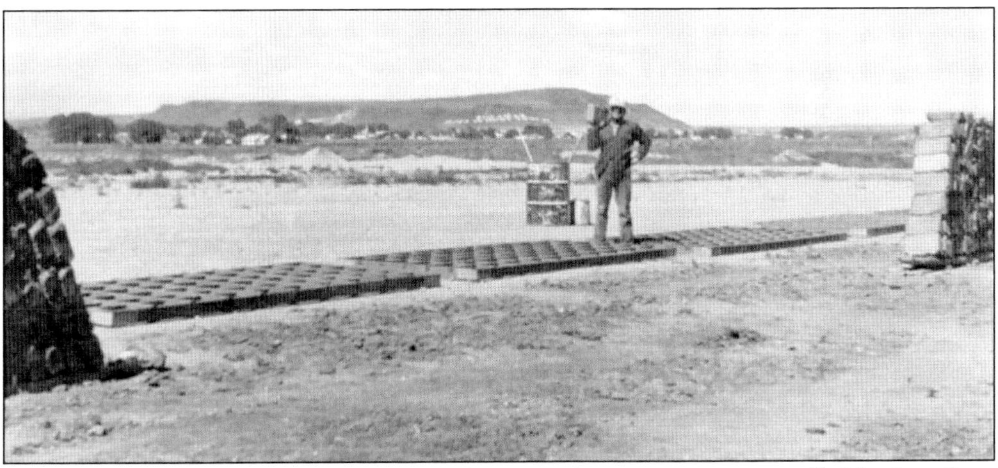

Abie Valdez owned and operated an adobe plant east of San Luis in an area called La Corrillera. Adobes are unfired clay bricks that are fabricated by pouring a mixture of earthen clay, water, sand, and straw into a rectangular wooden form. The bricks are removed from the forms and dried on the barren ground for two weeks. Abie Valdez had a mechanical operation that accommodated about 60 bricks at once. The standard brick produced was 10 by 12 by 4 inches and weighed around 16 pounds. Valdez sold his adobe bricks to builders throughout New Mexico and southern Colorado. (Courtesy of Iva L. Gallegos.)

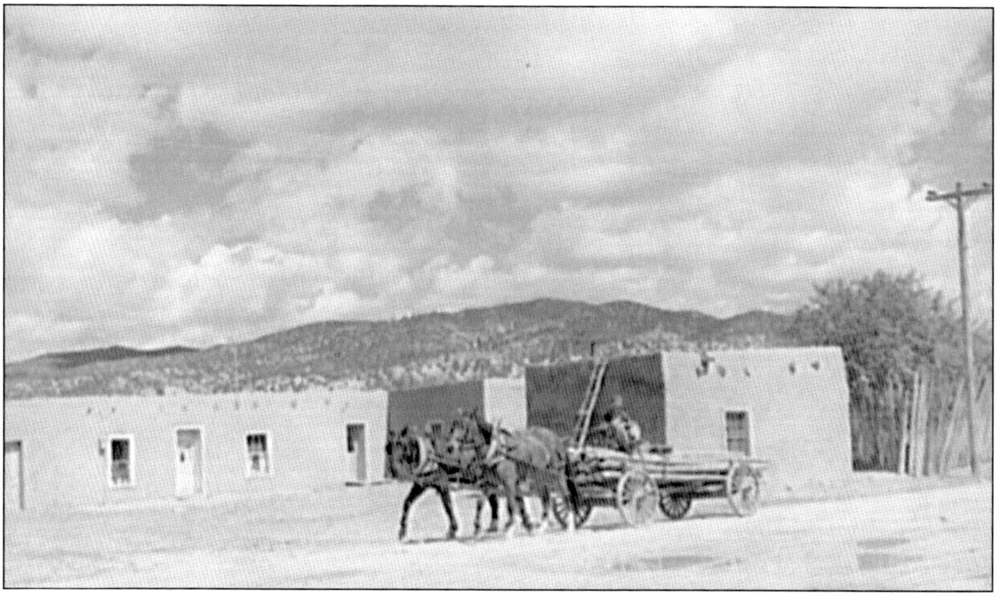

This scene in October 1939 depicts a sleepy village in the Culebra basin in southern Colorado. Two workhorses pull a wooden wagon that carries *latillas* (thin logs) used for constructing a roof. The adobe buildings in the background are a plaza rectangle with individual rooms joined together. The flat-roofed adobe building has vigas placed on the roof structure. Notice the wooden ladder on the side to climb up to the roof. (Photograph by Arthur Rothstein; courtesy of Farm Security Administration, Library of Congress.)

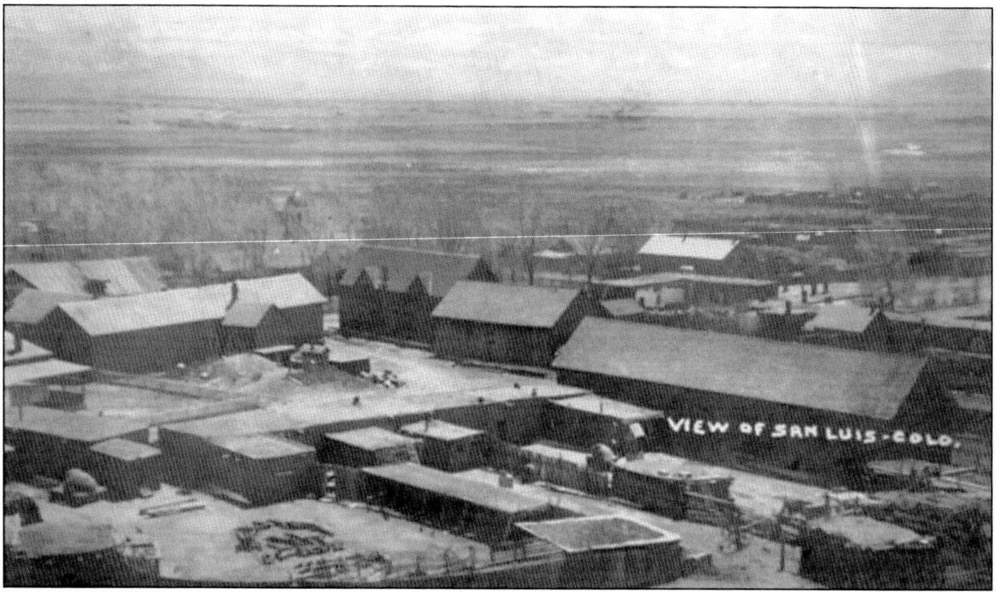

This view of San Luis in the 1920s is from San Pedro Mesa looking east toward the Sangre de Cristo Mountains. Seen are many of the original adobe placitas with a common wall and individual rooms joined together. Also shown are plazuelas. Also in sight is the back of the Gallegos store and the Dario Gallegos home. Around the house are the white picket fence, a couple of hornos used for baking, and corrals to house the farm animals—all elements of life in San Luis de la Culebra. (Courtesy of Huberto Maestas.)

Five

La Gente de la Culebra

The story of San Luis and the Culebra basin is a blend of Moorish and Spanish, mestizo and Indian. It is the expansion of European and Latin culture, Spanish law, and native peoples who have contributed to the cultural identity of a community. Spanish influence predominates the region, with the rivers and mountains named by the Spaniards who explored these lands.

Explorers told astounding stories of hunting buffalo and deer and abundant fishing in the fertile lands north of the New Mexico Territory. The search for wild game and fish and the promise of land by the land grant system brought the early pioneers and their families up into the Sangre de Cristos. This land was unspoiled for grazing of cattle, goats, and sheep. It was not only the harsh winters and short growing season but also the Utes that discouraged settlements. Fortunately, the perseverance of the early pioneers has allowed descendants to recount stories of their ancestors' paths to survival, such as the agreements with the Utes to plant crops but leave after the harvest. Also told is the account of *criados* (Indian captives) who were taken into Spanish families as slaves. According to Castilian law, owners were to practice charity toward their slaves and treat them as one of the family.

Like the pastoral *pobladores* (settlers), their descendants live in now 100-year-old adobe homes, gather wood for heat, hunt deer, raise cattle and sheep, farm the land, and grow crops. The bounty from those crops sustains a unique way of life. *Familia* is spending time with grandparents as they pass on generations of tradition through food, music, and land use practices. An example is the use of *yerba buena* (wild spearmint) for cooking, medicine, tea, and arts and crafts. The *capulín* (chokecherry) makes a delightful jam and syrup, and its bark makes an herbal cough syrup.

The Spanish colonists brought deeply rooted traditions within the church. Spiritual support was given to the family in both sadness and joy. That sense of place endures in the people living in the region who share a common faith, with baptisms, marriages, and burials. The interdependency and responsibility to one another exists while the extended family remains strongly bonded to one another and the community.

San Luis is a seedling of Colorado. It is not a compilation of buildings and places but a collection of people who make up a culture. Today, many have ties to the oldest town in Colorado, and though they may have never lived there, they still call San Luis home. The following photographs express the close ties that bind family in the Hispanic tradition.

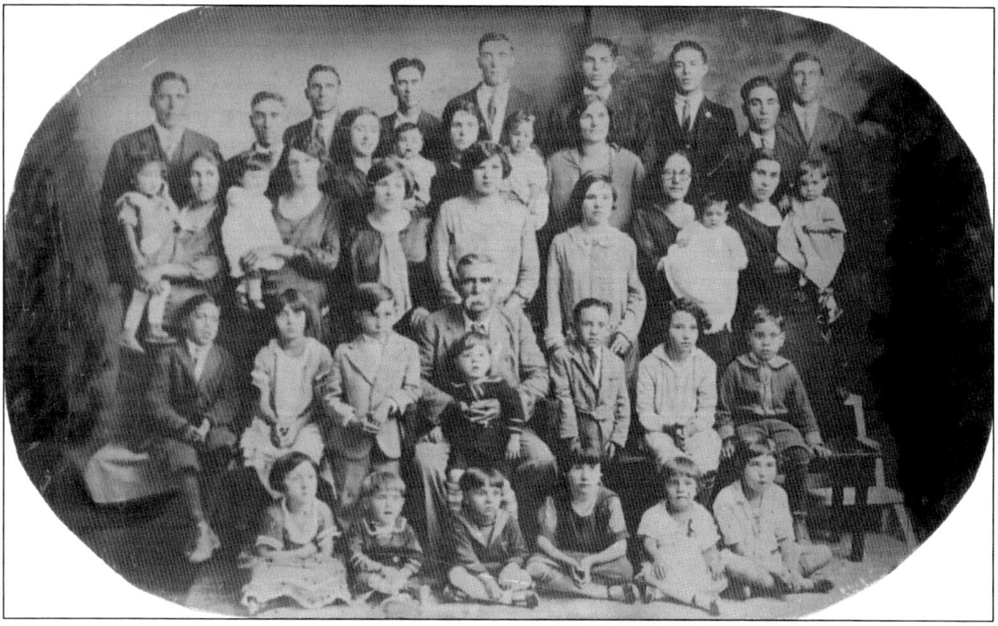

This c. 1926 Vigil family photograph illustrates the generations that come together to celebrate family events. Pictured from left to right are (first row) Cora Trujillo (Vigil), Adolfo Montoya, Fares Valdez, Clarita Vialpando (Vigil) Maggie Lopez (Sanchez), and Trinidad Montoya (Vigil); (second row) Bernabe Aragon, Beatrice Vialpando, Emilio Valdez, Carlos Lopez (holding Julio Trujillo), John Montoya, Inesita Medina, and Maxemiliano Aragon; (third row) Joaneva Montoya (Valdez), Adelina Lopez, Teddy Cruz (Valdez), Adelicia Valdez (holding Anna [Martinez]), and Soledad Lopez (Trujillo) (holding Stella [Roybal]); (fourth row) Rufina (Lopez) Aragon (holding Tia Cora), Fidelia Lopez (holding Alica Montoya), Deluvina (holding Orly), Maclovia Vigil (holding Stella [Sanchez]), and Severa Lopez (Montoya); (fifth row) José Luis Aragon, Antonio Vigil, Juan Andres Valdez, Leandro Montoya, José Lopez, José Montoya, Felique Montoya, Ralph Lopez, and Mariano Lopez. (Courtesy of Larry and Rita Vigil.)

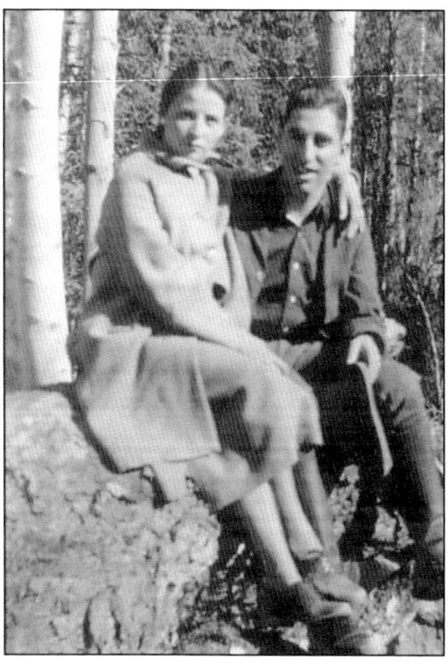

This endearing photograph of Emma Vigil and José Maria (Joe) Espinoza was taken at La Sierra when they were dating in the 1930s. Joe was born on December 8, 1911, and passed away in 2004 at the age of 92. Emma was born on May 18, 1917, and is 97 years old in 2014. The Espinozas owned and operated El Patio Inn and Emma's Hacienda Restaurant "Food of the Southwest" in San Luis from 1942 to 2012. In the inn's beginnings, Joe's brother Manuel helped run El Patio Inn and Bar. The bar and restaurant has been operated by five generations of the Espinoza family. (Courtesy of Emma and Joe Espinoza family.)

Pictured is José Maria (Joe) Espinoza at the Golden Gloves Tournament in Denver around 2000. He sang the national anthem at the tournament for many years. Espinoza brought boxing clubs to San Luis from New Mexico and Colorado to compete with his boxers. He coached local boxers who went on to become No. 2 champions of the world in the featherweight division in the Olympics and U.S. National tournaments. (Courtesy of Emma and Joe Espinoza family.)

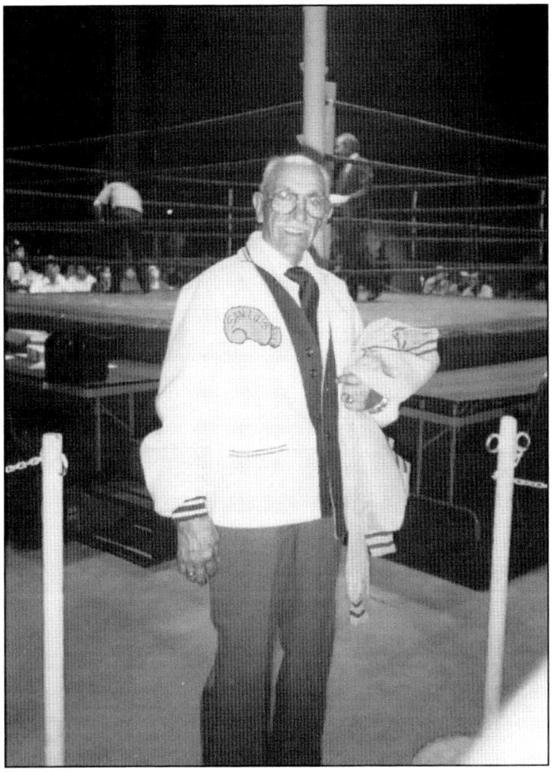

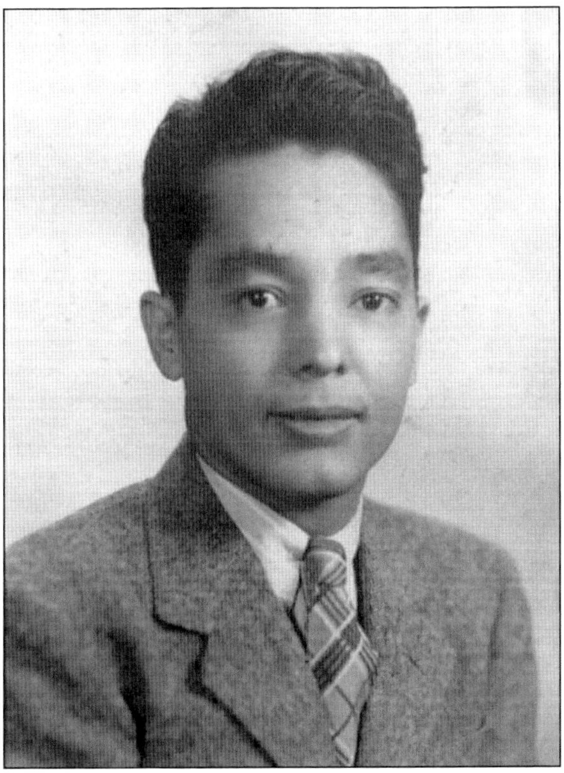

Pictured is schoolteacher and boxing coach Filomeno Sanchez. Sanchez taught boxing in the San Luis area for many years, naming the boxing arena "El Madison Square Garden del Valle de San Luis." There were two boxing clubs, El Club del Dr. R.C. Diaz and El Club de Don Meliton Maxwell. The boxers he coached were known to be the best in the San Luis Valley. (Courtesy of Frankie Sanchez.)

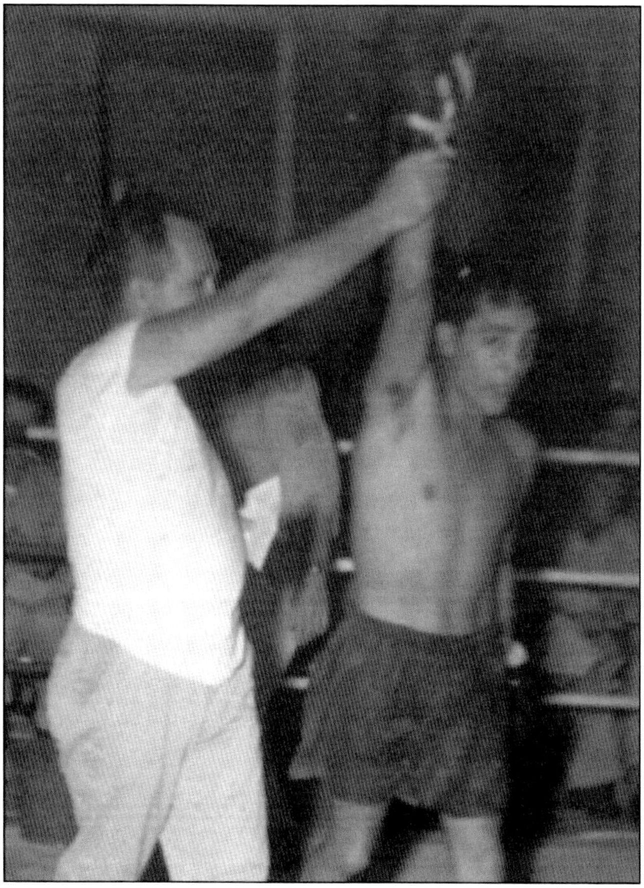

This photograph of Filomeno "Phil-O-Meno" Sanchez was taken in 1945 when he won the Southern Pacific Boxing Championship at the bantamweight division at 119 pounds. The young Sanchez returned home from the Navy to teach boxing to youngsters in the Culebra area. He was from La Corrillera, just east of San Luis. (Courtesy of Frankie Sanchez.)

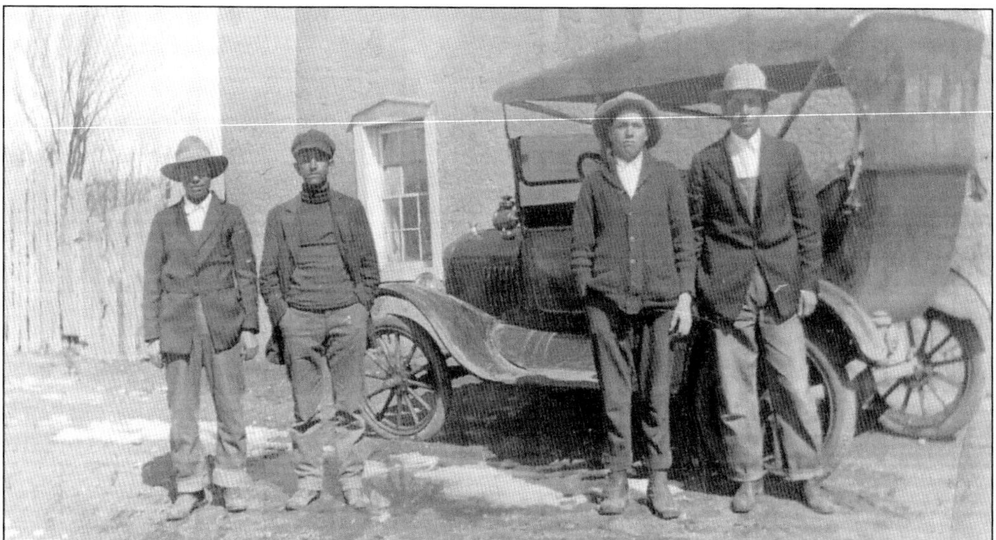

From left to right, Eutimio Vialpando, Placido DeHerrera, Rosalio Vialpando, and Porfirio Vialpando pose in front of an old Model T convertible and an adobe building in Chama around 1920. (Courtesy of Brenda Vialpando)

Pictured here in 1901 are the children of Francisco Gallegos and Ursula Garcia Gallegos. Clockwise from top left are Lucinda, born on May 15, 1894; Maclovio, born on September 11, 1900; José Alarico, born on July 9, 1896; and Diego Antonio, born on June 11, 1899. (Courtesy of Hope Gallegos Yost.)

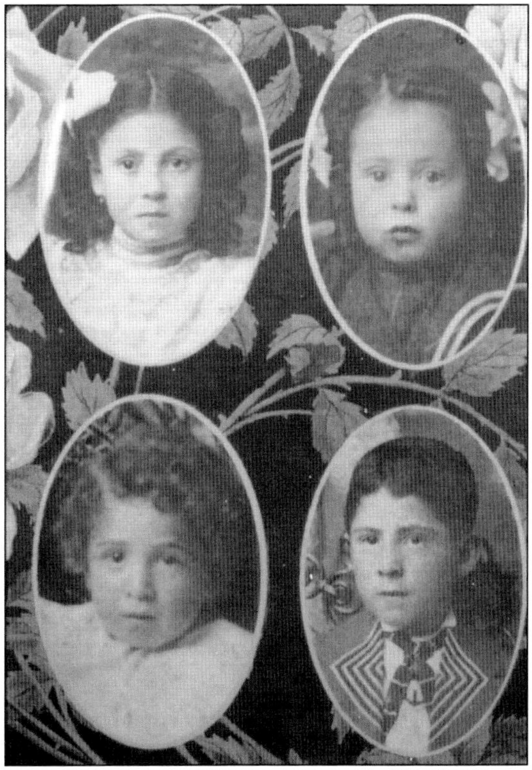

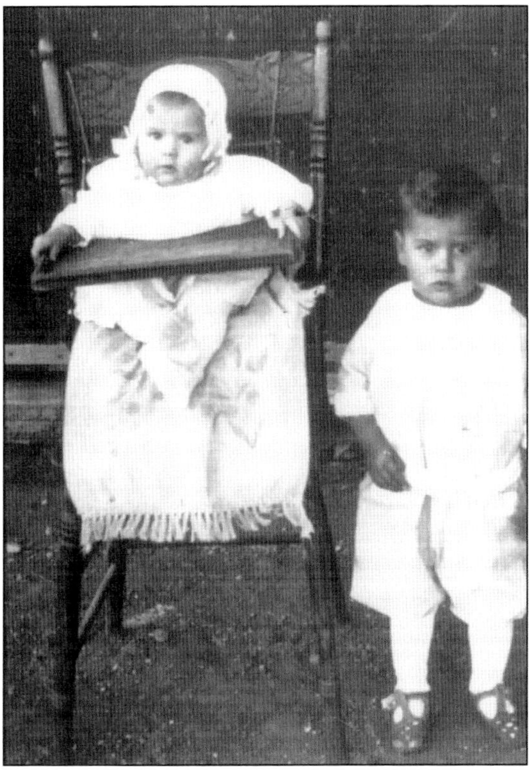

This cute photograph of siblings Anne Trujillo (Little) and big brother Sam Trujillo was taken around 1923–1924. The children's parents are Abel Trujillo and Eloisa DeHerrera Trujillo of San Luis. Anne is seated on what appears to be a small colcha. Sam worked for a college in Sacramento, California, and passed away at the age of 90 years. Anne is 90 years old in 2014 and is a retired nurse from the Camarillo State Hospital in California. (Courtesy of Julia Valdez.)

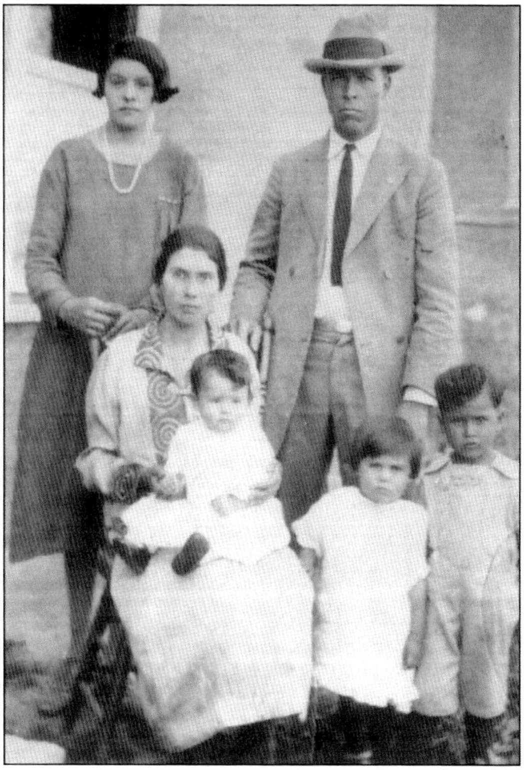

This c. 1925 family portrait shows, from left to right, (first row) Eloisa DeHerrera Trujillo holding baby Julia Trujillo (Valdez), daughter Anne Trujillo (Little), and son Sam Trujillo; (second row) Josephine Olivas and Abel Trujillo. Olivas was Abel Trujillo's cousin from San Acacio. (Courtesy of Julia Valdez.)

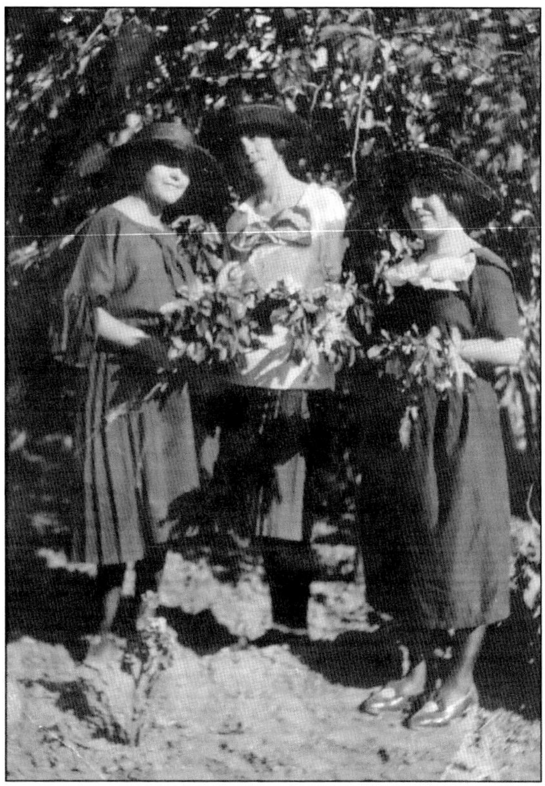

These lovely friends are pictured holding bouquets of flowers near a backyard garden in Chama around 1924. Dressed in the Gibson girl style of the 1920s, these stylish young women are, from left to right, Ada Sanchez, Lucy "Luz" Vialpando, and Cedalia Cruz. (Courtesy of Beatrice Marquez and Libby Rivera.)

This young man leaning on a car in the early 1950s is Donald Maestas, born on May 1, 1928. Donald loved to drive fast cars or cars fast—he wrecked over 10 cars on the same turn in San Pedro. He was a Korean War veteran who received commendation for his bravery in hand-to-hand combat with a bayonet. He was a farmer and rancher who loved being in the Ventero, an area of windy farmland south of San Luis where he raised his cattle and sheep. As a mayordomo for the acequias for over 40 years, he was knowledgeable about the acequia culture, the water, and the land. (Courtesy of Olivia Maestas family.)

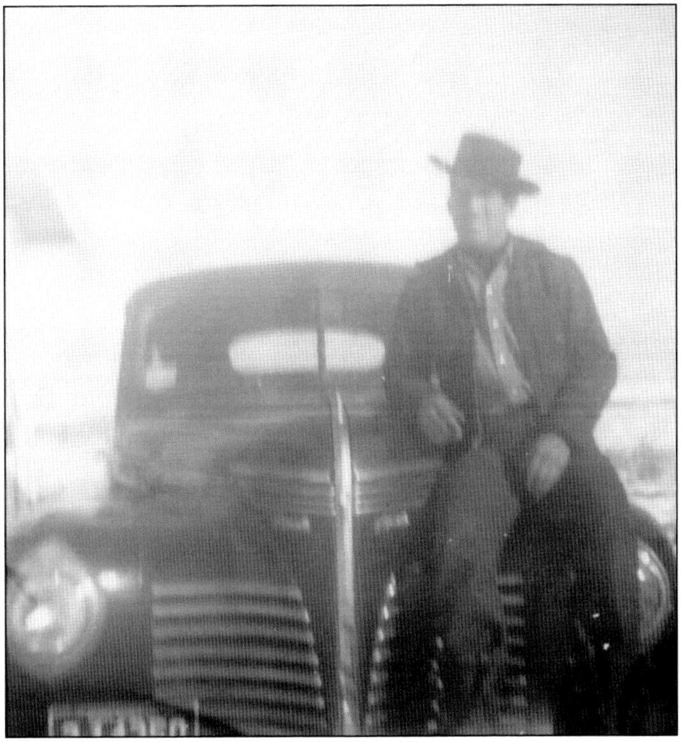

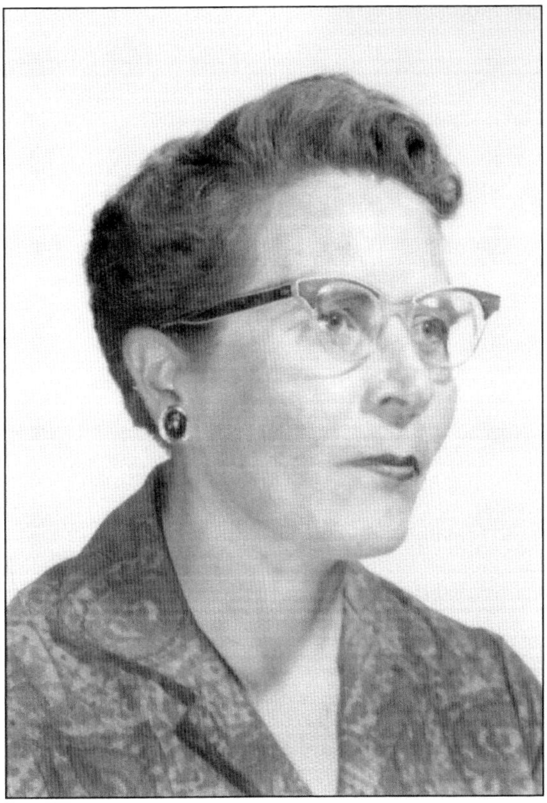

This is Bridgette Maestas Olguín, born in 1918. She married J.M. "Jimmy" James Olguín in 1947. They met when she taught school at the San Luis Institute of Arts and Crafts in the 1940s. They raised five children: Carla, James, Monica, Carmen, and Loretta. Her family later owned and operated the Olguín SAV-U-MOR store in San Luis. Mary Cordova Olivas was the Olguín family's nanny. (Courtesy of Richard Olivas y Cordova.)

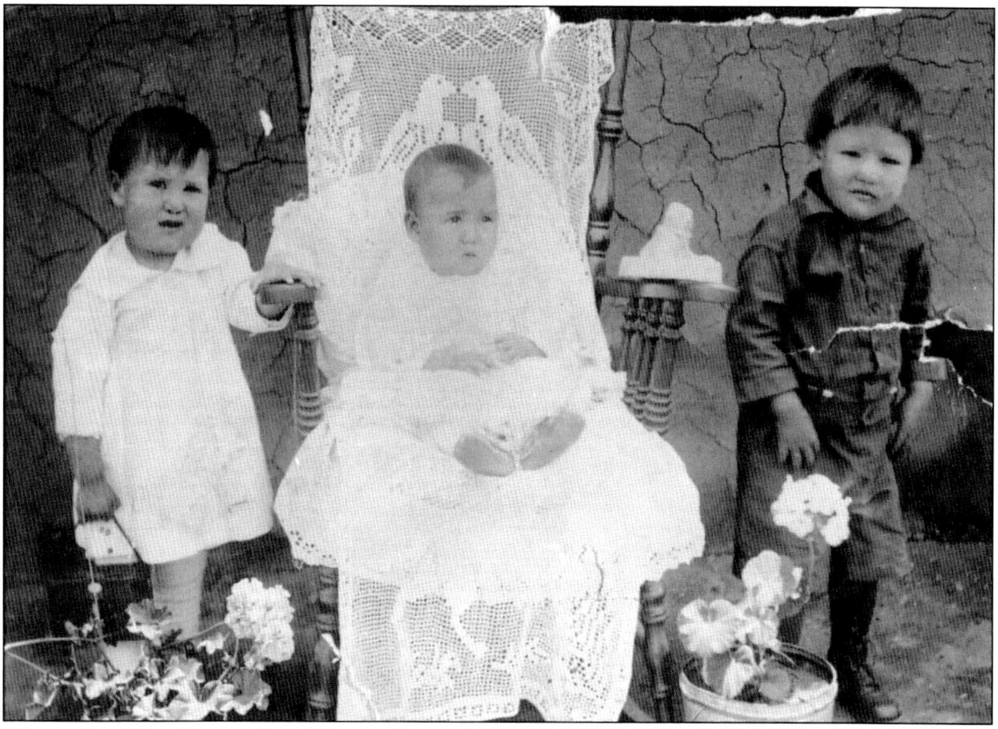

These adorable siblings, from left to right, are Casilda Atencio (Vigil), born in 1922; baby Estella Atencio (Aragon), born in 1923; and Estevan Atencio, born in 1920. They are the children of Amarante Atencio and Aurelia Valdez Atencio. The photograph was taken in front of their parent's adobe home in Cañon de Chama in 1923. The baby is seated on a beautiful crochet coverlet. Crochet pieces were used to decorate household items such as chairs, tables, and windows. (Courtesy of Clarence and Casilda Vigil.)

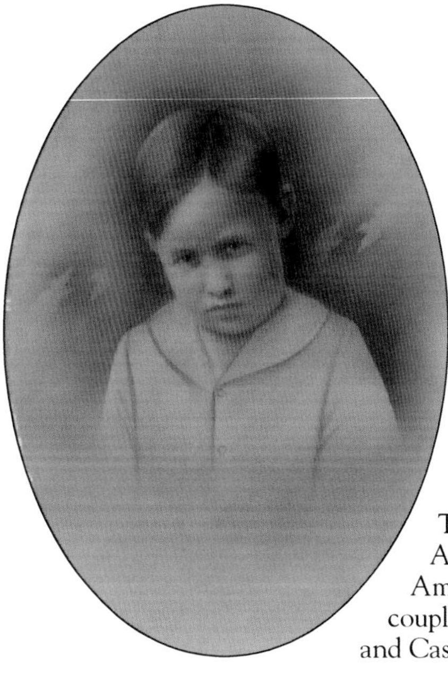

The shy little boy in this picture is eight-year-old Amos Atencio. He was the youngest of six children born to Amarante Atencio and Aurelia Valdez Atencio. The couple was married on April 26, 1920. (Courtesy of Clarence and Casilda Vigil.)

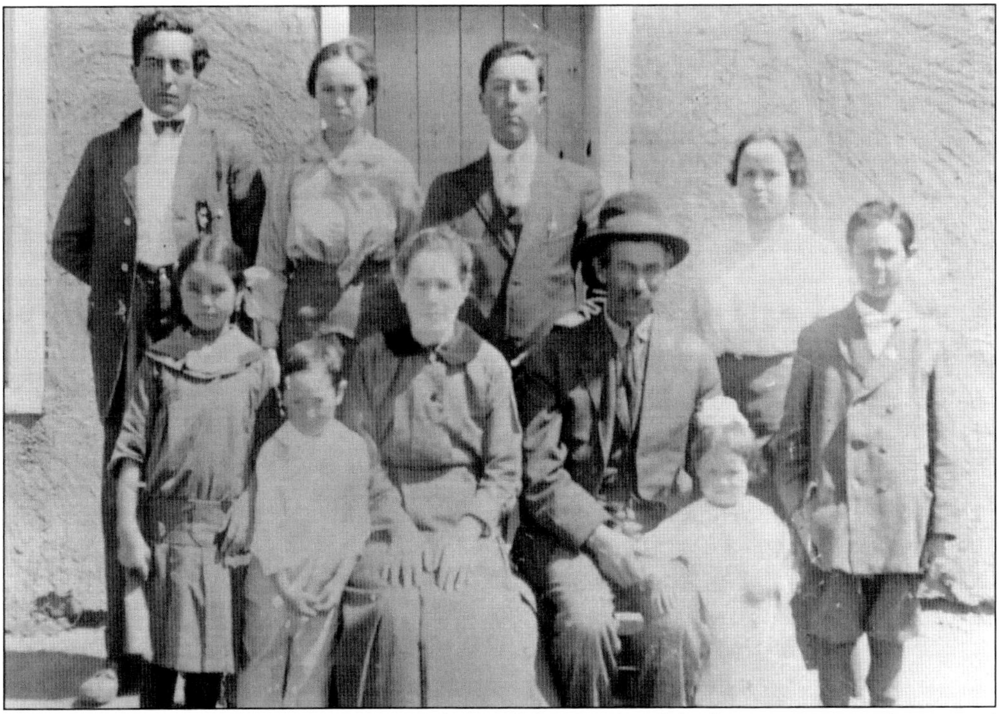

This Olivas family portrait was taken in front of the family adobe home in San Pedro around 1916. Pictured from left to right are (first row) Gasparita Olivas, Rogerio Olivas, Gregorita Valdes, Gabriel Olivas, Susanita Olivas, and Felix Olivas; (second row) Epifanio Sanchez, Inez Olivas, Rafael Olivas, and Lucia Olivas. The family's adobe home was somewhat of a feature in the neighborhood. The father, Gabriel Olivas, planted an orange tree inside the house. Neighbors called it La Casa del Árbol. He kept the room with the tree locked so no one could go inside. The tree never bore fruit but nonetheless grew beautiful and large. The home is presently owned by David Pacheco. (Courtesy of Richard Olivas y Cordova.)

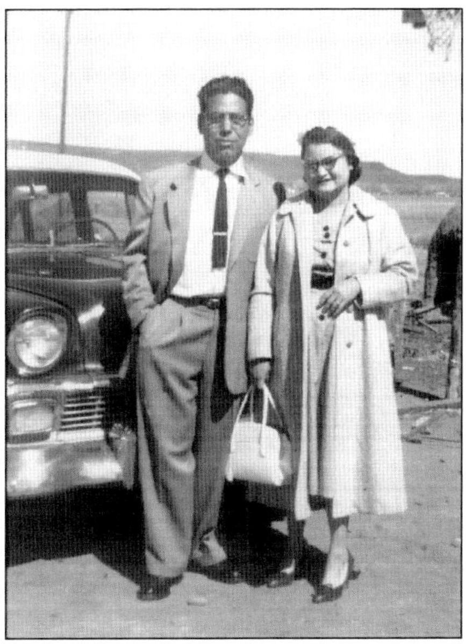

This couple is Prudencio Chacon and his wife, Belinda Valdez Chacon. The 1930s photograph was taken on their family farm one mile east of San Luis. Both husband and wife were enterprising individuals. He owned and operated a shoe shop, and she owned and operated a secondhand store called Belinda's Bargain Store. She carried antiques and many household items. Belinda's was a popular place to shop even before thrift store shopping became trendy. (Courtesy of Dora Vialpando.)

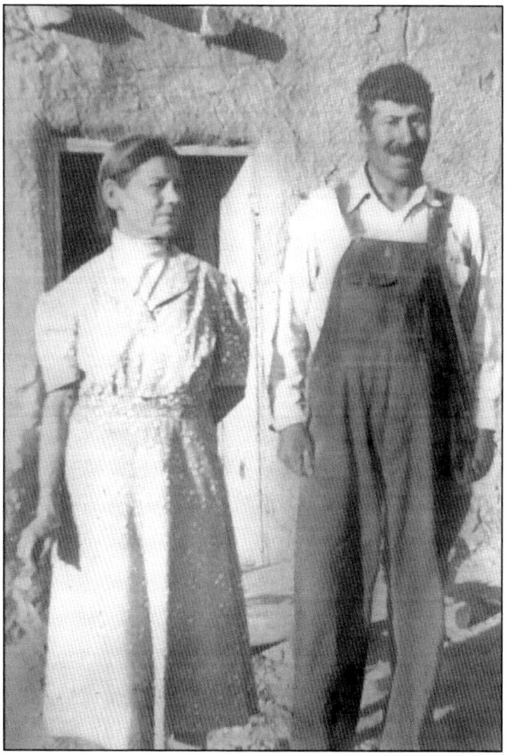

Pictured in front of their adobe family home are Leonardo Chacon and his wife, Maria del Rosario Martinez Chacon, in the 1930s. The couple farmed the land and raised animals in the area east of San Luis called La Corrillera. (Courtesy of Dora Vialpando.)

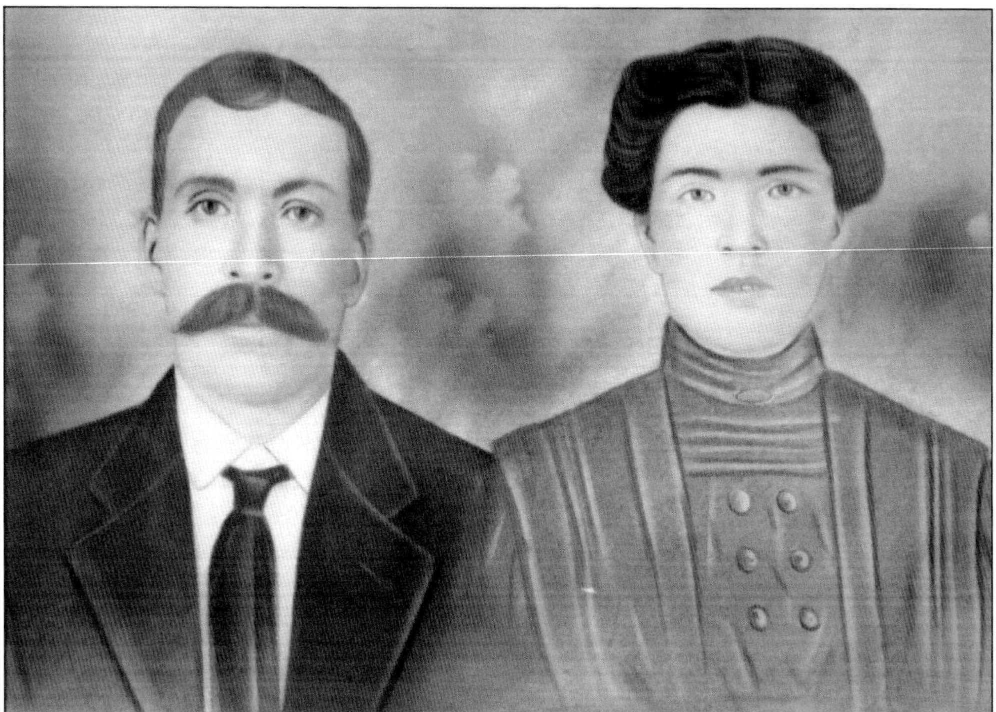

This striking couple is Samuel and Felisita Vialpando. They lived in Chama. Samuel was a farmer and his wife tended to the household and children. (Courtesy of Dora Vialpando.)

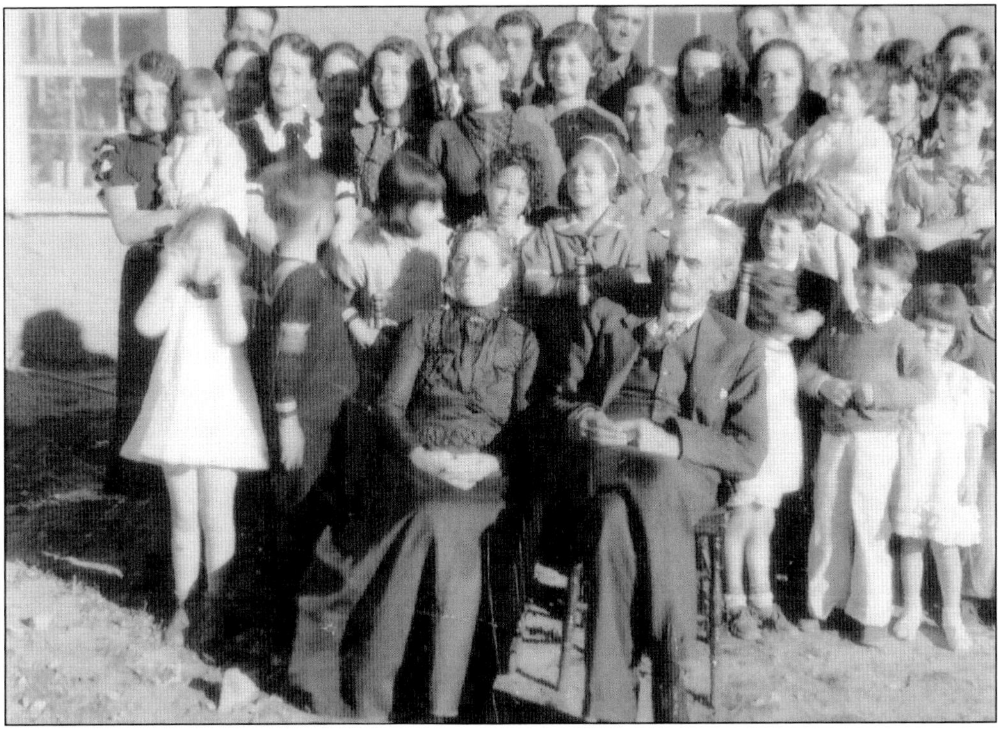

Maria (Mary) St. Clair Choury and Armand Choury celebrate their 50th wedding anniversary in 1937 surrounded by their seven children, their grandchildren, and their great-grandchildren. Mary was a teacher and homemaker while her husband Armand, a farmer and rancher, was elected to the position of Costilla County treasurer for 35 years. At the age of 16, Armand became a graduate of the University of Paris in Bourgeois, France. He enlisted in the French army at the age of 17. Armand made a significant mark in the San Luis area as a businessman and politician. (Both, courtesy of Henrietta Mascarenas.)

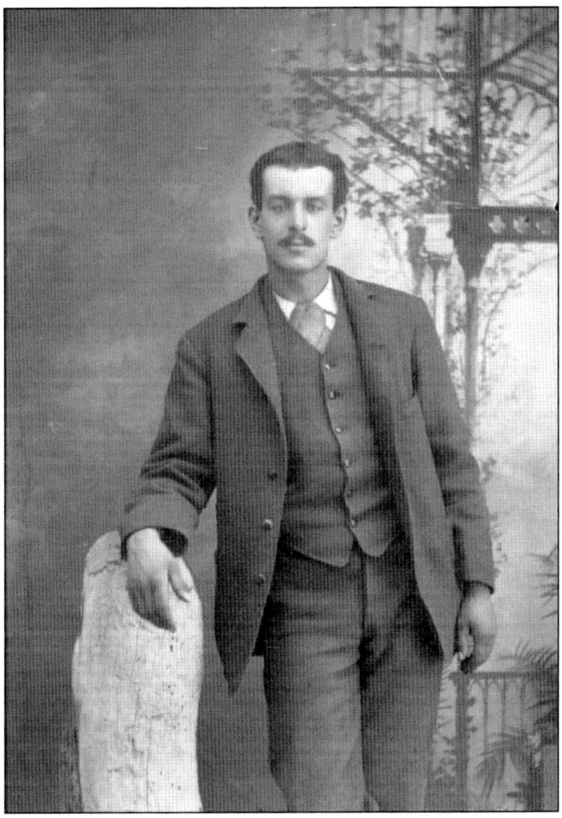

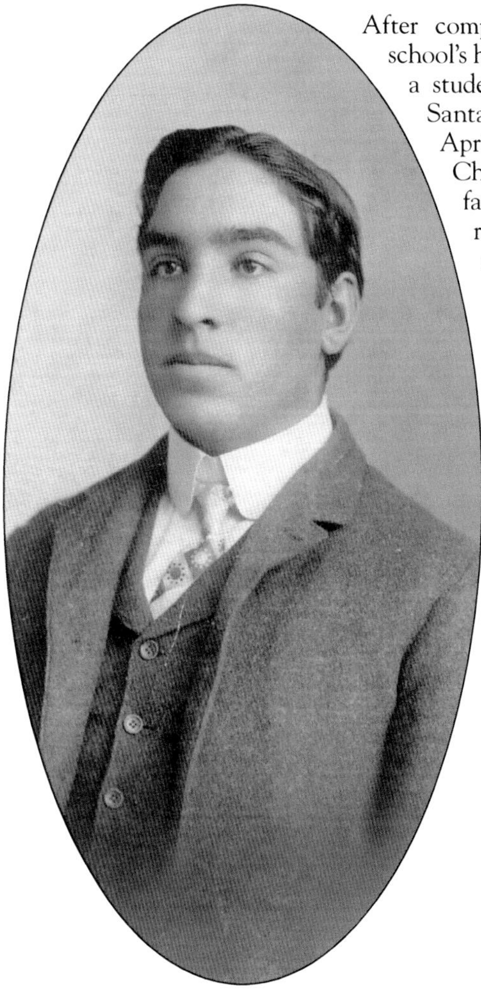

After completing the eighth grade, the San Luis–area school's highest education level, Emilio Lobato Sr. became a student at Sacred Heart College (St. Michael's) in Santa Fe, New Mexico. This photograph was taken on April 17, 1904. At 17 years of age, Emilio returned to Chama to run the Chama Mercantile Store with his father, José Francisco Lobato. Although he never received a high school diploma, he was a well-respected businessman and politician. (Courtesy of Henrietta Mascarenas.)

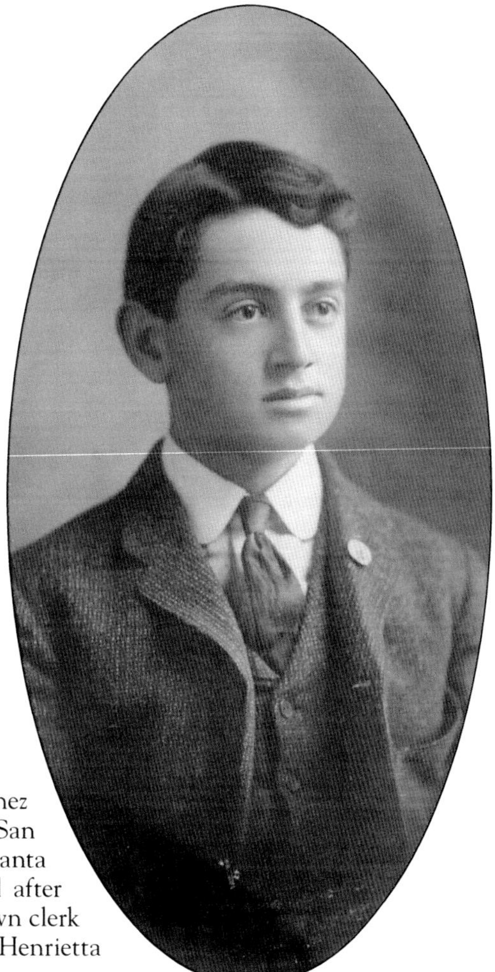

This school photograph of the young José Sanchez was taken on April 17, 1904. A local boy from San Pedro, he attended Sacred Heart College in Santa Fe, New Mexico. Sanchez Reservoir is named after him. He is the great-grandfather of San Luis town clerk Mary Jo Sanchez-Manzanares. (Courtesy of Henrietta Mascarenas.)

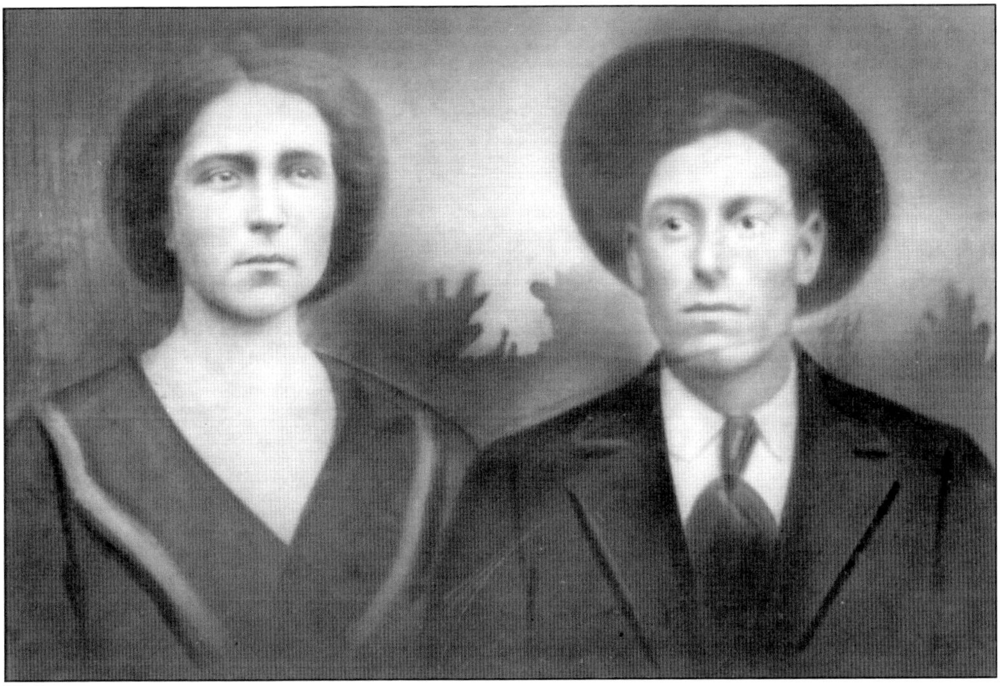

Pictured here around 1920 are Francisquita Vialpando Mascarenas and her husband, Fred Mascarenas, from Chama. The couple raised seven children: Lilia, Gaspar, Fred, Steven, Clorinda, James, and Josephina. (Courtesy of Henrietta Mascarenas.)

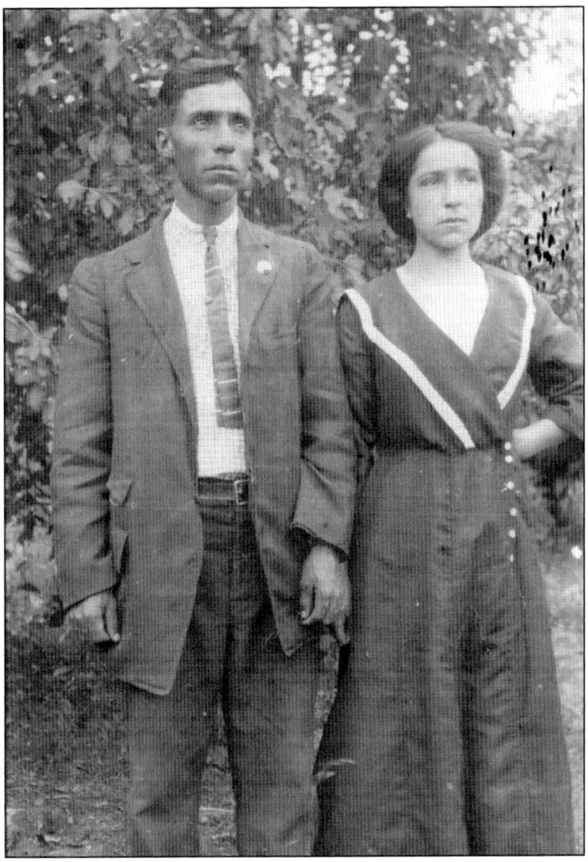

Pictured here are Francisquita Vialpando Mascarenas and her brother Eutimio Vialpando in the early 1920s. The siblings posed for this photograph on the family farm. (Courtesy of Henrietta Mascarenas.)

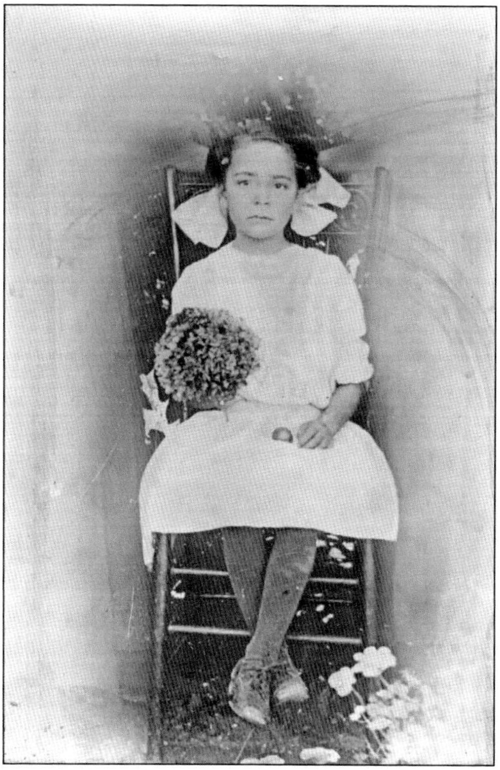

Seated on a chair with a big white bow is seven-year-old Manuelita de Jesús (Lucy). Manuelita de Jesús was born on August 11, 1904, to Alejandro Vialpando and Beatrice Mascarenas Vialpando in Chama. She is affectionately called La Luz by friends and family. She was baptized on August 14, 1904, at Most Precious Blood Church by the Rev. J.S. Garcia. Her godparents were Juan de Dios Vialpando and Crestin Lopez. She married Anastacio José Valdez and raised five children. Lucy Vialpando Valdez, "Grandma Lucy," was the author's paternal grandmother. (Courtesy of Beatrice Marquez.)

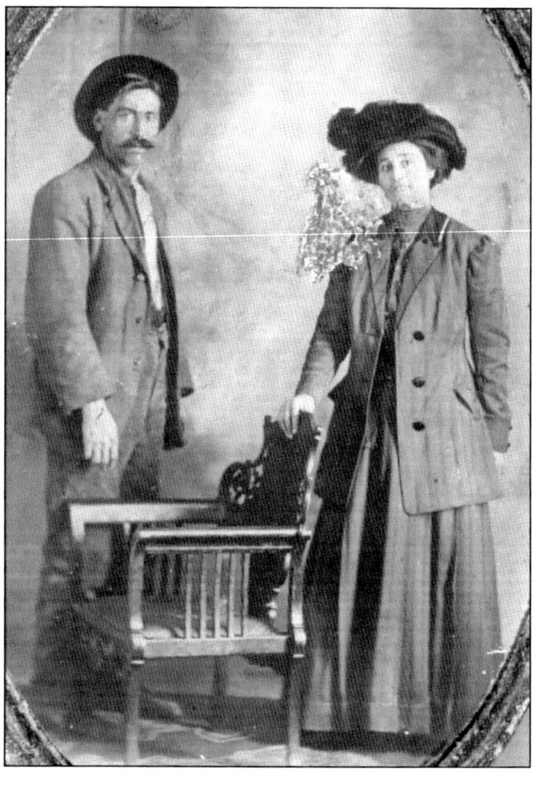

This classic portrait of Alejandro Vialpando and Beatrice Mascarenas Vialpando was taken around 1900. Alejandro and Beatrice had two children, Manuelita de Jesús (Lucy) and Ciria Vialpando. He was a farmer and rancher, and she was a homemaker. (Courtesy of Beatrice Marquez.)

This photograph of three-year-old Evan Arthur Valdez was taken in Cañon de Chama around 1935. Evan is one of five children born to Lucy Vialpando Valdez and Anastacio José (Joe) Valdez. He loves farming, but his first love is education. A well-admired and respected educator and school administrator, he retired after 34 years. During the Korean War, Valdez served with an intelligence unit with the 1st Infantry Division in Europe. During his term as an officer to American Legion Post 142, he was instrumental in the building of the housing development in San Luis. He served Costilla County as the veterans' service officer for 32 years. Valdez is a member of the Knights of Columbus. (Courtesy of Evan A. Valdez.)

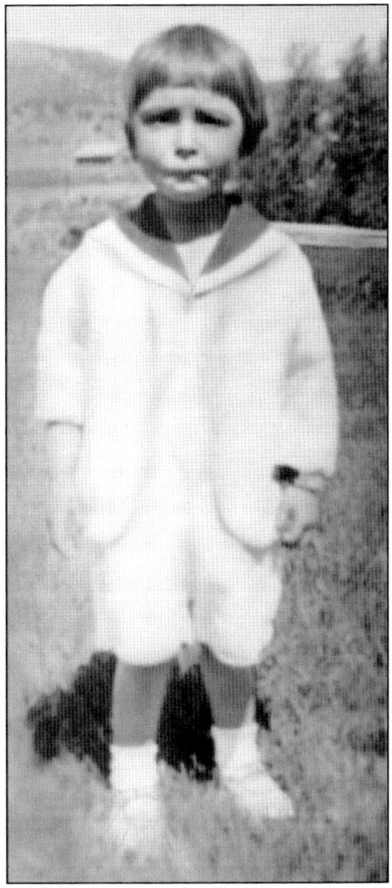

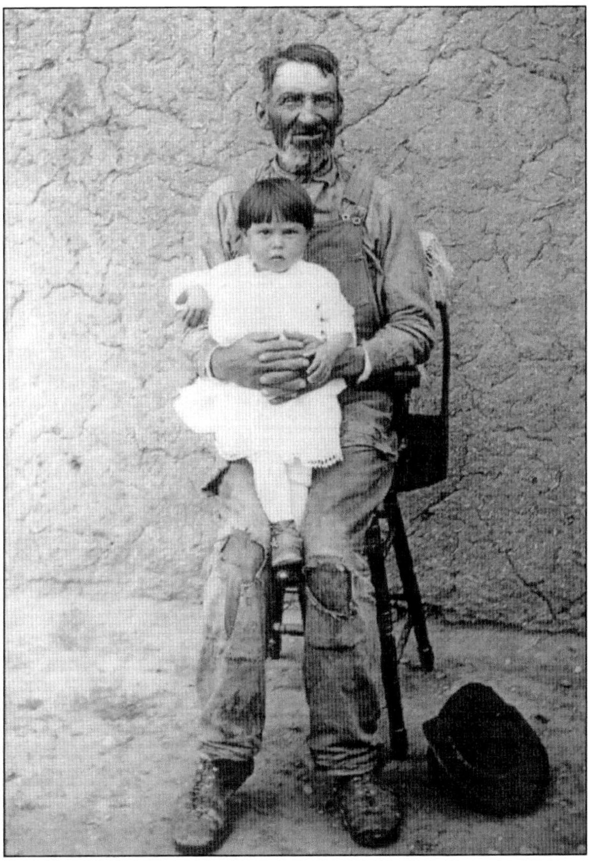

This grandfather and his granddaughter are pictured in front of an old adobe home in San Luis de la Culebra. The image of the settlers of the Culebra shows that life was not easy. They had to build homes out of the natural materials of dirt, straw, and wood; plant and harvest crops; make many of their own clothes; weave or crochet their textiles, rugs, and coverlets; hunt and preserve their food supply; and, because of long distances, make travel plans to go from place to place to take care of the children. (Courtesy of Evan A. Valdez.)

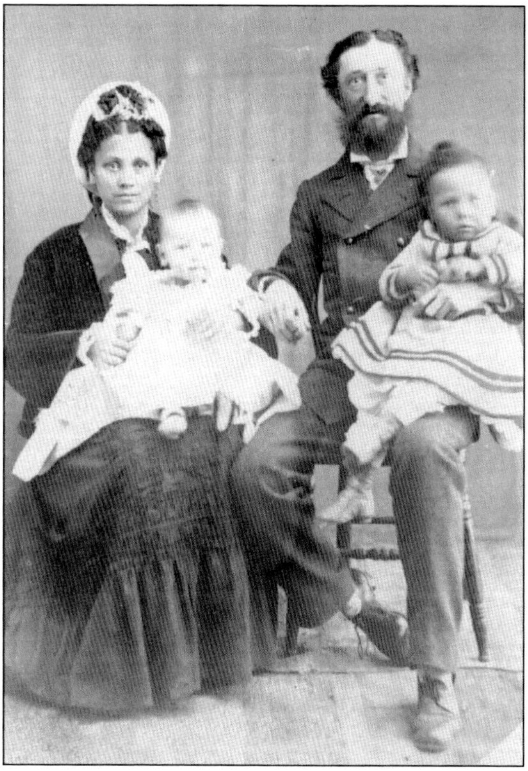

The beautifully dressed people in this photograph are Mr. and Mrs William Sabine. Mrs. Sabine is holding Beatriz Jaramillo Gallegos. The child William Sabine is holding is unidentified. The event is the christening of little Beatriz; the Sabines became Beatriz's godparents. When she grew older, she told her grandchildren stories of how they would run into the forest when the Indians attacked. Beatriz is Theresa Vigil's maternal grandmother. (Courtesy of Theresa Vigil.)

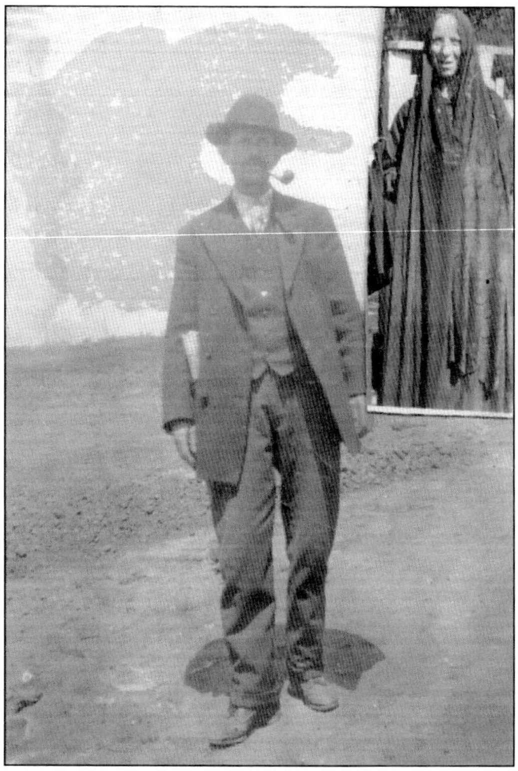

These two photographs are of couple Raymundo Gallegos and Beatriz Jaramillo Gallegos. Their son Luis Tomas Gallegos carried this picture in his wallet during his tour of duty during World War II. The descendants of the Culebra villages continue to proudly serve their country. Luis Tomas Gallegos kept the photo of his family close to his heart so they would always be with him. He served valiantly as a soldier, and returned home honorably discharged. (Courtesy of Theresa Vigil.)

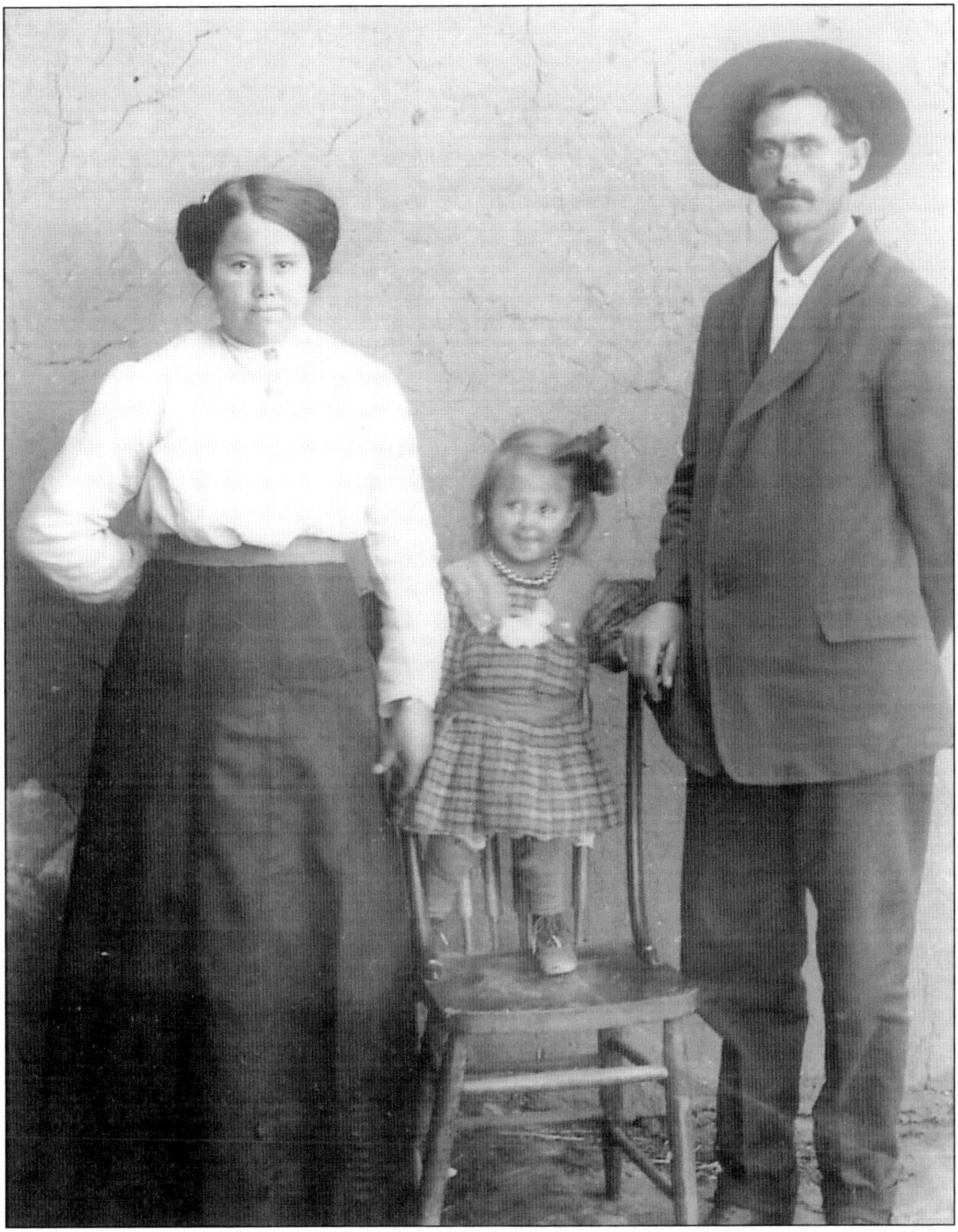

This endearing family photograph taken around 1912 shows Francesquita (Lobato) Olivas, daughter Maclovia, age two, and Candido Olivas. Candido was the son of Blas and Ignicita (Zamora) Olivas, who settled on the family farm in 1863 with the Carlos Beaubien Land Grant. The picture was taken on the side of the family home. That same homestead is a Centennial Farm, having been owned and operated by five generations of the same family (Ida Manzanares Valdez) for over 100 years. (Courtesy of the Candido Olivas Sr. family.)

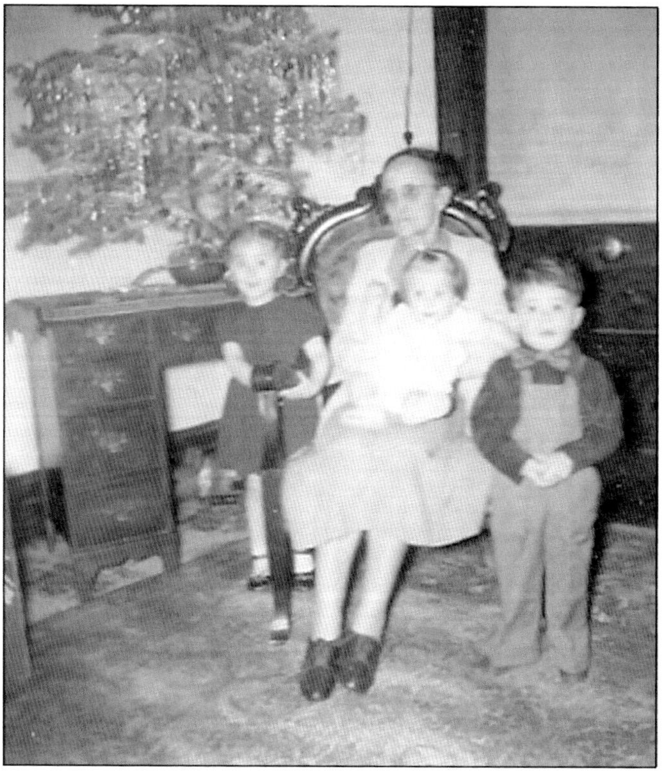

Everyone loves spending time at Grandma's house, and the Olguín family are no exception. Grandchildren tell of happy memories spent at the Olguín home. Grandmother Beatriz owned the Olguín Mercantile next door, so the grandchildren split their visits between home and business. This picture was taken in December 1952 inside the Olguín home. Grandmother Beatriz, born in 1887, is holding seven-month-old Monica. On the left is three-and-a-half-year-old sister Carla, and on the right is two-year-old James M. Olguín III. (Courtesy of Monica and Carmen Olguín.)

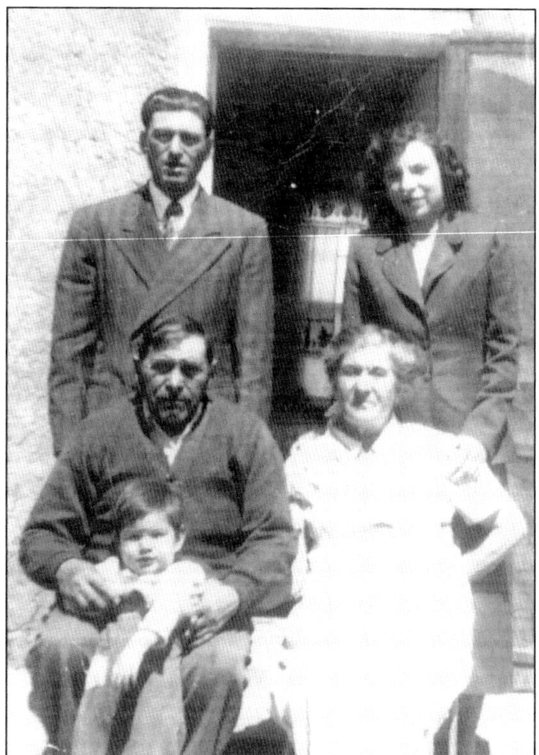

Pictured around 1952 in front of their San Acacio home are, from left to right, (first row) Aniceto, born in 1885, and Eufrasia Martinez, born in 1887; (second row) their son Petrolino and his wife, Flora Martinez. Two-year-old grandson Issac Valero sits on Aniceto's lap. Issac is the son of their daughter Ana Martinez and Ruben Valero. The Martinezes were married on January 3, 1909, at Most Precious Blood Parish in San Luis, officiated by Rev. J.S. Garcia. Aniceto was a farmer, and Eufrasia was a homemaker. (Courtesy of Wanda Vigil.)

Pictured is one-year-old Delfina Martinez around 1913. Born in 1912, Delfina was the eldest of 10 surviving children born to parents Aniceto and Eufrasia Martinez. (Courtesy of Wanda Vigil.)

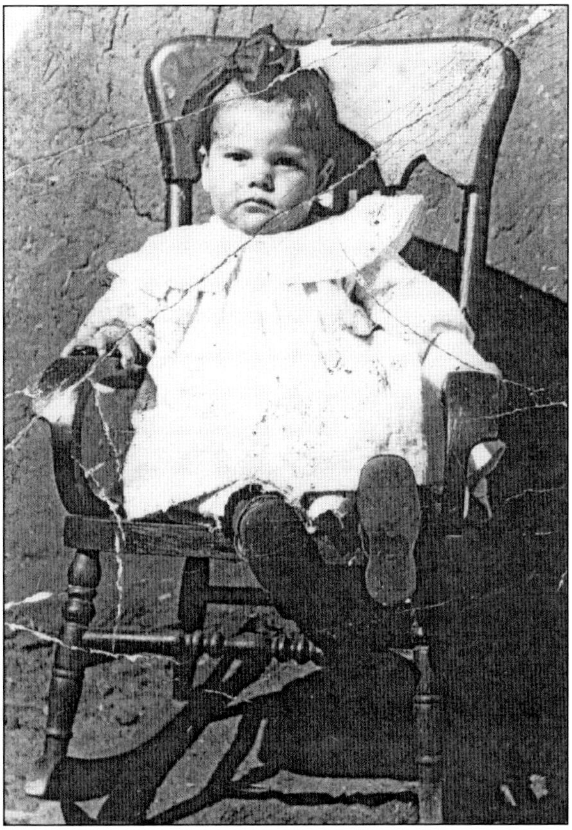

Sisters Rose and Josephine Cardenas are pictured in the 1930s. Rose married Sam Medina from Arroyo Hondo, New Mexico, and they had one son. Together they operated Sam's Covered Wagon bar and restaurant for 46 years. Around 1958, they purchased the Riverside Dance Hall from the SPMDTU and opened up the Tin Cup Café. Josephine married Meliton Maxwell and raised four children. She worked with her husband in the family grocery store and later worked as a mail carrier from Fort Garland to El Rito de San Francisco, about 26 miles each way. The Maxwell store burned down around 1940. It was located at the site of the present-day Padilla Liquor and Gas Station. (Courtesy of Eugene and Josie Lobato.)

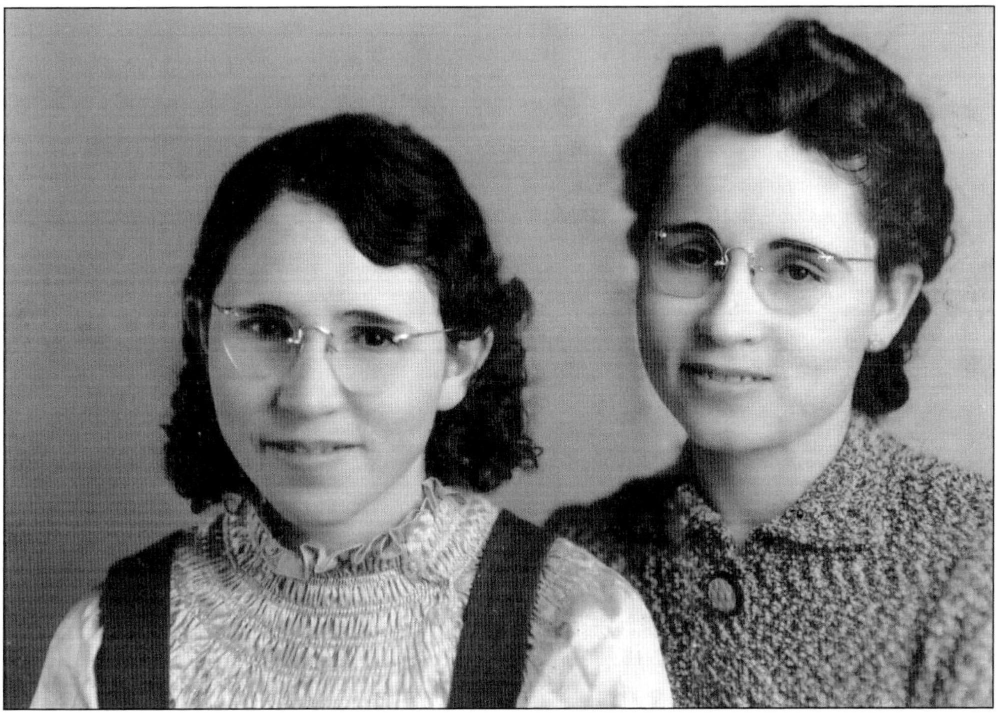

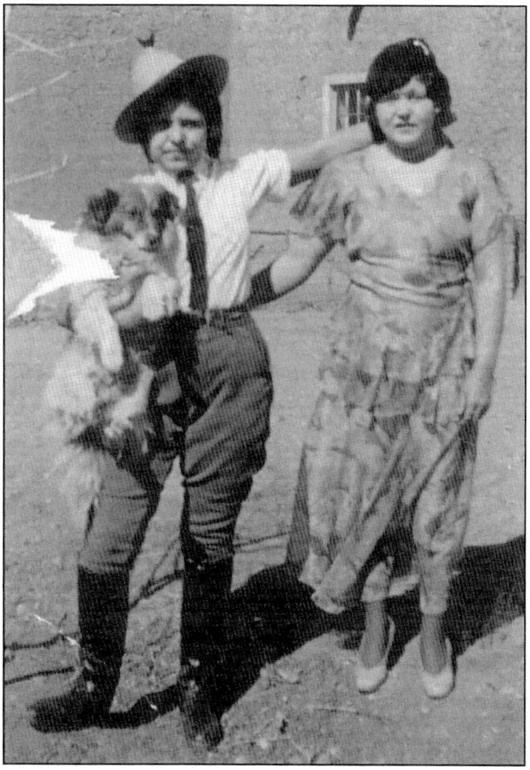

Pictured here are two of the Martinez sisters, 18-year-old Celestina, born on December 27, 1916 (holding a dog and dressed in riders uniform), and 20-year-old Maria Benina, born on July 15, 1914. Maria Benina married Esequiel Santistevan in San Acacio. They had three children: Johnny, Sammy, and Cecelia. (Courtesy of Wanda Vigil.)

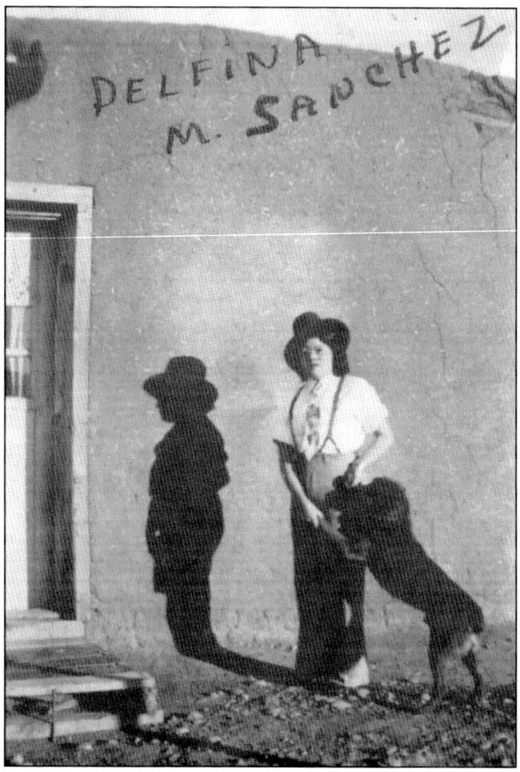

This photograph of 18-year-old Delfina Martinez, born in 1912, and her dog was taken around 1930 in front of her parent's adobe home. The shadow against the wall adds an artistic element to the photograph. Delfina married George Sanchez in San Pablo in 1935. Together they raised six children: Mabel, Arthur, Richard, Virgil, Billy, and Freddie (who passed away in 1951). (Courtesy of Wanda Vigil.)

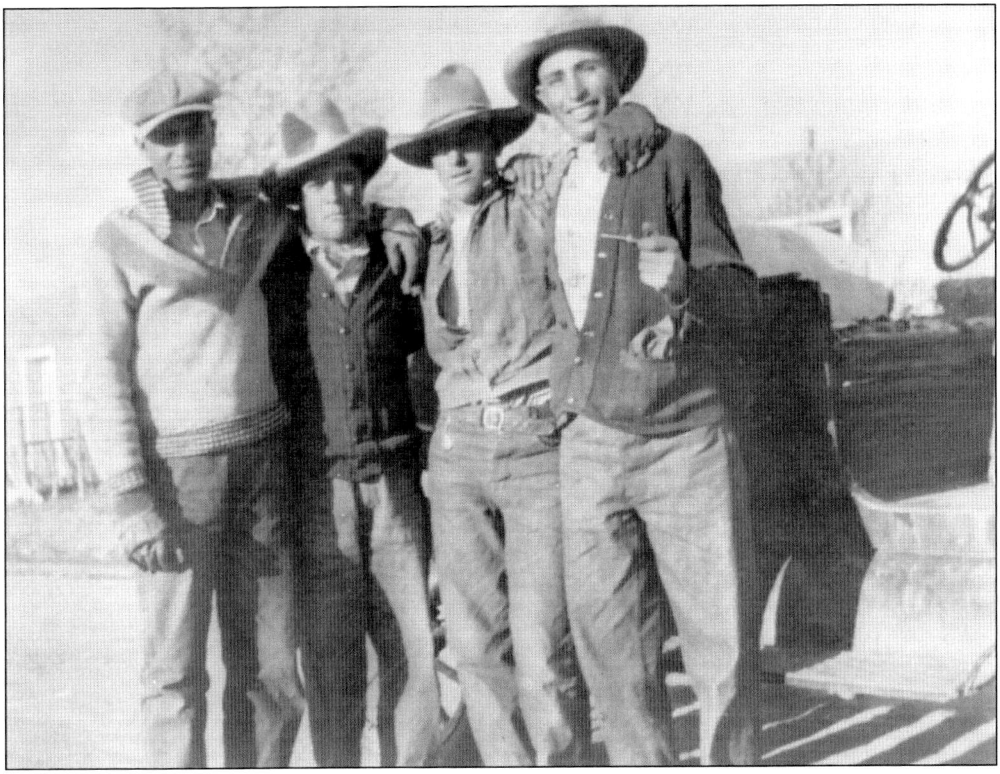

Pictured from left to right are Fermin Vigil, Ben Madrid, Patrick Jaramillo, and Demostenes Vigil. The photograph was taken in San Luis in the 1940s. They were a group of hardworking, steadfast young men who loved a challenge. During the WPA era, Demostenes Vigil participated in the weaving revival project in San Luis and worked on the building of the bridge and stone wall around the San Luis Institute of Arts and Crafts. He also was a carpenter, handyman, and stonemason. He would take the lava rock used to build the bridge in town and carve the shapes in the stones to fit. (Courtesy of Demostenes Vigil II.)

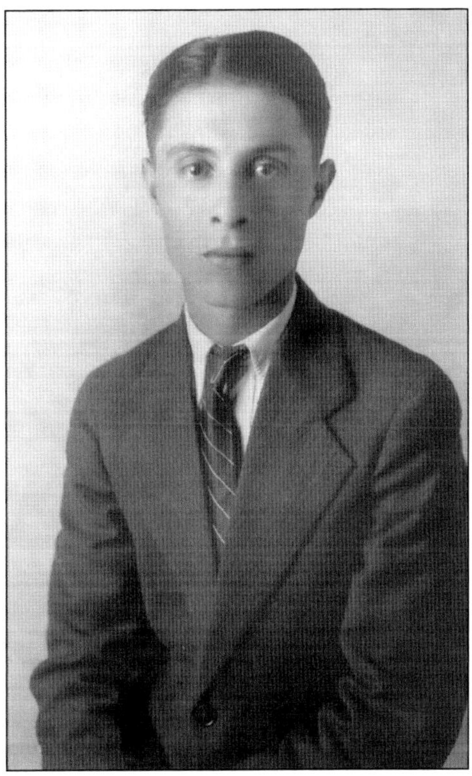

This formal graduation picture is of 18-year-old Meliton Garcia from Mercy High School in 1929. Meliton, born in 1910, served as Costilla County clerk and recorder. He also was employed as county clerk deputy for other elected officials, including his brother Alfonso Garcia. His tenure for Costilla County lasted close to 40 years. (Courtesy of Conrad and Acela Garcia.)

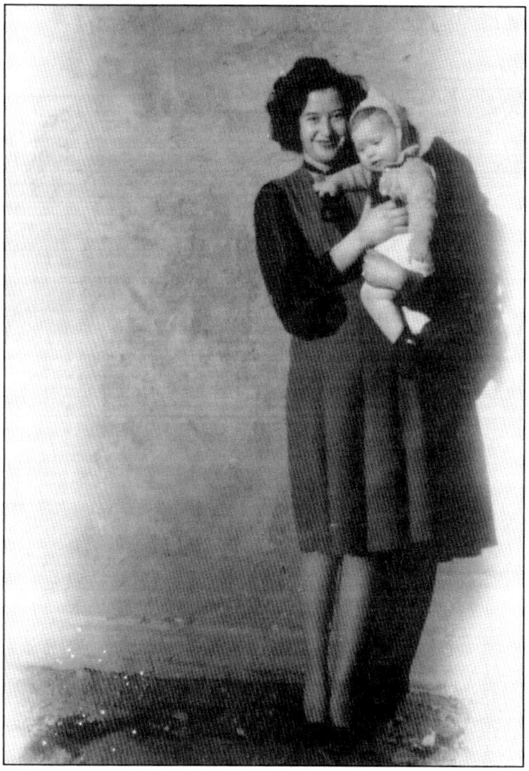

Big sister 16-year-old Yvette Sanchez (Gallegos) is shown holding her baby brother, three- to four-month-old Conrad, in June 1947. The photograph was taken next to their parent's home in front of the Costilla County Shop in San Luis. Yvette grew up to be a beloved schoolteacher in the San Luis and Colorado Springs school districts. Her little brother grew up to work for General Telephone in California for over 33 years until his retirement in January 2000. (Courtesy of Conrad and Acela Garcia.)

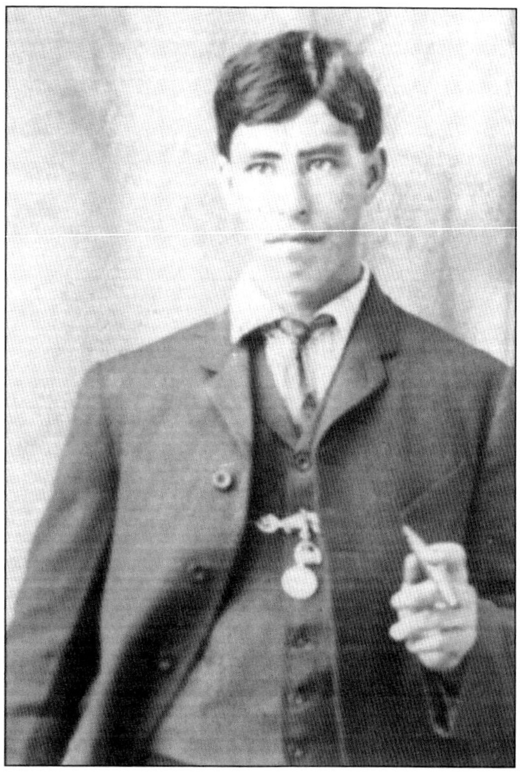

This handsome young man is Henry Medina, born in El Rito de San Francisco in the late 1800s. Although he never smoked, he thought it would be fun to pose with a cigar, giving him a look of distinction. He worked for the mines in Walsenburg, where he met his wife, Selicita, to whom he was married for 55 years. He was employed by the Santa Fe Railroad for 51 years. Being a butcher by trade, he returned home to San Luis to open a meat market in the early 1920s. It was located in the green house just north of the county shop. He cut meat on the weekends and returned to his railroad job on the weekdays. The store was built by his son-in-law Meliton's grandfather Pilar Mondragon. Pilar Mondragon traded the store building to Henry Medina for a brand-new Model T pickup. (Courtesy of Conrad, Acela, and Sam Garcia.)

The handsome gentlemen in this 1920s photograph are Esequiel Manzanares (left) and Marcoz Manzanares. They were from the Culebra villages, possibly the San Pablo or Los Fuertes area. The picture was found in the belongings of Eduvigen Vialpando Jaquez Esquibel, born on June 14, 1895. (Courtesy of Charlie Jaquez Jr.)

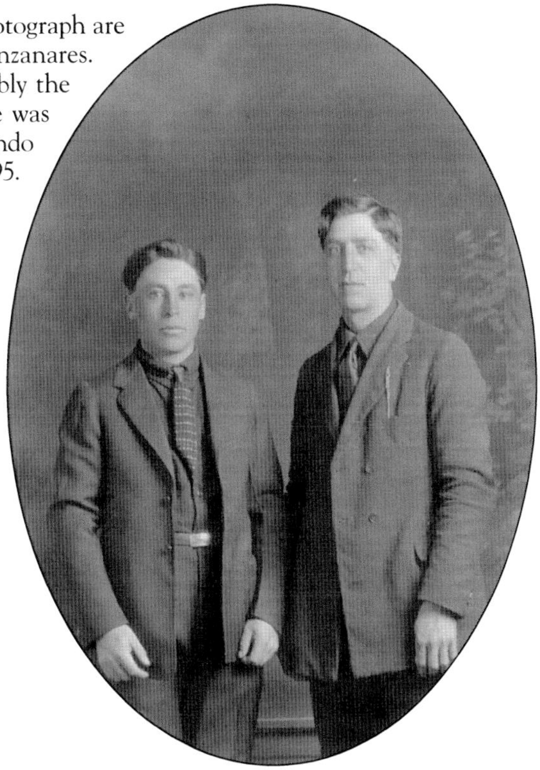

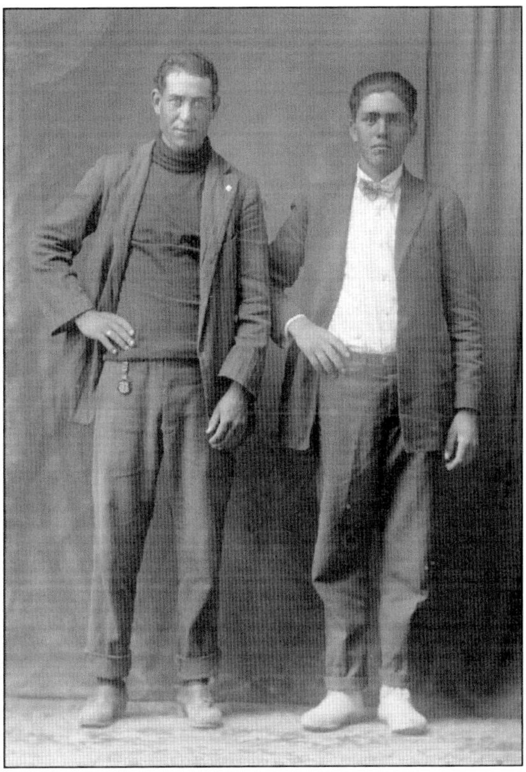

The two men in this picture are Ismael Sanchez (left) and Rosalio Vialpando, born on August 27, 1900. The young men were from Chama. Rosalio Vialpando is the brother of Eduvigen Vialpando Jaquez Esquibel, born on June 14, 1895. This photograph was found in a hope chest that belonged to her. She is Charlie Jaquez Jr.'s grandmother. (Courtesy of Charlie Jaquez Jr. and Brenda Vialpando.)

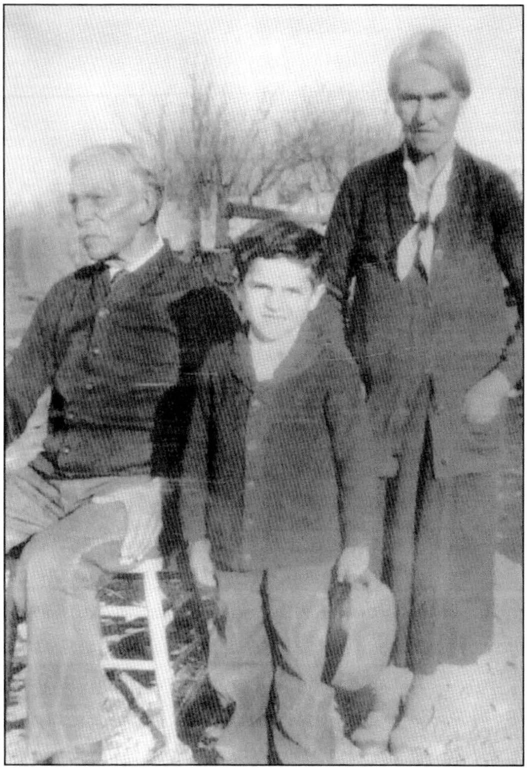

Jose Francisco Lobato and his wife, Crucita Sanchez-Lobato, are pictured with their grandson José Lobato Jr. in the 1930s. José had a horse named Costello, which he always loved riding. Mrs. Crucita Sanchez-Lobato was the first non-Indian woman born in Chama in 1866. (Courtesy of Henrietta Mascarenas.)

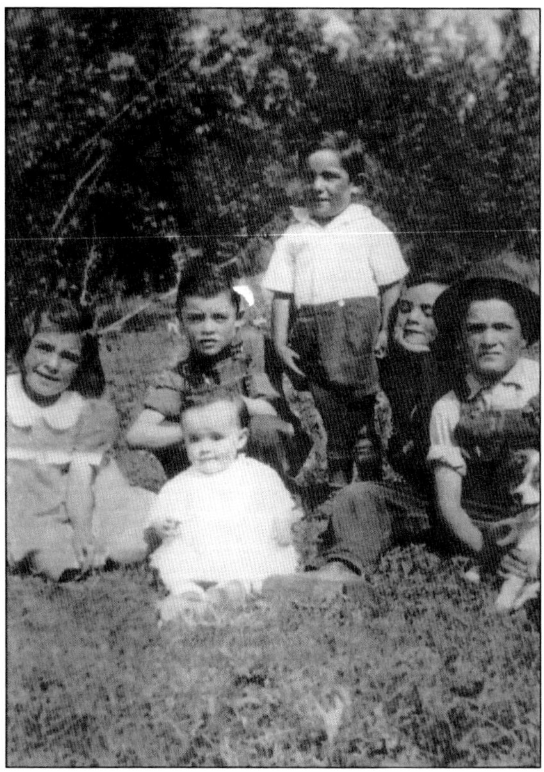

Taken in the 1930s, this loveable photograph of six siblings shows (from left to right) Eva, Jennie (baby), Carlos, Bonifacio "Bonnie," Moises, and José Francisco Lobato. They are the children of Ernestine Sanchez Lobato and José Presentacion "J.P." Lobato of Chama. (Courtesy of Adolfo Lobato.)

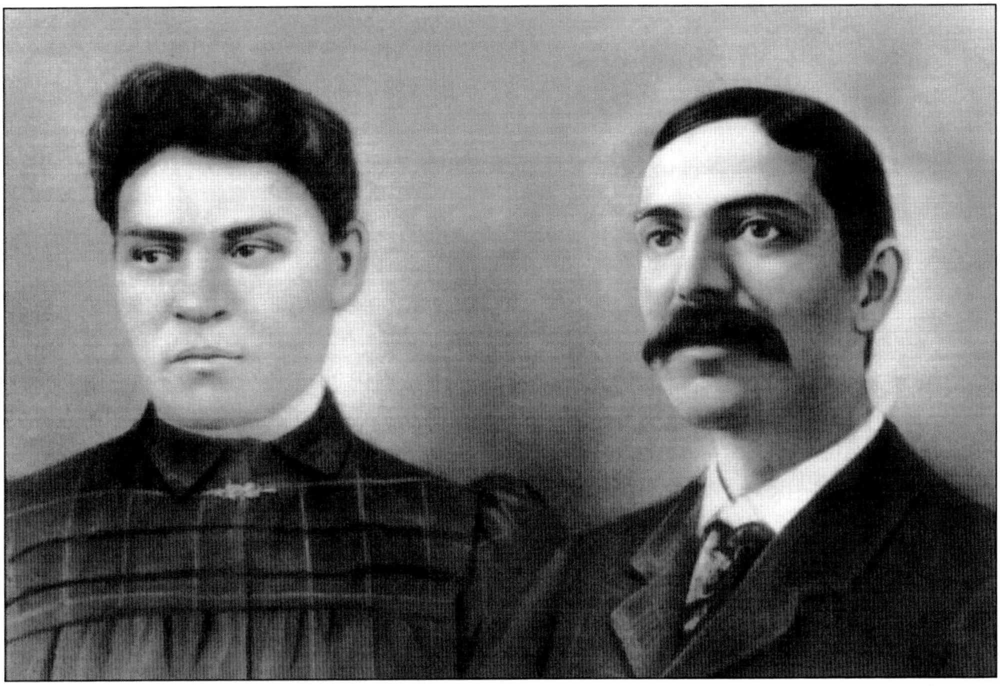

This is a portrait of José Francisco Lobato and his wife, Crucita Sanchez-Lobato, around 1890. José was born in 1865, and his wife was born in 1866. He was 25 years old when this photograph was taken. He owned and operated the Chama Mercantile Store. (Courtesy of Adolfo Lobato.)

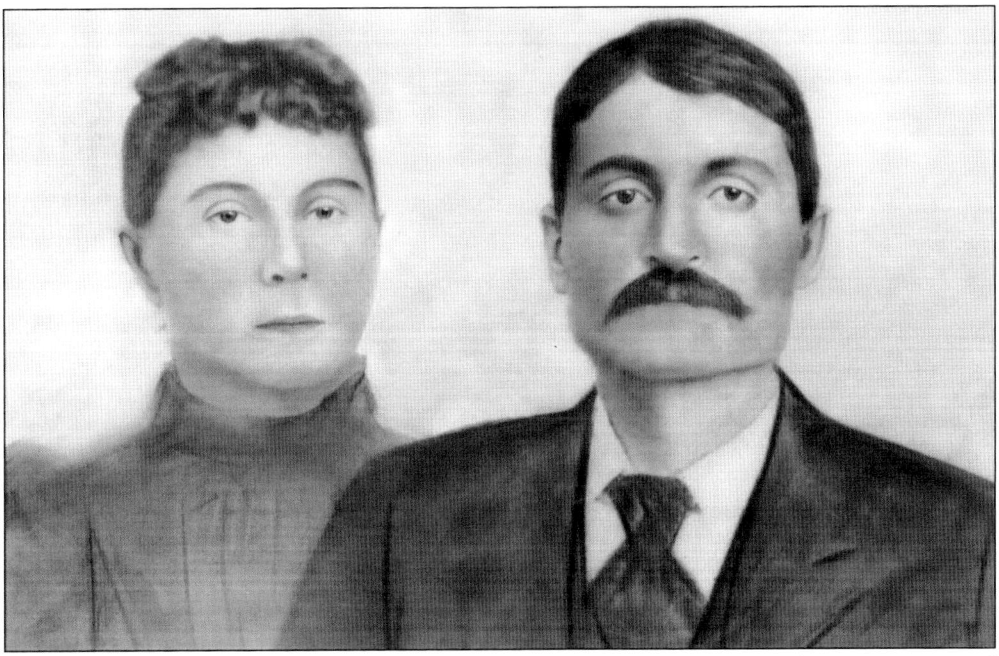

This couple is José Maria Taylor and Sarah Riegenberg. Her family came from Germany and up from South America to settle in Mora, New Mexico. Her husband was from San Francisco (El Rito), Colorado. They met in New Mexico and settled along the Culebra River to farm and ranch. They are Adolfo Lobato's great-grandparents. (Courtesy of Adolfo Lobato.)

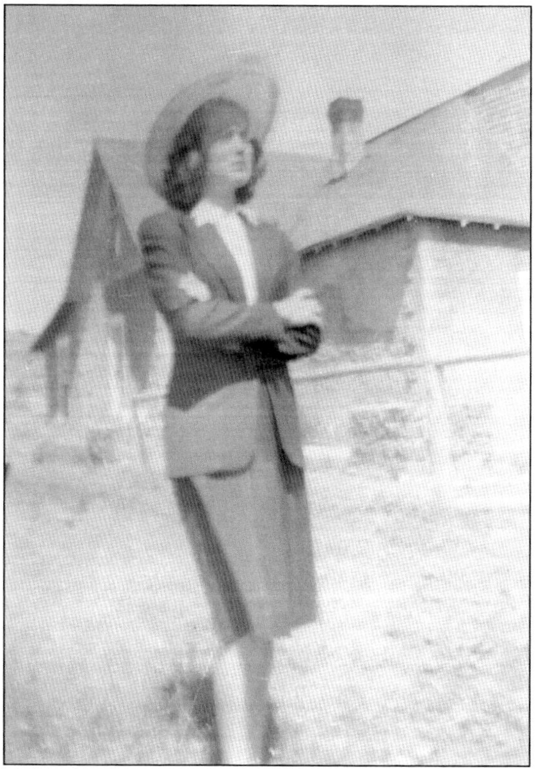

At left, in the late 1940s, when she was in her late teens, Celina Mondragon (Trujillo) posed in front of her parent's home in Los Colonias, Colorado. Below, around 1925, she is about one and half years old. She married Alonso Trujillo and raised five children. She worked for many years under director Marbella Vigil Smith as a case worker until her retirement from the Costilla County Department of Social Services in San Luis. (Both, courtesy of Pat Trujillo VanZandt.)

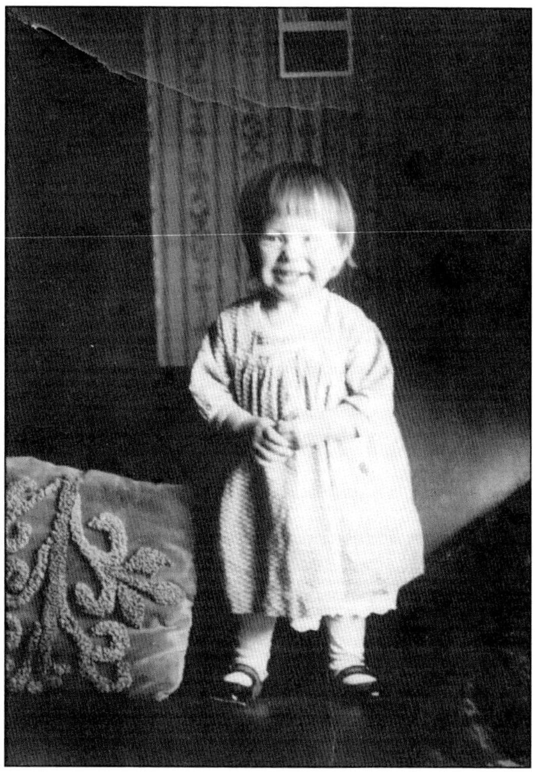

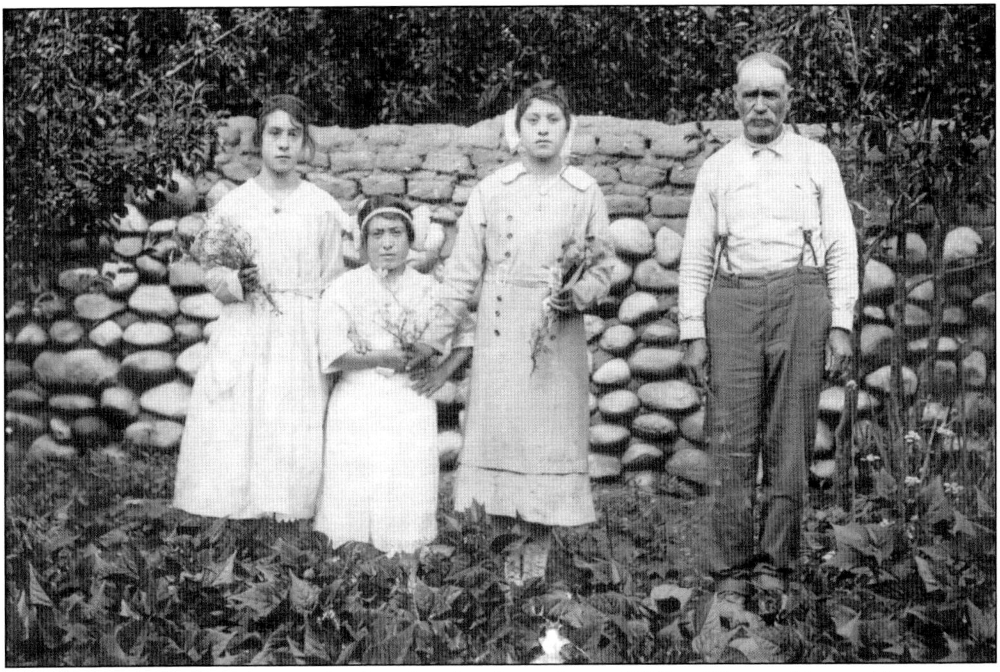

This photograph was taken in the Sanchez family garden in 1923 in Chama. Pictured from left to right are Reina Roybal, Lucy Sanchez (Ortega), Isabelita Sanchez (Vialpando), and José Manuel Sanchez (Isabelita's grandfather and Lucy's father). The girls are holding flowers grown in their backyard, with a river rock and adobe fence behind them. (Courtesy of Brenda Vialpando.)

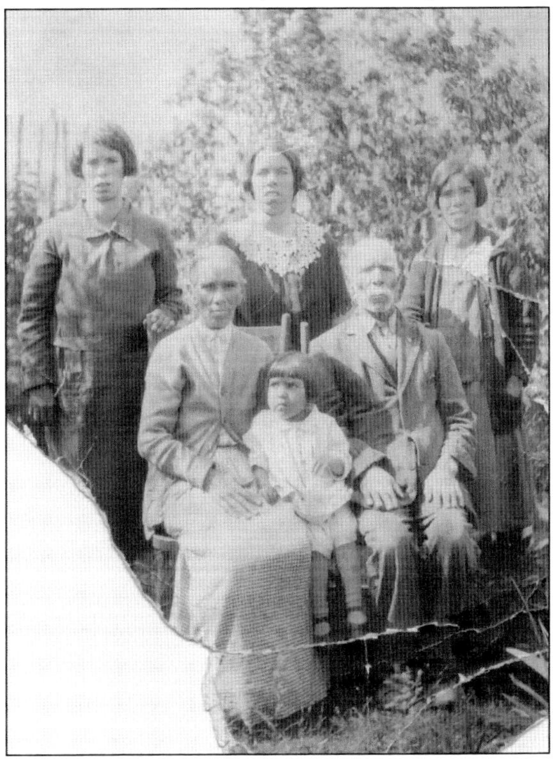

Pictured in this 1922 Lopez family photograph are, from left to right, (seated) mother Isabelita Sanchez Lopez, granddaughter Cleotilde Vialpando, and father Rumaldo Lopez; (standing) sisters Delfina Lopez Vigil, Elvira Lopez, and Julianita Lopez Vialpando. (Courtesy of Brenda Vialpando.)

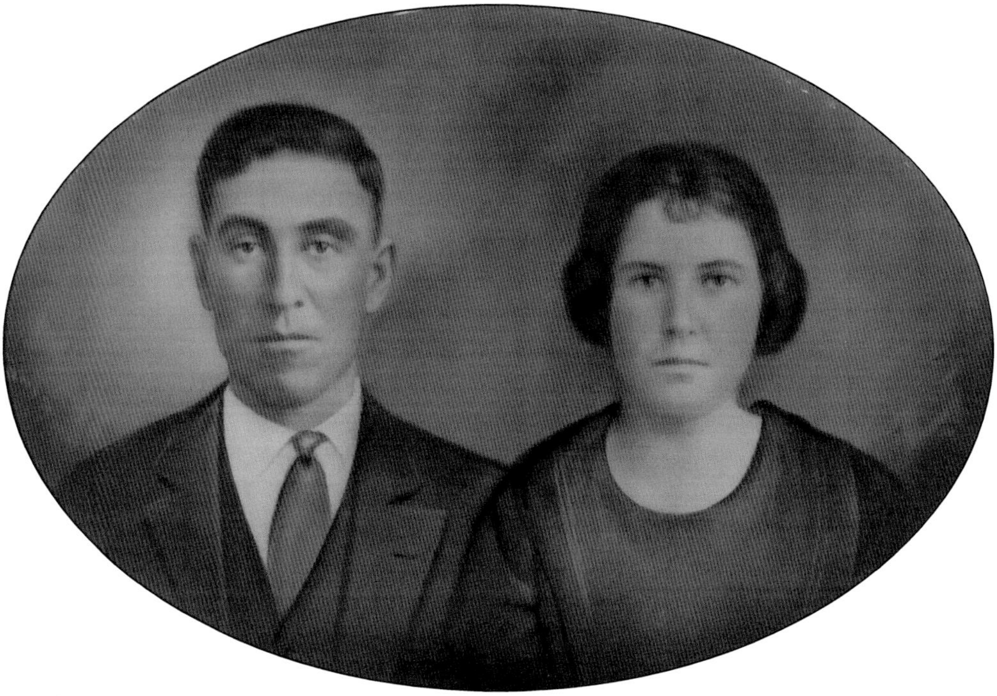

Rancher, farmer, and carpenter Antonio Isidro Vigil and his wife, Maclovia Lopez Vigil, are pictured in this 1910 photograph. The couple were married on September 9, 1908, in Chama. Mrs. Vigil was a homemaker and avid gardener. The trees planted on their land in Cañon de Chama are still being cared for by their grandson Larry Vigil, who inherited Maclovia's green thumb. (Courtesy of Larry and Rita Vigil.)

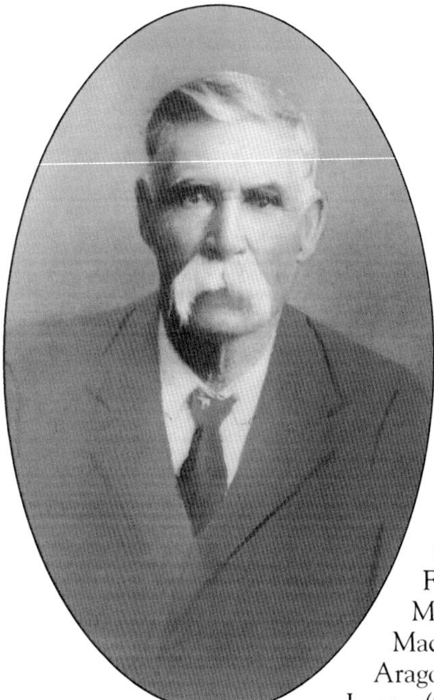

The man in this photograph, taken in the late 1800s, is farmer and rancher Carlos Lopez. His parents were Francisco Lopez and Maria Alta Gracia. He married Maria Inez Atencio on March 12, 1888. He is the father of Maclovia Lopez Vigil, Severa Lopez Montoya, Rufina Lopez Aragon, Soledad Lopez Trujillo, Adelina Lopez, and Rafael Lopez. (Courtesy of Larry and Rita Vigil.)

The first daughter of Maclovia Lopez Vigil and Antonio Vigil is baby Clarita Vigil (Vialpando). She was one year old when this photograph was taken. Clarita married Rosendo Vialpando and they raised 12 children. (Courtesy of Larry and Rita Vigil.)

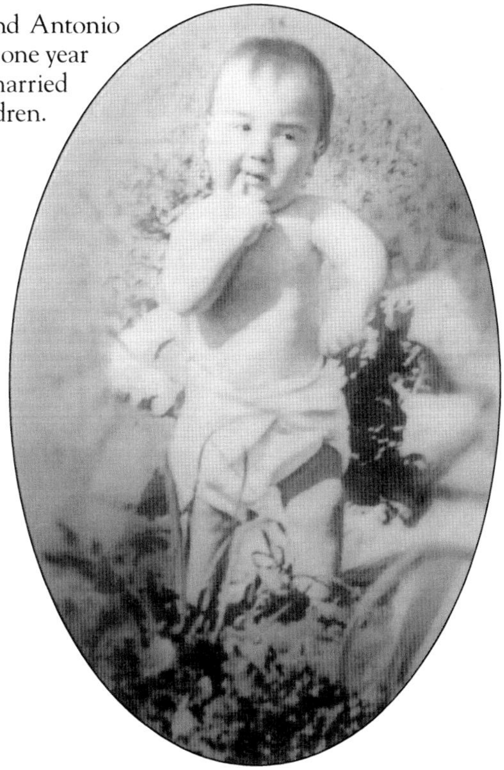

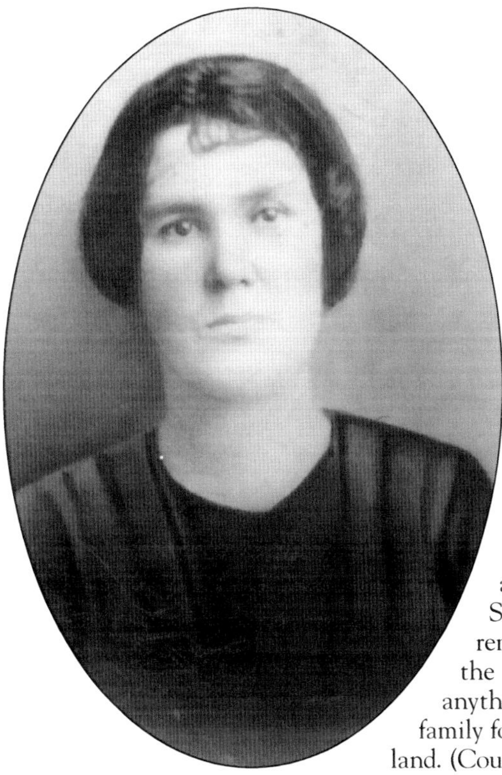

This beautiful portrait is of Maclovia Lopez Vigil. She was a homemaker who grew beautiful gardens, flowers, and crops in Canon de Chama. She loved the outdoors. Her gardens of flowers and plants grew lavishly, and her crops of vegetables grew plentiful. She was a talented carpenter, and her children remember her always fixing the windows, redoing the floors, and even the roofing. She could cook anything, mend anything, and fix anything. Her family fondly recollects her talents and her love for the land. (Courtesy of Larry and Rita Vigil.)

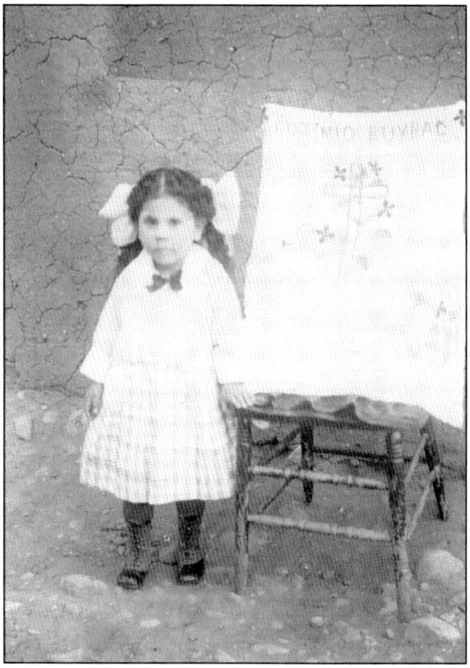

This little girl with button-up boots and a big white bow in her hair poses in front of an old adobe home. She stands next to a chair with a small colcha draped over it. It might have been a colcha stitched as a baptism cloth or memoriam banner. It has stitched flowers and leaves that surround a stitched cross in the center. The name on the small tapestry reads, "Eutimio Roybal." (Courtesy of Charlie Jaquez Jr.)

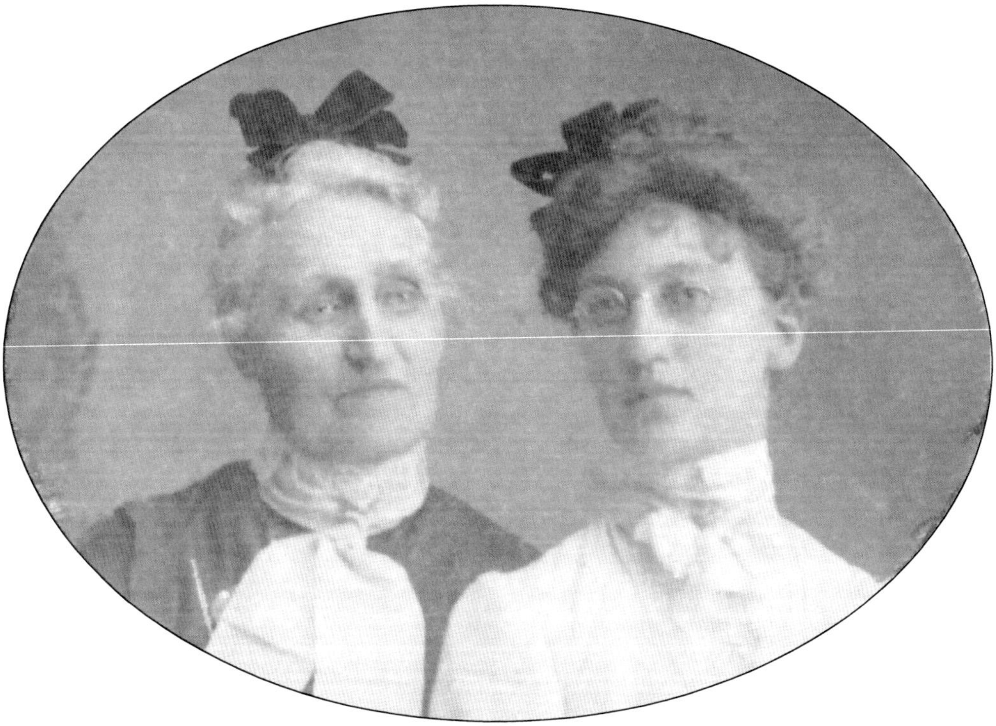

These two women were schoolteachers who taught in the San Pablo school in the early 1900s. The picture was found in the belongings of Eduvigen Vialpando Jaquez Esquibel, born on June 14, 1895. On the back was written, "Las primeras maestras de tuve en San Pablo." The note translates to "The first teachers I had in San Pablo." The San Pablo schoolteachers taught students from fourth to eighth grades. (Courtesy of Charlie Jaquez Jr.)

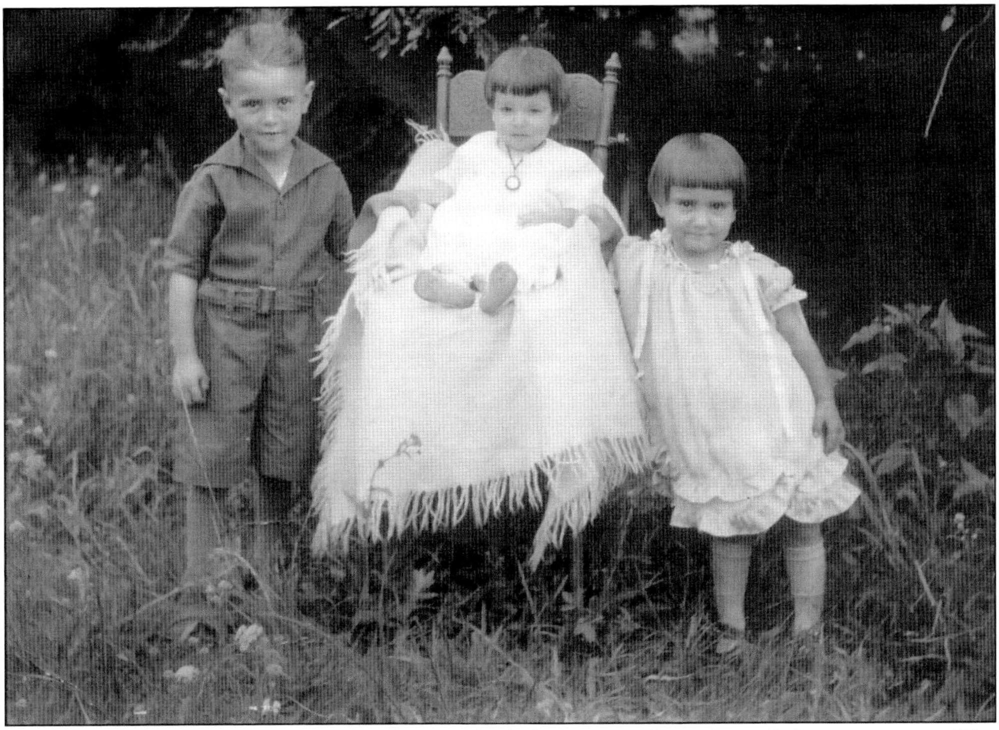

This lovely picture of three siblings shows a little boy posing happily with his two sisters. The baby in the center sits on a white jerga, or rug, a textile usually woven by the grandmother or mother. (Courtesy of Charlie Jaquez Jr.)

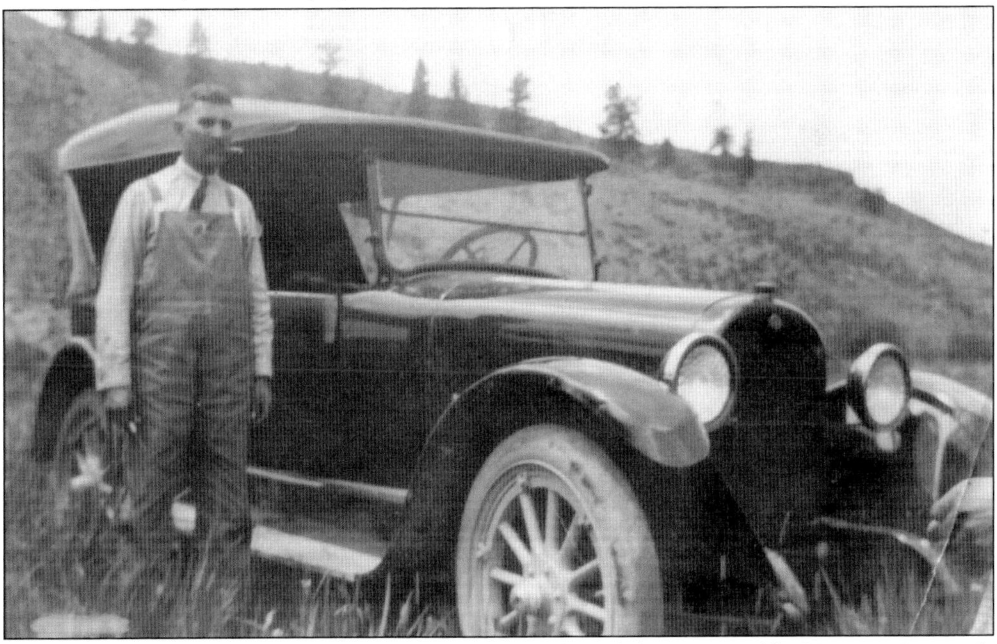

Jose Julian "J.J." Lobato is pictured in front of his Ford Model T convertible. He owned a ranch three miles east of San Luis on which he raised cattle and sheep. He also served as Costilla County treasurer in 1920 and Costilla County judge in 1925. (Courtesy of Hope Gallegos Yost.)

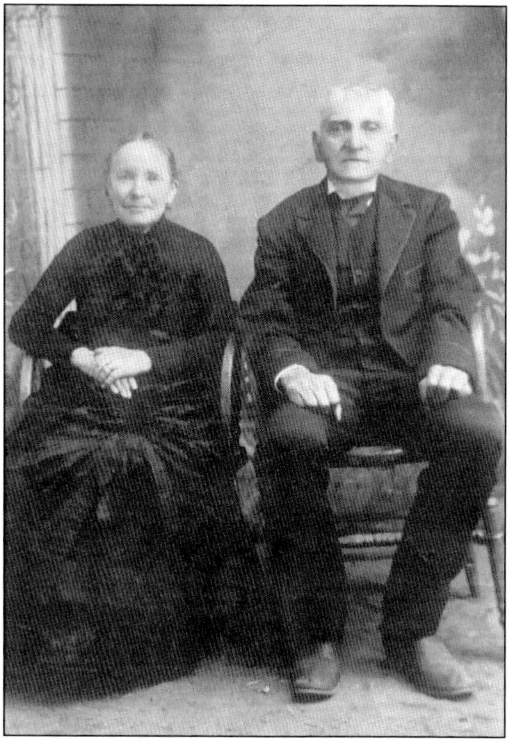

This portrait is of Placida Baca Gallegos and her husband, Eluterio Gallegos. They were married on November 10, 1864, in San Luis. Eluterio farmed with his father-in-law, Juan Antonio Baca, on land that was part of the original Sangre de Cristo Land Grant. (Courtesy of Hope Gallegos Yost.)

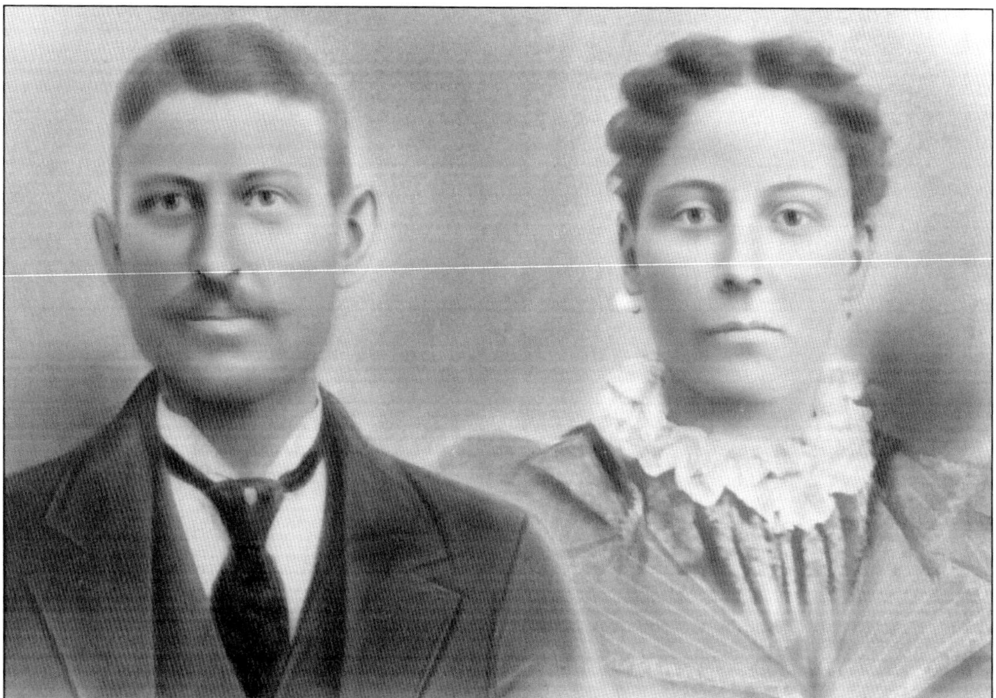

This portrait is of the couple Francisco Gallegos and Ursula Garcia Gallegos. They were married on January 30, 1893, in San Luis. Francisco raised cattle and sheep and farmed vegetables with the help of his sons. (Courtesy of Hope Gallegos Yost.)

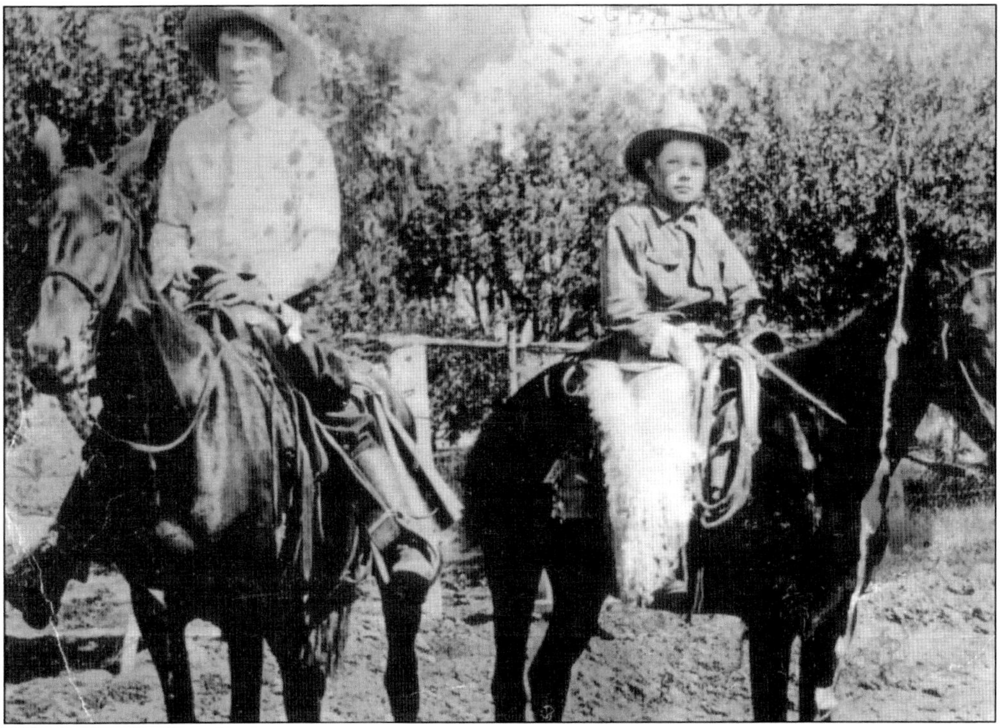

Local residents Seturino Lucero and his 12-year-old son Julian enjoy a backpacking trip together around 1917. The photograph was taken near La Urraca (the Magpie) area near El Rito, New Mexico. Later, Julian was credited for helping build the volcanic rock fence around the San Luis Institute of Arts and Crafts. (Courtesy of Eugene and Josie Lobato.)

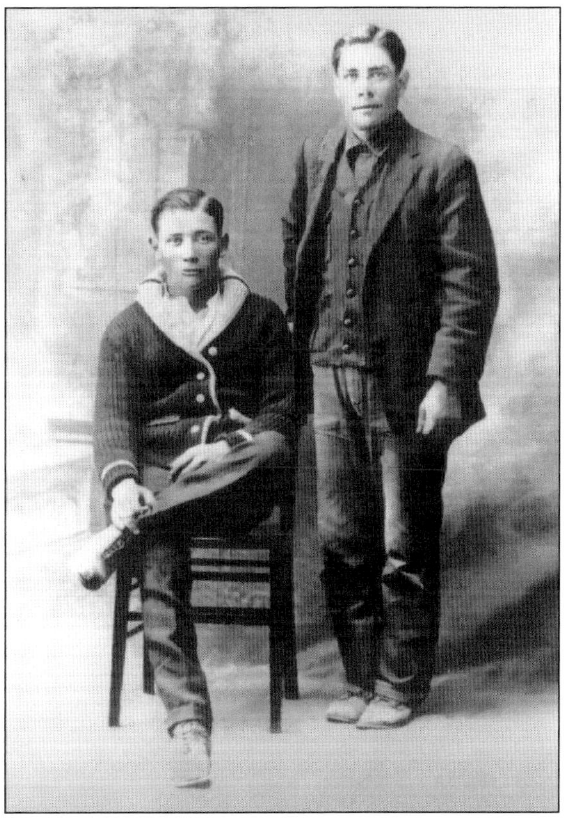

Taken in 1922, this photograph shows Seturino Lucero (standing) with his 17-year-old son, Julian. Mr. Lucero was a sheepherder who worked for J.P. (Jose Presentación) Gallegos. When his wife died during childbirth, Seturino raised his three-year-old and two-year-old children. The baby was given to the family of his boss, J.P. Gallegos, to be raised. (Courtesy of Eugene and Josie Lobato.)

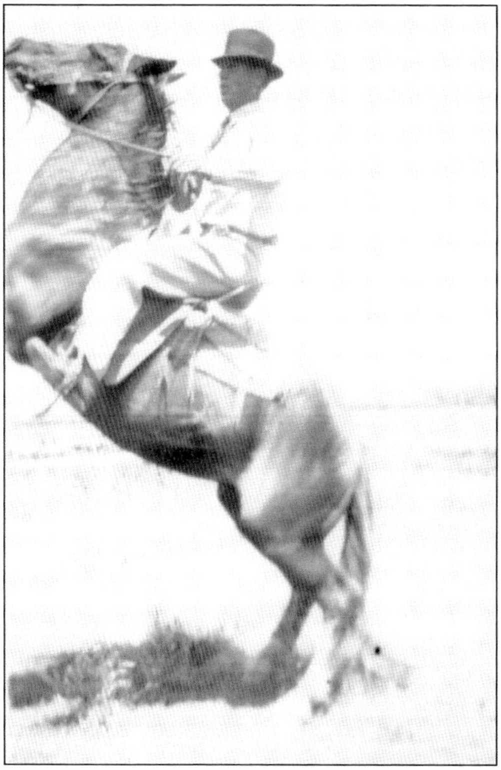

Pictured here is rancher and farmer Francisco Mondragon on his horse, which is rearing up, in Colonias west of El Rito de San Francisco, on the family ranch in the 1930s. Mondragon was an avid rider. According to his grandchildren, "He loved his horses." (Courtesy of Pat Trujillo VanZandt.)

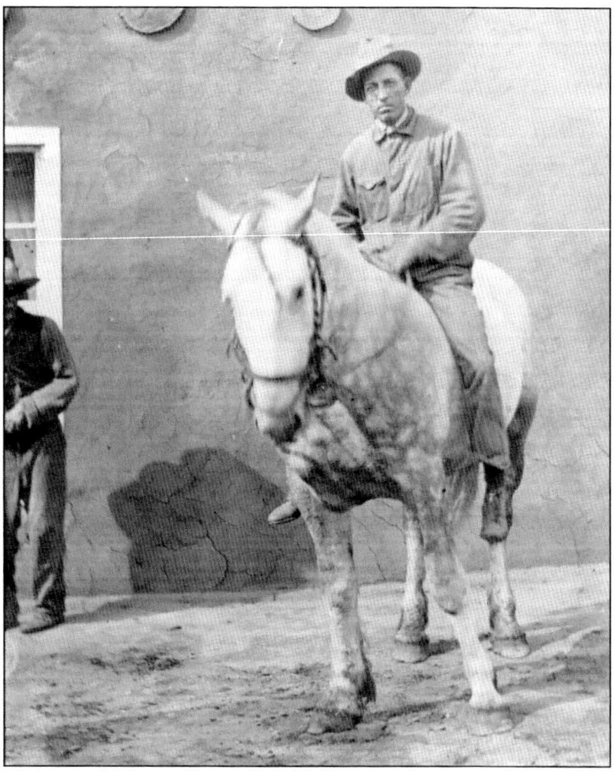

Farmer and rancher Eluterio Esquibel poses on his horse in San Pablo, Colorado. Tall, dark, and lanky, he is remembered as an easy-going man. A trait well suited for his profession, as Eluterio was the San Pablo veterinarian. There was usually no money exchanged for his services; instead, he bartered for grain and other goods. He was also known for his skill in shoeing horses, getting his supplies from blacksmith Leroy Payne. (Courtesy of Charlie Jaquez Jr.)

Bibliography

Baker, Fred R. "Oldest Colorado Store Marks Centennial." *Denver Post*, June 25, 1957.

Centennial High School Student Project. *ADOBE Magazine* 1, no. 1 (Spring 1974); 1 no. 2. (Summer 1975).

Colorado Society of Hispanic Genealogy. *Hispanic Pioneers in Colorado and New Mexico*. Denver, CO: Alliance Press LLC, 2006.

Garcia-Simms, Charlene, Maclovio C. Martinez, and Maria Mondragon-Valdez. *Celebración San Luis 150 Years*. Pueblo, CO: El Escritorio Publications, 2001.

Gibson, Chas E. Jr. "Further Information from San Luis and Vicinity." Microfiche. Stephen H. Hart Library & Research Center, History Colorado, 1934.

Gifford Spurck Associates. Historic Structure Assessment, Costilla County Courthouse. Used with permission, Ben Doon, Costilla County administrator, 2002.

Green, Robert Kino, Maria Mondragon Valdez, and Dana Maestas. "The Utes of San Luis," "The Early Commercialization of San Luis," and "The Sacred Community of San Luis." *La Sierra Newspaper*, Special Edition, July 27, 2001, 5–13.

Jaquez, Freddie. *A History of the Most Precious Blood Parish Chapel*. Research in Chicano Studies, prepared for Wilma Gomez Stump, Adams State College, Alamosa, CO, 1976.

Lopez-Tushar, Olibama. *The People of El Valle: A History of the Spanish Colonials in the San Luis Valley*. Pueblo, CO: El Escritorio, 1997.

Martinez, Maria C. "Juan Ramos Valdez: His Ancestors and Descendants." *La Sierra Newspaper*, 6.

Martinez, Maria C. and Kenneth Gardner. "Ferdinand Meyer: Picturesque Figure of Pioneer Days in Costilla—San Luis Areas." *La Sierra Newspaper*, April 11, 2014, 16.

Mondragon-Valdez, Maria. *Casa del Senor: A Brief History of Sangre de Cristo Parish Church and Its Missions*. San Luis, CO: self-published, 2001.

Olivas y Cordova, Richard de, and Maria C Martinez. *Spanish Colonial Americans*. Denver, CO: self-published, 2003.

Simmons, Virginia McConnell. "Early Hispanic Textile Tradition in the San Luis Valley." *San Luis Valley Historian* 27, no. 1 (1995): 2–18.

————. *The San Luis Valley: Land of the Six Armed Cross*. Boulder, CO: Pruett Publishing, 1979.

Teeuwen, Randall, Maclovio C. Martinez, Marianne L. Stoller, and Ron Sandoval. *La Cultura Constante de San Luis*. San Luis, CO: Sierra Printing Inc., 1985.

Valdez, Maria. "La Sociedad Protección Mutua de Trabajodores Unidos." *San Luis Valley Historian* 13, no. 2 (2001): 5–23.